MONEY
CONFIDENCE

MONEY
CONFIDENCE

ADVICE FOR WOMEN
to Take Control of Their
Financial Freedom Now

CRYSTAL OCULEE

GREENLEAF
BOOK GROUP PRESS

This publication is designed to provide accurate and authoritative information in regard to the subject matter covered. It is sold with the understanding that the publisher and author are not engaged in rendering legal, accounting, or other professional services. If legal advice or other expert assistance is required, the services of a competent professional should be sought.

Published by Greenleaf Book Group Press
Austin, Texas
www.gbgpress.com

Distributed by Greenleaf Book Group

For ordering information or special discounts for bulk purchases, please contact Greenleaf Book Group at PO Box 91869, Austin, TX 78709, 512.891.6100.

Design and composition by Greenleaf Book Group and Sheila Parr
Cover design by Greenleaf Book Group and Sheila Parr
Cover image © Elnur / Shutterstock

Cataloging-in-Publication data is available.

Print ISBN: 978-1-62634-439-6

eBook ISBN: 978-1-62634-440-2

Part of the Tree Neutral® program, which offsets the number of trees consumed in the production and printing of this book by taking proactive steps, such as planting trees in direct proportion to the number of trees used: www.treeneutral.com

Tree Neutral

Printed in the United States of America on acid-free paper

17 18 19 20 21 22   10 9 8 7 6 5 4 3 2 1

First Edition

IMPORTANT DISCLOSURES

Information provided herein reflects the views of the author as of the publication date of this book. Such views are subject to change at any point, and neither the author nor 9Q Ventures, LLC shall be obligated to provide notice of any change. Information contained herein is provided for informational purposes only, and nothing presented herein is or is intended to constitute investment, tax, or legal advice or a recommendation to buy or sell any types of securities. No investment decision should be made based on any information provided herein.

The author has not taken into account the investment objectives, financial situation, or particular needs of any individual investor and is not responsible for the consequences of any decisions or actions taken as a result of information provided in this book. There is a risk of loss from an investment in securities, including the risk of total loss of principal, which an investor will need to be prepared to bear. Different types of investments involve varying degrees of risk, and there can be no assurance that any specific investment will be profitable or suitable for a particular investor's financial situation or risk tolerance. Mutual funds, exchange traded funds, new issue bonds, and annuities have offering documents (e.g., prospectus and statement of additional information), which outline the investment strategies, fees, risks, and conflicts pertaining to the applicable investment. It is very important for an investor to read the offering documents to fully understand the investment. Options also carry risks and are not suitable for all investors. Prior to investing, an investor should read: "Characteristics and Risks of Standardized Options," which can be obtained from any exchange on which options are traded, at www.optionsclearing.com, or by calling 1-888-OPTIONS, or by contacting your broker/custodian.

Asset allocation and portfolio diversification cannot assure or guarantee better performance and cannot eliminate the risk of investment losses. To the extent that they are mentioned, it is important to understand that annuities are intended for retirement or other long-term needs. They are intended for a person who has sufficient cash or other liquid assets for living expenses and other unexpected emergencies, such as medical expenses. Annuities are not FDIC-insured, and any insurance and annuity product guarantees are backed by the financial strength and claims-paying ability of the issuing company. Past performance is no guarantee of future results. Some of the information provided herein was obtained from third-party sources believed to be reliable, but such information is not guaranteed to be accurate.

Any forward-looking statements or forecasts are based on assumptions only, and actual results are expected to vary from any such statements or forecasts. No reliance should be placed on any such statements or forecasts when making any investment decision. Any assumptions and projections displayed are estimates, hypothetical in nature, and meant to serve solely as a guideline. Accordingly, you should not rely solely on the information contained in these materials in making any investment decision.

In Memory of My Grandmother

This book is dedicated to every woman who has worked hard to support her family, every woman who has kept going regardless of the struggles she faced, and who kept saving even though at times it all seemed to go into a "black hole." I hope that within the pages of this book you will find hope, wisdom, and empowerment to plan a better retirement. I hope you'll be able to stand up to whomever or whatever it is that's trying to hold you back.

CONTENTS

ACKNOWLEDGMENTS

As the famous saying goes, it takes a village.

This book was inspired by the stories of many women I met throughout the years. Even though—for their privacy—their names are fictitious, their stories are real. I would like to thank all of them for their inspiring and, in some cases, heartbreaking stories, and I know they will want any woman who reads this book to be aware of the "wolves" that can, in the blink of an eye, wipe away hopes and dreams.

First, and most important of all, I want to thank my husband, who has always been there for me. He has encouraged me every step of the way. His motivation and his genuine you-can-do-it attitude truly inspire me every day. Without his support, strength, and motivation, this book would not have been possible. Thank you with all my heart and soul. You are a remarkable person!

I want to thank my parents for teaching me to be the strong woman I am today. Without them, I might never have understood the importance of being independent!

I want to thank my staff, who were with me every step of the way—from book design to editing to all the work that goes on behind the scenes. I offer my sincerest thanks to Mae Talle, who organized me above and beyond to help me achieve my deadlines for this book—her effort to make this book the best it can be was beyond enthusiastic, and Silvia Park, who offered her support and many nights of long debates on subject matter.

I want to give my heartfelt gratitude to my client and dear friend Alice Bryant, who helped with editing and who was an incredible sounding board for many of the topics, including helping me come up with the cover idea. I appreciate how selfless her kindness was, and it has been an absolute pleasure to have someone so amazing in my group of counsel.

I also want to thank my editor, Sally Garland. Sally, thanks for all of your hard work, dedication, and belief in our mission to empower women.

Finally, I want to thank all the women who will read this book and will choose to take control of their financial futures. Nothing makes me prouder than that, as I know that together our voices will shake down all the wolves in the financial industry, and we will be a force to be reckoned with. After all, it is you, the reader, who will help us pass this empowerment message along and make a difference in your life or someone else's!

PART ONE

THE ENCHANTED
WALL STREET AND THE
SLEEPLESS BEAUTY

Chapter 1

WHEN IT COMES TO MONEY, TOUGHEN UP!

"With the new day comes new strength and new thoughts."
—Eleanor Roosevelt

I t was a crazy busy but beautiful day in downtown Los Angeles. The streets were crowded, full of honking cars and lots of noise, as a colleague and I made our way across the street to the convention center. We were attending an industry conference, and we couldn't wait to get inside and away from the sweltering heat. As we walked up to the center, we were stopped by the sound of someone screaming. We saw—just a few yards away—a woman fighting with a man. She held on tightly to her purse and yelled at the top of her lungs, "Give me back my purse! I'm not giving you my money!" Someone was obviously trying to rob her, but she was so direct, intimidating, and was making so much noise that the man must have gotten scared, since he let go and took off! She was one tough lady!

Then we noticed a teenage girl standing next to her. We later found out she was the woman's daughter. The girl was not moving, was clearly shaken up, and had tears welling up in her eyes and a completely lost look on her face. To our surprise, as the girl began to cry, the woman turned to her and said, "Oh, stop your crying! You've got to protect what's yours! You think I'd let some scumbag take what's mine after I worked hard for my money?" In a nutshell, the mother was telling her daughter to "toughen up," meaning it was important that she take her money seriously and not let anyone yank it away from her. Granted, I think in hindsight, she could have risked both their lives by resisting, so maybe her choice of action wasn't the best in that situation—but then again, they were on a crowded street and not in some dark alley.

We asked if they were all right and if they wanted us to call the police, but the woman looked at us and said, "Hey, I did what I had to do! As you can see, there were no knights in shining armor coming to my rescue," hinting at the fact that on that crowded street, not one man stepped in to help her. She proceeded to tell us that she didn't resist the robbery only because of her valuables, but because she didn't want her daughter to think it was ever OK to be a victim.

Her words resonated with me, but for a different reason. It wasn't only because guys walked by pretending not to notice so they wouldn't have to get involved. It was because this woman had come to *expect* that no one would help her, and in this instance, she simply took care of the situation herself—no knights in shining armor required. She didn't roll over and give up. She didn't stand there paralyzed with fear. She did what she had to do and took care of herself. And that took confidence.

Her actions stuck with me for a long time. I started to wonder how many women we all know, of all ages, who are still waiting for their knight in shining armor to come to their rescue. And I'm not talking about a situation like a robbery, where there is real, physical danger, but everyday financial situations where women allow themselves to be victimized, either because they are too afraid to confront a bad situation or they don't know how to do it. I'm not talking about simply paying bills and balancing checkbooks, but managing their wealth with the same ease they pick out a new purse. I'm talking about managing their money and their retirement portfolios exactly how *they* want to. Doesn't the retirement portfolio do essentially the same thing as your purse—hold your valuables? We make sure that our purses have zippers so nothing falls out and everything is protected, and we like having different compartments so we can access our wallets or our keys when we need them. But as much attention as women give to protecting the relatively inconsequential valuables in their purses, they generally don't put even half that much effort into protecting their retirement money! Why? Because they keep thinking that somehow, everything will turn out all right. And—of maybe even more concern—they don't even realize most of the time they're thinking that way.

Since that day, I set out on a mission to explore the stories of women who could have stood up for themselves but didn't—and what they lost as a result. These women weren't robbed in the physical sense—no one stole their purses. They lost something much more valuable—their retirement savings—and with it, their ability to have the kind of life they had not only wanted, but had worked hard to achieve. The enchanted Wall Street destroyed their dreams, and their knight in shining armor (their financial advisor) didn't ride in on a white horse to rescue them, but in fact did the exact opposite. Why didn't these women stand up for their lifetime earnings like that feisty woman on that street in Los Angeles? In short, most women lack money confidence.

Confidence comes from knowledge. If you value a good purse, then you probably have spent time researching brands, going into stores and touching the materials, trying on various purses for fit and style. You might talk to your friends about the bags they love and why. You probably have an impressive collection. So when it comes time to choose a new purse, you're not afraid or intimidated—you're confident! A salesperson won't be able to convince you to buy a bulky purse when you know you love smaller handbags. You know what works for you.

The same is true of money confidence. Right now, you're taking the first step in an exciting journey of gaining knowledge about your finances. As with your first handbag, it will take time to understand the different brands—or in this case, the different investment products out there. But it's not rocket science! Even though you might not become a stock market genius, you will gain enough basic information to give you the confidence you need to make smart decisions about your future. As with a purse, you might not know how to make one, but you can easily spot the difference between a fake leather purse and one made of genuine leather. The same is true with managing your finances.

You're probably wondering why more women don't have money confidence. The busy lives that so many women have today is one reason. Women never truly stop to take care of themselves. They are so dedicated to everyone else in their life and to those individuals' best interests that they forget about their own. Because women have been busy saving the day for their loved ones, it's natural they would assume someone would step in and save them when it comes to their financial future. Since we're nurturers by nature, it is natural for us to think our financial well-being will be nurtured as well. That's a nice thought, but not a realistic one. We have to be our own nurturers. It's as simple as that. We don't need to change the core of who we are. Nor do we need to learn to be financial advisors. All we need to do is take charge and take control of our own financial management.

I'll never forget that crazy day in Los Angeles, where I was inspired to see there is still hope for women out there to stand up for themselves and to learn to think differently about themselves and their future. They just need to know that they can, and should, stand up to anyone, like that tough lady did. She spoke her mind, fought like hell, and didn't let anyone take advantage of her!

Chapter 2

THE BEGINNING . . .

" . . . some day you will be old enough to start reading fairy tales again."
—C. S. Lewis

I was about eight years old when I noticed a common thread among the women in my family. They were all especially thoughtful, intelligent, and outspoken—women whose voices could literally shake up a room and demand attention. They were strong, opinionated, and always commanded respect, but all of them would go to their husbands to ask for money to pay the bills, do the grocery shopping, or go to the salon. It was as if the man were a walking, talking ATM. It's funny how we perceive things when we are children, because we don't really know what is right or wrong, or why things happen the way they do. So I assumed that if Mom did something, then because I was a girl, that's what I was supposed to do as well.

I remember when I started receiving my allowance, I would collect it, take it to my room, count it, write down the amounts in my journal, and then—give it to my dad for "safekeeping." My dad didn't understand why I would turn around and give my allowance back to him within an hour. He was even more confused when I would proceed to make "withdrawals" from him ("the ATM") and get just enough money for a doll or candy or whatever my heart desired. I remember him telling me several times, "You know, this is your money, and you can keep it with you. That's why I gave it to you in the first place." To which I would respond, "Well, Mom doesn't keep her money with herself, so why should I?" I could not for the life of me see why he wanted me to keep my money in my room. Having him safeguard it for me seemed like such a no-brainer that I was always confused why he would make such a silly suggestion!

At about that same age, my grandfather passed away. Up to that point in my life, his death was the hardest thing I had ever faced as a child. He was like a second father to me and I loved him very much. I stayed with my grandparents during the summers and I loved to hang out with Grandpa, who was the best storyteller ever. He didn't get annoyed (or at least he didn't seem to) by the silly questions I asked about how cars worked and why the sky was blue—or about all the other wonderful stuff that seems so strange when you're young and the world is amazing and filled with excitement.

But this story is more about my grandmother, a doctor with a multifaceted intellect who spoke several languages and could easily outdebate almost anyone.

On his deathbed, my grandpa asked my dad (his son-in-law) to please take care of Grandma and make sure she would be OK. So my grandma moved in with us, and Dad now had another member of the family to look after. He handled Grandpa's funeral arrangements and the onslaught of paperwork that comes with sorting out finances after someone's passing so my grandma didn't have to figure it all out while she was grieving. Dad also took over of all of my grandma's bills, and as she used to do with Grandpa, she would then go to my dad to get "spending money." She was lucky, because my dad took care of her well and did his best to make sure she was truly comfortable. She lived a long life (she passed away at the age of ninety-six), and her golden years were spent in comfort, with her family helping her in whatever she needed, financially and physically. I didn't realize how truly lucky she was until much later in life, when I found out that she had spent most of her money by the time she was about eighty, and for almost two decades after that, my dad took care of her financially. I am still proud of how my father handled this situation, because he never abandoned her, didn't try to shove her off on other relatives, and wouldn't even let her go to a nursing home until she insisted on it, at the age of ninety-six! But again, she was lucky.

As much as these events taught me about the value of family and the importance of being there for the people you love, I can't help but feel that things could and should have been different. There was no reason why my grandma could not have taken care of herself or planned her retirement in advance. She was an intelligent and confident woman, far from a shrinking violet, and at the time of my grandpa's passing, she was in her mid-seventies, still healthy and full of life! She could have easily managed her own money, made her own budget, and had complete independence. But she didn't do any of that.

The years passed, and by the time I was a teenager, I thought I knew everything. I was still withdrawing money from my personal ATM (my dad), but I was getting more and more lectures from him, especially when I overdrew on my "account balance" (and rightfully so many times). That was when I asked myself, "Hey, why do I need a bank that talks back?" and asked my dad to help me open my first real checking account. Since I was older, and the little allowance I had received before no longer worked for me, I started babysitting and tutoring. I added more and more to my bank account because I had to prove to my dad that he was wrong, and that I indeed *knew* what I was doing! Hey, I was no longer his carefree little girl. So I watched my spending closely and paid my "bills" on time. I even tried to convince him that because I was so responsible and paid all my teenage bills on time, that he should buy me a pager. (Yes, you remember, we didn't always have smartphones with cool apps; we only had the coolest invention of the time—pagers!) Well, unfortunately my dad didn't think that was a necessary purchase and told me that when I became a doctor, he would gladly buy me a pager! (Become a doctor? Yuck! The medical field was too bloody and gross, thank you.) "No thank you," I told him. If I could stand the sight of blood, then I'd become a vampire, not a doctor! At least I would always look young and live forever!

Making more money and saving it became important to me. I had to show the bank (my dad) that I no longer needed him for *any* loans. Well, he would still have to pay for the rent, the food, the cable bill, and everything else, but other than that, I could totally survive on my own. So I saved and spent wisely. I paid my own teenage bills and never asked him for any more money. Although he wasn't always happy with the stuff I bought, he was proud of my initiative, and I was thrilled!

On a serious note, having my parents say no to me whenever I wanted to buy some silly teenage thing is what pushed me to become more serious about my money, to budget, and to plan ahead. I didn't make all that much money with my babysitting gigs, and like most teenagers, I was faced with the constant dilemma of having to decide what clothing accessory or gadget I absolutely couldn't live without. So budgeting became a must. Eventually, I realized there was no reason why a girl cannot, or should not, do this. The sun didn't stop rising in the morning because I was handling my own money, and even though I'd make mistakes from time to time, the world didn't end, and my dad never had a problem with what I was doing. So why was it that my mom still didn't know how to pay a bill, or why did she still come to Dad for money? She had a part-time job but handed her paychecks over to her husband. I didn't get it!

My confusion about why women didn't put more energy into managing their own money wasn't confined to the women in my immediate family. When I was in my early twenties, I saw my parents going through a difficult time trying to help a close family friend who became a widow at the age of fifty-one. She was a homemaker with a fourteen-year-old son, and her husband suddenly passed away from colon cancer that he didn't even know he had. He went to the emergency room one evening because he felt ill, and died a few days later. No warning, no time to prepare, no time to really say good-bye. Everyone was in total shock and a state of disbelief. He had a small taxi business, and his wife had never worked a day in her life. She thought he had handled everything and planned for such a situation. But as it turned out, he was a procrastinator (like most people) and obviously didn't expect to die so young, so he hadn't planned ahead. He had never bought life insurance, and because he was a business owner, he didn't have a pension plan. He had barely paid into Social Security, and now his widow was left with nothing but a couple of taxicabs and a huge mortgage. Unfortunately, she didn't know how to run his business so there was no money coming in, and because they had no real savings, she lost her home and had to move into a tiny place. Because she was not savvy and didn't have any work experience, she had to accept a minimum wage job in a retail store. She barely got by.

It was sad watching how the anger she and her son had for their late husband and father prevented them from grieving the right way. They went from burying the person they loved, who took care of everything for them, to struggling to stay afloat, with absolutely no time to cope with their sudden loss. The truth is, I get that—yes, maybe the late husband should have thought of all those things. But I could not understand back then, why was it *his* responsibility to do everything? Why didn't his wife at some point say, "Hey, how are we protected? How much is in our savings? What is our debt?" Why was she not involved? Is it fair to assume that because he was a man, he should have had it all figured out? What if he didn't think about it? What if he, like her, lived day to day and ignored the big picture? Again—not becoming involved was her choice, too.

That is when I said to myself, "NO MORE!" At least in my family, this helplessness and dependence would end right here—with me. I told myself that I would *never* be like that. I saw this dependence as a weakness—something not worthy of intelligent women. I saw it was a choice, a choice that somehow throughout these women's lives, they had decided to make.

But even afterward, when I was all grown up and living in the real world, I noticed the same thing. Except now I saw women taking the exact same approach that they took with their husbands or fathers with their financial advisors. They didn't communicate with people who managed their money, they didn't ask questions, and didn't show much interest in how their money was invested. Instead, they had complete trust that their advisor was taking care of everything for them. They had that same he-will-take-care-of-me-and-I-have-nothing-to-worry-about attitude!

So why is it that women continue making these choices? When I started working in finance, I began to see a common thread in all these scenarios. It was not because of career; housewives and professional women alike were making the same choices. Neither was it because some were more educated than others. The common thread seemed to be nothing more than habit, a habit they had learned from their mothers and grandmothers and which was amplified by the culture around them. Their upbringing taught them one way to look at their money, and they never broke that habit—perhaps because they didn't feel confident in themselves or their abilities to take control. They feared they would make a mistake and mess it all up!

I also noticed that often women made these choices because of the relationships they had with the people handling their money. They held tight to the assumption that "my husband, my dad, my advisor knows what is best for me." That assumption was like an emotional security blanket they could pull over themselves so they wouldn't have to deal with situations that made them feel uncomfortable, lost, and confused. When they combined the blanket with a what-I-don't-know-won't-hurt-me attitude, they were all set to enjoy the joys of ignorance and the bliss of not worrying—even though they had plenty to worry about.

The problem is that we grow up with so many unrealistic representations of the world around us—so many damsels in distress who are saved by handsome princes—that we think everything will somehow work out. We think everything will always turn out for the best. But ignorance about our finances is like a beautiful swan that grows into an ugly, fire-breathing dragon when it's abandoned and neglected. It's a monster that cannot be put down once it rears its ugly head and shows its true colors. It hides behind a fake sense of security, and when it finally shows up, it's hard to break away from its grip, because by that time it's likely too late to do anything about it. We have to face this monster early, because that's the only way to control it.

Think of all the stories we are told when we are kids—"Cinderella" is a great example. What do we learn? Let's just buy a pretty dress, do our hair all nice, go to a ball, and everything, including our financial well-being, will be taken care of by Prince Charming. Yay! Life's easy! Now, don't get me wrong. Fairy-tale endings are great, as long as you have people around you who can help shape you into an independent woman who can take care of herself. But the problem is that, too often, positive, strong influences don't exist, and we grow up into adults who still have those same fairy-tale mentalities. We are surrounded by women who may not be the best examples of good money managers, and we follow in their footsteps unconsciously. Maybe Mom is too comfortable letting Dad take care of all the finances. Or maybe we're watching episodes of shows like *I Love Lucy*, and we see that Lucy is bad with money, so we think that's normal. And if you think things are completely different today, you haven't watched some of those ridiculous reality TV shows and what they are teaching young girls today—be petty, materialistic, and completely misunderstand what it means to be independent. (No, "annoying" and "independent" are *not* the same thing!)

Our environment and upbringing have definitely contributed to the scary statistic that shows so many women nowadays having a difficult time managing their money. The sad part about this is that as women are living longer, and often alone (after a divorce or after becoming widowed), they are literally running out of savings during their retirement. They end up spending their so-called golden years living Social Security check to Social Security check, without any freedom and with little independence. But it doesn't have to be this way.

As you read the stories in this book about women who went through tough moments and made their own mistakes, keep in mind the tough woman in the first chapter. Anytime you come across a story in this book that you can relate to, think of how much better such situations will turn out for you if you approach them from the perspective of "Give me back my purse! I'm not giving you my money!" and you don't allow people to take advantage of you. Standing up for yourself can be tough, but anytime a solution to your problem sounds too scary or too complicated to face, I want you to think of what the smart woman said to her daughter. But this time, imagine her pointing at you and saying, "When it comes to your money, toughen up!"

Because you can do anything you want, standing up for yourself and your retirement is, after all, a choice. This is at the heart of money confidence.

The stories of the women in this book are real, but their names have been changed to protect their privacy. They hope their stories will help reshape your attitude toward your financial future, so you can approach situations similar to theirs in a much more productive way than they did. The thing is, many of the advisors who ultimately damaged these women's futures, and other advisors who have hurt their clients' futures in the same way, are not necessarily evil monsters. They're just humans who adopted bad habits. Some have a lazy attitude toward their jobs, and that attitude affects their clients' well-being in a negative way. Some advisors are uneducated or inexperienced in their financial field. Some are greedy, some are incompetent, and some are too self-centered to understand the details of what they are selling and how those products can potentially affect their clients. Others are young salespeople right out of college, working for big firms with big names, and pushing whatever the analysts in their headquarters are promoting, and who do not understand the consequences of their actions. For others, this is a side gig. They're CPAs who got financial licenses to sell financial products on the side. Some lawyers do the same thing. As we all know, a person cannot truly be a jack-of-all-trades. But unfortunately, anyone who can pass the test can go out and start advising. So please keep in mind when I refer in this book to your financial advisor or your financial professional, I'm referring to anyone who fits into an advising category—whether it's an actual financial advisor (regardless of experience level), a broker, or another professional who sells investments on the side.

As you continue reading, keep in mind that I will first share the women's stories and talk in detail about why we, as women, are where we are in the eyes of society and the financial industry. As you keep reading, you will find chapters with solutions and advice on how these women could have handled some of the situations and scenarios more effectively. I hope you will apply these lessons to your own situation. You will learn about financial concepts, decision-making techniques, how to take control of your finances, and how to never let these not-so-happy endings happen to you.

Also, as you see references to Wall Street throughout the book, keep in mind that I am referring to the financial industry in general, not the actual Wall Street in New York or the New York Stock Exchange. It's a way to refer to the overall financial industry that's supposed to help you build your future but often ends up crashing down on top of you.

It is my sincere hope that by reading this book and hearing about the women I have met throughout my career and the lessons I learned trying to help them, you will become more comfortable in dealing with the beast of inaction and you will come to better understand your strengths and weaknesses. I hope you will learn from their mistakes and that this book will help you become more involved and more aware of your relationship with your money, money management, and your advisors.

Chapter 3

A RUDE AWAKENING

"Fairy tales since the beginning of recorded time, and perhaps earlier,
have been a means to conquer the terrors of mankind through metaphor."
—Jack Zipes

S ince we all love fairy tales, let me tell you a quick story about a fair
maiden I once knew.

Once upon a time, in a faraway land, there lived a fair maiden who
dreamt of an early retirement so she could live her life to the fullest. She didn't come from a wealthy family but was an extremely
hard worker and diligently contributed money into her retirement
account, or a "401(k)" as it was called in this fairy-tale kingdom.
The fair maiden had great dreams for her golden years: traveling,
taking up new hobbies, relaxing in the hot sun with cold piña coladas (yum!), and living life to her heart's content. In fact, she didn't
simply *hope* for financial independence but was *sure* she would reach
her goals—after all, she regularly set aside money into her retirement account and had a financial advisor she thought was as concerned about her retirement as she was.

From time to time, the fair maiden would check in on her
nest egg to marvel at the amount of money she had accumulated,
and each time it seemed she was getting closer and closer to her
dream of real financial independence. In fact, she had grown so
accustomed to seeing increases in the value of her account that her

dreams seemed almost within reach. The magical stock market was ever increasing, and her account followed suit. When her net worth had surpassed the million-dollar mark (after all, she had been diligently contributing to her 401(k) for over twenty years), she could hardly believe her eyes. *Looks like all of my hard work is finally paying off,* she would think while imagining what the hot sand would feel like beneath her feet on the tropical island where she was going to take her first overdue vacation.

Unfortunately, as in most fairy tales, evil was lurking—an evil in the form of account fees, stock market volatility, and an ugly toad pretending to be a diligent financial advisor.

When you think about it, childhood for a girl is quite a sham, almost like a Ponzi scheme. Growing up, we're told a whole bunch of things and given all these promises about the world—that we later find out aren't true. We're steeped in magical stories about heroes and villains, and all the warm and fuzzy fluffiness that comes with them. But what we should notice about these magical worlds is that they are clearly defined. There are good people and there are bad people, those who only want to help us and those who only want to take advantage of us, and it's always easy to distinguish between the two: The good characters in these stories are almost always handsome and flawless, while the bad ones are usually fat, ugly, and have crooked teeth. And if that's not enough, these fairy tales teach us—incorrectly—that life is inherently fair, that at the end of the day, good will triumph over evil, that everything will turn out fine, and that the handsome prince will come riding in on a beautiful white horse and we'll live happily ever after. Imagine, for a second, that if instead of ending like the perfect love story, the prince decided to tell Cinderella that he didn't really like her, and gave her some lame excuse. How differently would that have shaped your outlook on life at an early age? Now, I'm not saying that the best solution is to destroy fairy tales for kids— that would be downright evil. But what I *am* saying is, "Think about the difference in perspective!"

It's no wonder that many of us go through a somewhat angry and rebellious phase when we become teenagers. Sure, some of it is because of the changing hormones in our bodies, but a huge part of it is because we start seeing the world for the complicated and disappointing place it can be sometimes. The real world clashes with how it was originally presented to us when we were young girls. We realize that people can be mean and selfish, and our relationships with others aren't always clear-cut. In real life, it's often truly difficult to tell who has your best interests at heart or if someone doesn't care about you at all. After all, in real life, selfish people don't always look ugly and don't always have crooked teeth.

Unfortunately, as much as we hate to admit it, even as we mature into intelligent and independent women, these childhood stories continue to affect our way of thinking and shape our judgment for the rest of our lives. Let's be honest, ladies, no matter what your age is and no matter how silly it may seem at times, we still like to believe that our life will turn out like a magical fairy tale. There's a reason why movies like *Kate and Leopold*, *Ever After*, and *Enchanted* are so successful! We *want* to believe that good will triumph over evil, and that the world *is* inherently fair and full of wonder. And maybe you're not exactly thinking of a knight in shining armor, or maybe the knight in your life turned out to be a bit of an ugly toad (who, no matter how much you kiss him, never seems to turn into a handsome prince), but we all like to stop and pretend from time to time about how wonderful it would be for our dreams to somehow come true.

Now, there's nothing wrong with stopping to dream once in a while, because that's what makes life magical—even if only for a moment. But unfortunately, this same way of thinking can often cloud our judgment by lulling us into a false sense of security and into the belief that at the end of the day everything will turn out all right—even when we should know better. This it's-not-that-big-of-a-deal mentality causes us to turn a blind eye to things that would otherwise eat away at our sense of logic. I'm not talking about when your husband or boyfriend decides that giving you a toaster on your birthday is a great idea; I'm talking about how this mentality can cause major problems when we apply it to serious topics that will have a truly profound effect on how our lives turn out—like our decisions about planning our income in retirement, or not taking the time to understand that the mere fact of being a woman virtually *guarantees* that you will miss out on hundreds of thousands of dollars' worth of earnings, pension, and Social Security benefits.[1]

I am not here to tell you to "shape up" and start penny-pinching so you can save more money. Nor am I going to tell you to start using coupons, to cut back on your morning lattes, or to find some other feel-good ways of saving more of your hard-earned dollars. Instead, I'd like to show you how to take control of your future in a much more meaningful and productive way by helping you understand the dynamics of your retirement planning not only from a financial perspective, but from the perspective of choices—the choices you make every day regarding your relationship with the financial professionals in your life and your inner relationship with money. Choices that can either help you grow your wealth or forever leave you lagging behind. Even more importantly—choices that will determine how you feel about yourself and your future.

So here is how the fairy-tale story at the beginning of this chapter ends:

The deterioration of financial markets in 2008 destroyed nearly two-thirds of this fair maiden's portfolio. By the time she realized what was happening, instead of having over a million dollars for retirement, her portfolio had shrunk by over 60 percent, and she now had less money in her account than she contributed over the years. Her early retirement plans were forever ruined. She wouldn't be able to take all those vacations that she wanted, her piña coladas would have to be regular pineapple juice, and the worst part—she would *have* to continue working way past her expected retirement age.

The real human tragedy of her situation was that her dreams weren't destroyed because she was careless with her spending or didn't earn enough at her job, but because she made the mistake of blindly trusting someone with her money without realizing that no one else truly cared about her dreams and what she wanted. She didn't review her portfolio allocations, didn't understand the risks of the investments she was placed into, and hadn't the slightest idea of what fees she was being charged, because she thought someone else was taking care of it for her. Her kind nature and a desire to avoid asking tough questions for fear of confrontation or for fear of seeming dumb caused her to place one of the most important aspects of her life—her retirement plan—into someone else's hands, without understanding the sad reality that no one cared about her nest egg as much as she did. And because no one cared, no one took the steps to protect her retirement portfolio from significant downside investment risk exposure.

The sad truth behind this story is that it happens every day. It is a story I have seen all too often over the years as a financial advisor. Hard-working, intelligent, independent women made all the right career choices but had their retirement plans completely ruined because they trusted someone with their entire nest egg and either were afraid to ask questions because they didn't want to look silly, or simply trusted that the person with the title of "Financial Advisor" or "Pension Specialist" or "401(k) Manager" cared about their future as much as they did themselves.

Chapter 4

CAN YOU HEAR ME?
CAN YOU HEAR ME NOW?

"Whatever words we utter should be chosen with care,
for people will hear them and be influenced by them for good or ill."
—Buddha

S leeping Beauty fell into a sleep that saved her from death—thanks to her trusty fairy godmother's power to fight back against a fatal curse. When she fell asleep, she left behind a family, a social life, a set of expectations about the world, and the role she played within that world. She was hidden away until she reached young adulthood and was about to burst into the world as an individual rather than as a part of her father's household. Sleeping Beauty stayed in her perfect youthful state, suspended for a hundred years, until the dashing Prince Charming came to her rescue. (Honestly, I'm already thinking that these hundred years of restful sleep sound fantastic, but add in the never aging part, and I'm looking for the sign-up sheet!)

Crashing through overgrown weeds and entering a castle that had been snoozing for a century, Prince Charming rescued Sleeping Beauty from her hundred-year slumber with true love's kiss. But when she awoke, she found a world that was hard to understand. Outside of her castle walls, the world had moved on without her. Inside, her life had stayed entirely the same. Frozen in time, Sleeping Beauty's castle and its inhabitants had not progressed one day.

Although we may not seriously compare ourselves to legendary fairy-tale princesses (well, maybe once in a while), as women, we do often occupy two opposing worlds—one that has progressed forward and allows us so many opportunities, and another that is still frozen in time and sees us as passive observers of our own destinies.

As I mentioned before, I grew up around women who were opinionated and outspoken, women who were educated, and women who were successful professionals. Today, success for women is more attainable than ever before. Women are better educated, have better jobs, and honestly, are even more outspoken. So why is it that in the financial industry, we are still not being heard?

One Hundred Years Ago . . . and Now

Let's take a detour. Hop in a time machine, take your seat, fasten your seat belt, and let's take a ride through a quick historical timeline. Better yet—put on your *Titanic*-inspired dress, and let's stroll down memory lane. You won't have Leonardo DiCaprio coming to rescue you from freezing cold reality with a floating board; you will have to face the cold, hard truth on your own—good or bad.

The last one hundred years have made an enormous difference in the daily lives of women. Though many women had already started working outside of the home by the twentieth century, until the 1960s, they had no real protection in their workplaces. Laws were eventually passed to "protect" women, but they often did so by keeping women away from supervisory positions. In the last hundred years, lawmakers have increasingly worked to protect women's rights in the workplace in a more real and productive way. I'm guessing that's a result of the most important change of the last one hundred years—a woman's right to vote! With more women voters came more attention to issues unique to them and their financial lives. In the early 1960s, for example, the Equal Pay Act and Civil Rights Act promised women equal access to jobs and, when they got those jobs, equal pay for the same work as a man (a promise that's only been about 80 percent achieved).[2] And more recently, the Lilly Ledbetter Act of 2009 further strengthened the ability of women to seek better protections when it comes to gender pay inequality.[3]

Women like Lilly—women who fought so hard, but in so many cases, unfortunately weren't able to correct their own situations—raised a loud enough voice to give others a better opportunity in the future. What women like Lilly were telling the world was, "Give me back my purse! I'm not giving you my money! I'm not going to work hard for less, just because I'm a woman, and you can't steal from me just because you think it's ok!" And although the Lilly Ledbetter Act of 2009 was passed only a few years ago, many things have changed for women when it comes to money, especially if we go even further back and compare how things have changed. For one thing, the way a woman deals with her money has changed significantly in the last century. When you get a paycheck, you probably don't even think about the fact that you have complete control over what happens to the money you have earned. You might direct deposit it, divert some to a savings account, decide to buy an astonishing amount of delicious-smelling bath beads at your local Sephora (hey, you *earned* it!), or lump it all into a wad of cash and stick it under your mattress. The point is that today, whatever you choose to do with your money is *your* choice. That's because the law is on your side—today. But a hundred years ago that wasn't the case. Forget about being able to spend your money how you'd like; before the twentieth century, married women weren't even considered individuals! The way it used to work was like this: When a woman got married, she fell under the coverture laws, which essentially created a single family unit where the woman had absolutely no legal voice.[4] In the eyes of the law, she was considered her husband's dependent and was treated like one.

If you think that was a long time ago, think again; in Texas, until the late 1960s, the laws were written in such a way that they gave a husband sole control over any money earned by his wife.[5] While single women may have been a bit better off, married women, even in the late twentieth century, have been consistently considered totally incapable of managing their own financial destiny. That destiny was placed squarely in the hands of their husbands, to the extent that if a wife was going to be hired, an employer technically had the legal obligation to ask the husband's permission.

You might be thinking at this point, *Ugh! A history lesson? Jeez! What's next? Are we going to review geometry as well? Why is Crystal talking about all this stuff anyway? It was all a long time ago . . . definitely before Facebook: Of course the attitudes were old-fashioned and sexist.* Well, the reason it's important is because we have to understand how history shaped attitudes toward women, but even more importantly, we have to understand how history shaped women's attitudes toward themselves. Although it's sometimes unbelievable how far we've come in such a short time, in many ways, things have stayed much the same.

As far as industry and the law, we are definitely worlds ahead of where we used to be. Women can own property. We can take out loans and establish credit in our own names, married or single, without answering to anyone. We have the legal right to start a business, and many of us do. In fact, women own 29 percent of all businesses in the US, a percentage that has seen a huge increase over the last two decades.[6] And now, in 2017, the head of the Small Business Administration is—you guessed it—a woman. Women have definitely come a long way from the days of coverture laws.

But the problem that remains comes from the fact that laws are much easier to change than attitudes, and some attitudes are still frozen in time, like Sleeping Beauty's castle and its inhabitants.

Still Frozen in Time

The road to equality and to a real change in attitudes has been difficult to pave, and would still be a small trail if it weren't for the likes of Marie Curie, who won the Nobel Prize in 1911 for her work with radiation; Amelia Earhart, who flew across the Atlantic; Frances Perkins, who served as FDR's Secretary of Labor and the first female Cabinet member; Valentina Tereshkova, a Russian civilian cosmonaut who became the first woman to orbit the Earth; and Sandra Day O'Connor, the first woman to sit on America's highest court. Many other trailblazers helped break old stereotypes about what a woman could do. Throughout history, literally "binders full of women" bravely challenged expectations, traditions, and critics—and they did these things at a time when it wasn't acceptable for a woman to stray too far from the kitchen. Their sacrifices and toughness are what got us to this point in time, where more and more women are becoming doctors, lawyers, professors, soldiers, scientists—and they continue to push the boundaries of what is considered acceptable for a woman to do with her life. Now, a new generation of women moves even further ahead.

Think about this: In 2010, nearly half of all law students were women,[7] and 34 percent of practicing physicians were female.[8] Three women now sit on the United States Supreme Court, three women have served as Secretary of State, female CEOs head up Fortune 500 companies, and women can be found in every profession from the ranks of the military to the halls of government. It's mind-boggling how many changes have taken place in such a relatively short period of time. The next several decades will probably be an even more amazing ride, as women continue challenging traditions and building a completely different world for the next generation.

But attitudes can take a long time to change, because we learn so many of our values when we're young, and these worldviews, even if misguided, shape our perceptions of what we can and cannot do. I remember when I was a kid playing make-believe with my cousins who, by the way, were almost all boys (I have over twenty cousins and only four are girls!). We would sit around and play one of those silly games where we would guess what we would become when we grew up, and I would always yell out, "Financial advisor!" Ok, just kidding . . . I didn't really say that. I would say that I wanted to be an astronaut. Something about space always fascinated me; I've watched every *Star Trek* episode. But in any case, whenever I would say it, my cousins would burst out laughing, saying that girls couldn't be astronauts. Of course, we were only kids at the time, and it was a silly game. But it's amazing how day by day, the things that all of us children heard at school and on TV shaped our attitudes, and we weren't even out of elementary school yet! Even in my early twenties, when I was certain that I would work in the financial field, some of my family members tried to discourage me because they didn't think it was a woman's job, and they didn't think anyone would take me seriously. This wasn't a hundred years ago, by the way.

These same attitudes continue to affect us on a daily basis, even when we're all grown up. Let's be truly honest for a moment: Even if you have a great job where you're happy, and even though no one can tell you what to do with your life, you probably have the same attitude toward your finances as your grandmother had. I mean, sure, you've probably got a 401(k), you've got your bank account and your credit cards, and when you go to the mall, no one tells you whether you're allowed to buy something. But for most women, that's pretty much where their money confidence stops. Like my grandma, and my mother's friend who lost her husband early, women still don't often get involved in the big picture when it comes to their wealth. I see this problem on a daily basis, and it's true for women of all walks of life.

Choosing to Be the Scullery Maid

We all know the Cinderella story. It's a part of our cultural consciousness. Cinderella loved her father, and her father saw the greatness in his daughter, whose mother had died. Determined to give her everything he could, he decided that what she really needed was a mother—someone to help her grow up into a strong woman. So he married a woman who had two daughters of her own. But rather than creating a happy, blended group, à la the Brady family, this fairy-tale marriage instead created a literal family feud (talk about a reality show!). The death of Cinderella's father made everything even worse, as she was permanently separated from the inheritance that was rightfully hers and was forced to work as a scullery maid. Cinderella only escaped this horrible situation by means of a glass slipper and a prince with a lot of determination and time on his hands.

Imagine instead a world where Cinderella had legal access to her inheritance and the gumption to go after it. Instead of sleeping in the attic and cleaning toilets, Cinderella might have drawn up an eviction notice for her stepmonster and taken back her room from her stepsisters. She would be managing her father's estate, hiring and supervising staff, and interacting with that determined prince as a landowner rather than as a desperate and penniless maid. But that's about as far from our comfort zone as we can get. Updated versions of this fairy-tale, even the ones that embrace a strong Cinderella, only let her near her money when some twist of fate convinces her that she deserves it.

Cinderella's sad tale of financial desperation isn't that far-fetched. Historically, women have always been at the mercy of the men in their lives, which led to real situations of poverty and hopelessness. So it makes sense that a woman's fear of being victimized by someone who has access to her money would become a kind of cultural Big Bad Wolf. Mixed fairy-tale metaphor aside, the fear at the heart of all of these bedtime stories has ironically become a self-fulfilling prophecy. The truth is that we really could be evicting, land-owning, smart-aleck Cinderellas, because the law is now on our side. Yet we keep choosing to remain scullery maids, leaving our glass slippers in the closet, apparently waiting for a later, better occasion to put them on. Since we all know there's no time like the present to wear a fabulous pair of shoes, this failure to act must be rooted in something much deeper. Either we still don't believe ourselves capable or we don't see how separated from our financial lives we truly are, but women simply do not take control of their money the way they can and *should*.

If you doubt this, I challenge you to ask a few girlfriends, neighbors, or coworkers about who handles their investments. I bet you anything you will hear mostly these three things: "Oh, my husband does it. I don't worry about that," or "Oh, I have my accountant for that," or "Oh, I have an advisor who handles my investments." Rarely will you hear, "I am in charge of my entire financial picture. I have an accountant who *helps* me with my taxes, and I have hired a financial advisor to *help* me grow my portfolio according to *my* goals. I ask my husband for his opinion from time to time, but I'm the one who makes the decisions about all my investments." That would be a rare answer and one you most likely will not get. Finding women who are *that* attuned to their finances is like looking for unicorns. Even if you *think* they exist somewhere, you can't be sure because you've never seen one. Trust me. Test it out, ask around, and make a list of the answers you get!

Scenes from Our Childhoods

A big part of financial hesitation on the part of women comes from growing up surrounded by cultural messages and family traditions that taught us how to deal with our money. Fairy tales and folk tales used stories about wolves, giants, and ogres as a way of subconsciously dealing with fears and worries. But in the process, these stories tried to teach women how to look, act, and behave. Nowadays, instead of fairy tales, we have television, which tries to tell us, over and over and in varied ways, how we should behave as women in society.

What do we see? Well, the quintessential portrayal of a woman and her money-managing abilities is Lucy Ricardo, who stays home (even before having children) and seems totally incapable of managing the small household budget that Ricky gives her. She's constantly overdrawing their account, spending frivolously, and receiving lectures from her husband about the need to be financially responsible (poor guy, he suffered so much). And when she really screwed up, Ricky didn't hesitate to give her a well-deserved spanking. Because that's how a grown woman should be treated by her much more intelligent husband: like a child. Because how else will she learn, right?

Portrayals of female business owners like Harriet Oleson on the incredibly popular show *Little House on the Prairie* often saw women constantly supervised and reined in by a long-suffering husband who was clearly more of the "adult" and had the cooler head for business. When we see women on TV today who are solely responsible for their family's financial success, their story usually involves a lot of hand-wringing and anxiety about how little they earn and how they're trying to make ends meet. Rarely are we presented with an example of a woman who seems to have the financial savvy or know-how to secure the resources she needs to get her financial act together.

In the same way, our childhood experiences taught us how women should interact with money. Maybe Dad went to work while Mom stayed at home, and because he earned the money, he made the financial decisions. It may have even seemed to us like Mom didn't care, so the lesson we learned was that we didn't need to be involved either. You likely didn't have in-depth financial talks at home, and your sole interaction with money as an impressionable child was probably a weekly allowance that was spent as quickly as possible on something completely frivolous. We may look back at those financial decisions with a mixture of envy and amusement—how excited we were to buy a tube of lipstick or a new magazine! How nice it was to have made money to spend on things we can't justify anymore! Our lifelong attitude toward money began early, and those lessons continue to influence our behavior to this day.

Recognizing Our Self-Fulfilling Prophecy

You look around at a world full of smart, savvy investors who are making the most of their money and wonder why you're not one of them. Trust me—many women share your feeling of financial disconnection and the feeling that their financial future is at the mercy of a crazy, volatile stock market, a sluggish economy, or an inaccessible advisor. (And they say women have mood swings! Someone seriously needs to talk to Wall Street!)

If in the last hundred years women have come a long way, one thing that still hasn't changed is a woman's lack of confidence about her own financial savvy. Like Sleeping Beauty's castle, in this area we've been unfortunately pretty much standing still. We are like a girl who knows in her heart that she can ride the bicycle all on her own but is still afraid to take the training wheels off. The financial industry has not made much effort to include us or ask us to be more involved. And why would they? After all, the financial industry is made up of people who grew up with the same male/female stereotypes as you did.

And when you *do* feel motivated to act in your financial life, ask yourself what reception you receive. Think for a minute about the last few major financial decisions you've made. Maybe you bought something big, like a car, a boat, or a house. People often joke about taking a man along when a woman is going to purchase a car so she'll get a better deal. "They'll see you coming from a mile away," someone snickers. I don't think a guy would need to take a woman along in order to be taken seriously. These kinds of attitudes drive me absolutely crazy, precisely because of how common they are and the fact that they are still perfectly acceptable. In fact, most of the time they're brushed off as some comical fact of life.

Trying to Take Control—and Failing

When women do talk to financial advisors (because they've decided to finally get some answers to their questions and tackle the uncertainty surrounding their financial situations), the reception they get is often very different than the attention and respect given to their male counterparts. Imagine for a minute that you visit your advisor's office

tomorrow with specific questions about the performance of your investments. Maybe you're concerned that you are not getting a large enough
return, or you want to be sure that you and your husband can retire early
enough to enjoy some years together and pursue your dreams. Instead of
showing you concrete numbers about your investments and their rates
of return (whether to encourage you to stick with them or to encourage you to adopt a different strategy), you'll probably end up getting a
broad explanation of what's going on with your portfolio, and hear that
you shouldn't worry so much because you have left your money in capable hands. Coffee and condescension, all in one short visit—until you're
back for a free refill of both the next time around.

Now that's efficiency for you!

The conversations below are those I've heard women recount over
the years about what happened to them during their visits to their financial advisors. I want you to imagine the following scenarios, play them in
your head, and ask yourself whether the reception you would get would
be all that different.

Mary's Story

This is a story from a woman named Mary, who describes an interaction
typical of those that took place when she and her husband would visit
their advisor.

> **Advisor:** Good to see you, Mr. Thomas! Did you see the stock mar-
> ket numbers today? Wow! What a day we had!
>
> **Mr. Thomas:** Hi, Bob [advisor]. Oh yeah . . . My goodness, Apple
> is just rocking.

(By the way, both sides are using typical meaningless jargon.)

> **Advisor:** So good to see you, Mrs. Thomas! Nice that you wanted
> to be a part of this.

(*Really?* "Part of this"? Umm . . . Earth to Bob: It's Mrs. Thomas's money
too . . . and her life . . . and her retirement. Heck, yeah, she wants to be
"a part of this"!)

Mrs. Thomas: Hi, Bob. So how is our portfolio doing?

Advisor: Oh great, really great. So Mr. Thomas, do you want to buy some more Apple shares?

Mr. Thomas: Well, you know, Bob, I'm not sure. Maybe I should just stick to what we have.

Advisor: True, but let's think about this: Apple is always good and I feel it going even higher. They're number one in the industry!

Mrs. Thomas: Umm, Bob, so what do you mean we are doing great? Are we on track with retirement? What's the plan?

Advisor: Oh, don't worry, Mrs. Thomas. We've got it all handled . . . [smile] . . . So, Mr. Thomas, back to Apple . . .

This may sound comical and you may be laughing, either a cynical laugh because you know exactly what Mary went through, or maybe a "No way!" laugh, because you're thinking that in this day and age such situations can't be real! *Crystal must be joking. This never happens anymore; not now!* Well, unfortunately, I've heard many versions of this situation—over and over again—and they *are* happening regularly, to women of all backgrounds. Their education level or how far they've gotten in their careers doesn't matter. Their only common thread is that they're women—women who kept trying to take more control of their finances, but whose efforts were as disregarded as those of some pesky Lucy Ricardo!

Let's look at another typical scenario.

Sandy's Story

Advisor: Hi, Sandy. How are you? So I heard you wanted to see me?

Sandy: Hi, Bob. I wanted to see you today because I wanted to reevaluate my portfolio. I'm concerned about whether it may be too risky because of all the recent news, and at this point I need to see if I am on track.

Advisor: Oh, don't worry about what they say on the news, that's not relevant to you, and you know we are on track.

Sandy: Actually, Bob, I am really not sure what my portfolio consists of at this point.

Advisor: Ha ha! Sandy, you know . . . mutual funds . . . and bond funds and some REITs. Typical, run-of-the-mill stuff we talked about before.

Sandy: Well, I know that, but I'm not sure how risky they are . . . and . . . [feeling uncomfortable that he is laughing and wondering, *Should I already know all this? Is this my fault?*].

Advisor: Well, they were based on that questionnaire that we did at the beginning. Don't you remember, Sandy? Ha ha! I know it's been awhile, but we did it . . .

Sandy: I know, Bob, but I'm not sure what I answered, and I can't really read my statements correctly as far as the fees and so forth . . . [feeling awkward at this point].

Advisor: Sandy, you know the fees. They have not changed since you started, and we manage your account diligently and everybody's portfolio goes up and down. You have to be able to have a tough stomach or you won't have any earnings. This is normal. Don't worry. Just let me handle it. We know what we are doing. Don't you trust me anymore? We've known each other for years now. Come on, Sandy . . .

(This is typical behavior, I may add.)

Sandy: Umm . . . Of course I trust you, Bob [not really . . .], but I was just wondering, I want to make sure I can retire according to my goals and needs . . . [feeling completely thrown off and guilty at this point].

Advisor: Don't you worry, we have it covered. You will have an amazing retirement!

If this hasn't happened to you, consider yourself lucky. And I really mean that. But I challenge you to ask your friends, your family, or your colleagues about their recent experiences. I bet you'll find that about one of every three women has experienced these feelings of dismissal, and that one of those women will be in your immediate circle.[9]

By the way, if you ever want to test out how seriously your advisor is taking your ideas, research an investment product that you think is a good fit for you, and then ask your advisor about it. If they give you alternative solutions, ask them why the solution they are suggesting is better than the one you came up with. If they don't give reasons *why* your idea is worse but go into extolling the virtues of whatever they suggested, you will quickly know that they immediately brushed off your suggestion without taking the time to understand what you wanted.

Mirror, Mirror on the Wall, Who Is Responsible for It All?

The most famous mirror in fairy-tale history, of course, is the one owned by the Evil Queen in "Snow White." Enchanted, the mirror had to repeatedly answer the Queen's now-famous question: "Mirror, mirror, on the wall, who's the fairest of them all?" Stroking her ego, and not wanting to get shattered with a brick, the mirror told the Evil Queen that, of course, she was the fairest. Who wouldn't love a mirror like that? A constant self-esteem boost and fashion advisor in one. I'll sign up now! But the Evil Queen only wanted to hear that preprogrammed response, and when she didn't hear it, she was unwilling to accept the reality of her situation.

In contrast, in the story of "Beauty and the Beast," when the Beast gave Belle an enchanted mirror so she could see her home once more, Belle saw the hard, uncomfortable truth. Far from the happy, thriving home she remembered and desperately wanted to see once again, the home she saw in that enchanted hand mirror was run down, and her once cheerful father was sick and lost without her. The magic that she found was the ability to see the truth—and then to do something about it. Yes, the truth was unpleasant, and yes, taking action wasn't easy. But without being honest with yourself, can you be truly happy?

Let's not be like the Evil Queen. Our mirror is not telling us we're the most beautiful or fashionable; our mirror is telling us that the relationship we have with our finances, detached and disconnected, is someone else's responsibility. And even worse, it's telling us that this is ok!

When it comes to the financial industry, many advisors aren't purposely evading questions or keeping their clients in the dark (some bad seeds may be, but most advisors are normal people). They, like you, have simply been immersed in the quicksand of the status quo. But that doesn't change the negative consequences of such attitudes on you.

Advisors have not seen any reason to change because most women haven't demanded to be heard, and the advisors have grown up in the same culture of "Dad takes care of the finances." So there's nothing truly pushing them to change their attitudes, because despite all of our progress, and the fact that we make up about half of the workforce,[10] women still often feel incapable of investing or managing their own money. They feel they have no option but to hand this responsibility over and that they have to accept the direction that someone else feels is best for them.

So what do we do now? Where is the path to money confidence? How can we find a true sense of empowerment? A woman with money confidence is free from the spells of witches and stepmonsters. She can clearly see her kingdom, and nothing will keep her from going after it.

Well, I would start with my favorite saying, which is—as you know by now—"when it comes to your money, toughen up!" Then, let's get to a real solution. It's time for us (you, me, all women) to claim our financial responsibility and change society's perception of women when it comes to our investment needs and the relationships we want with financial professionals. That means everything from refusing to laugh at stupid "Oh, you should take your husband with you or you'll get ripped off" jokes to simply investing more energy into taking care of our finances. These changes of attitude can't be legislated into our daily lives—they have to start with taking deliberate steps to gain confidence and reshape these attitudes. And the first place to start doing that is within ourselves.

I still hear my mom laughing and saying, "Why do I need to do all this? That is what I have your dad for." Nope. Not funny, Mom. Can you imagine if my twelve-year-old nephew heard this? What would he think of his future wife if she decided to be in charge of her own finances? How would he raise his daughter if he had one? We all have people in our own circle who grew up with these attitudes. But now it's time for them to change.

The Happily Ever After Starts with You

The bottom line is that if your financial advisor doesn't know your priorities (either because you feel uncomfortable sharing them or because he or she is not listening), then you are likely to end up with a result you don't want. As women's wealth and spending power increase, and life expectancies continue to rise, so will the need for solid financial plans. It's unavoidable. And no matter how much you trust your instincts, no matter how on the ball you are in other areas of your life, you need to be sure that your financial plan will get you where you want to be in your retirement.

The first step in gaining true money confidence is to abandon the worry that you'll offend an advisor by questioning their suggestions. It's time to abandon the idea that you don't have the right to clear, timely information when you ask for it. Somehow, we've grown up with the idea that when women want something done, they have to negotiate or charm their way into success. "You'll catch more flies with honey than with vinegar," they tell us. If you're an exterminator, maybe this advice is worthwhile. But who else is interested in catching flies? I don't know about you, but I want to get rid of those disgusting insects! So if you're a woman looking to steer her own financial course, then abandon the baking ingredients and make sure your financial professional is listening to what you have to say. It's your money, not a recipe for a scone. And if a more aggressive attitude is what it takes to get the results you need and to create the relationship you want with your advisor, then forget about being Miss Goody Two-Shoes—you need to toughen up!

This approach, by the way, goes for every other aspect of your life where money is involved. Whether it's buying a car or a house, applying for a loan, or negotiating your salary,[11] demanding respect can go a long way. Unfortunately, when a woman does demand respect, her tenacity is usually attributed to her being a bitch. When a guy is rude and says whatever he wants, he's called a "tough negotiator," but when a woman does the same thing, she is often characterized as a bitch. So, if I remember high school algebra correctly, I can set up this equation as follows: If women are equal to men (Women = Men), and in the same situation Man = Tough Negotiator while Woman = Bitch, then Bitch = Tough Negotiator. And by that formula, the logical conclusion is that if you want to be an even *tougher* negotiator, then you have to be an even bigger bitch. Math *is* fun!

And you know what? Honestly, bitch is a word that guys use when they don't have a real point to argue, can't come up with a valid reason to prove you wrong, but don't want to admit you're right. So they either blurt it out or think it, while rolling their eyes, as a way to make *themselves* feel better when they can't come up with a valid rebuttal. So if you happen to be in a situation where someone either dares to call you that or is obviously thinking it, then that's your validation that what you're saying is 100 percent correct.

Things to Keep in Mind

It is time for us to step up and be heard—first by ourselves, and then by society. Our new, changed attitudes can make it happen.

In the last hundred years, women have gained legal rights and social acceptance, and now we can seize complete control of our financial destinies. We have rights that were nothing more than a fantasy for hundreds of millions of women, for thousands of years. Yet, our complicated history of forced alienation from our finances, along with a cultural message that women were/are incapable of successful money management, has left women detached from our financial lives. This detachment led to similar inaction in financial professionals, who often see their female clients as a bunch of Lucy Ricardos, incapable of making intelligent decisions, and definitely not to be taken seriously. It's a perplexing, frustrating cycle, and one that only we can change through regular action and involvement in our finances.

The reality is that even though we now have extensive legal rights, women have remained complacent about their own money. In almost every other area of women's lives, they have demanded attention and forced change—in law, in politics, in healthcare—but in this key area, they are mostly mute. If women are going to take control of their own financial futures, if we are going to teach the next generation of girls that managing their money is indeed *their* responsibility, then we must step up and demand the attention and respect of the financial professionals in our lives—whether it's your financial advisor, the manager at your local bank, or your CPA.

It's time to be the gutsy Aurora, a sleeping beauty who prefers the modern world to her ancient kingdom; or the ingenious Rapunzel[12] who comes up with a battle plan, cuts off her hair, and makes a rope out of it to escape her tower. Stepping up and taking control of your own finances is not only possible, it's necessary. You can make your own fairy-tale ending, but you have to believe in yourself enough to try.

Chapter 5

WALL STREET VILLAINS

"If the lessons of history teach us anything,
it is that nobody learns the lessons that history teaches us."
—André Gide

I remember when I first set foot on Wall Street in New York. I was twelve years old, and I remember how excited my dad was when he was telling me all about it. "Oh honey, this is where all the action happens," he told me. He couldn't wait to show me the trading floor of the exchange. We went on a tour, and of course, it was a really interesting experience—for my dad. *Me*? I was confused about all the commotion, the excitement, and the yelling and screaming of the traders! Being a kid, I didn't fully understand what was going on. I thought it was one big playground where adults could scream and yell at each other and throw papers on the floor because they were excited about something! "Tag! You're it! You own this stock now! Ha ha! Now, try to tag me back and see if I'll buy those shares again at the same price!" It's ironic how innocent and fun it all looks from the outside, but in reality it can devastate lives with a push of a button or a crumpled piece of paper that is tossed away.

The glamorous kingdom of Wall Street—full of villains, ogres, and dragons, all cleverly disguised as handsome princes and brave heroes. With all the hype, glamour, and crafty deceit, it is extremely easy to be lulled into a false sense of security in the middle of such a wonderland. But you never know when your precious nest egg is going to be cracked open, cooked, and eaten by an ugly ogre. If only there were a warning sign big enough to actually see: "Enter at your own risk, no nest egg security guard on duty."

In this dazzling world of Wall Street, if we believe the blockbuster movie starring Michael Douglas by the same name,[13] we seem to have an unhealthy fascination with what we see as sexy. "Sexy" in the sense of the huge gains that are dangled like carrots in front of us; "sexy" as in wanting to be a part of that alluring and often impenetrable world where the big dogs play; and "sexy" as in the feeling of power and importance that comes from being part owner of a national or multinational business.

Most of us are too busy being captivated by the glory to notice the ugly monsters hiding behind the scenes. And over the years there have been plenty of these scoundrels lurking in the shadows. Let's revisit some of the once-upon-a-time, ugliest characters of Wall Street—those villains disguised as heroes.

We'll start by traveling back in time only a few years to consider a story that many of you will be familiar with. It's the story of Bernie Madoff, or as I like to refer to him, "The Prince of Madness."

In March of 2009, Bernard Madoff admitted to having defrauded thousands of investors of billions of dollars in a ridiculously massive Ponzi scheme. Although most of us are probably familiar with this story, it's important to understand exactly what a Ponzi scheme is. Let me try to explain it simply, because it really is quite simple. The Ponzi master, who outwardly appears to be a highly intelligent and enigmatic prince, convinces his subjects to jump on board the latest and greatest investment opportunity. And although these investors are not his subjects (as no one forces them to invest), they become beholden to the prince because he makes it appear he has figured out a way to consistently make money without too much risk. Of course, the prince never shares the details of his strategy, which makes him even more enigmatic.

By promising either excessively high returns with little risk or remarkably stable returns, he lures his faithful subjects into his evil scheme. After the first subjects invest, the prince fakes account statements showing sizable returns on investment, and even gives cash payouts to these investors to make the scheme look more real. But, of course, the payments aren't made from any actual investment growth, but from the investors' own money that they gave the prince originally. Investors see their account balances increasing and some nice payouts, and they think, *Wow, this prince must be using a magic spell! I still have my original principal in my account, and the prince gave me a nice chunk of money because he was able to earn a great return on my original investment.* What the subjects *don't* realize is that although the cash they received is real, the account balances shown on their paper statements are completely fake, because that money doesn't exist. They just got some of their own money back, and nothing else!

Of course, no one was screaming, "Give me back my purse! I'm not giving you my money!" Instead, the loyal subjects tell their friends and family about the wonderful investment they have found with the unbelievable returns, and encourage them to become investors, too. What drives this scheme are two things: The original investor wants to do something nice for his or her family and friends, and the original investor also wants to have some of the prince's enigmatic appeal rub off on him or her as well. The original investor wants to be regarded as being "in the know," like he originally regarded the prince. This works wonders for the evil prince's advantage: Instead of having to continue working hard on his image, his loyal first investor's subjects will do the work for him. They will sing his praise to anyone who will listen, free of charge.

The scheme continues, with the new investors' contributions being used to make dividend payments to the previous investors, and so on. Inevitably the scheme master uses some of the money to make himself look more impressive and believable—bigger castles (his offices), more servants (his assistants), and the finest clothes other people's money can buy. For this pseudo-prince, the beauty of a scheme like this is that his subjects' human nature plays right into his hands, and the human desire to be perceived as intelligent and special will sustain his ruse for a long time.

When his investors (who might as well now be his disciples) tell their friends about the amazing opportunity, and their friends express doubt, the investors will vehemently defend the prince, even if the deceit is obvious. Why? Because we all want to be in the know, and most of us crave the positive attention that comes from somehow appearing special. And most of all—we *hate* admitting our mistakes. That's human nature; we want to make believe we have something amazing at our fingertips, and even when the ugly truth is right there in plain view, we will sadly deny it so we can hang on to that amazing feeling a little longer (this is called cognitive dissonance). Without this uniquely human quirk, massive Ponzi schemes would be impossible.

Eventually, because all honeymoons end sooner or later, some people do become suspicious and begin to withdraw their account balances. Because the fake prince has to keep up appearances, he will pay their fake balances in full, but with other people's money. At some point, it becomes impossible to pay everyone because there simply isn't enough money available to pay the dividends, pay out account balances, and keep up the prince's lavish lifestyle, and the scheme crumbles in a roaring thud. Some people might get a portion of their money back, but it becomes such a tangled web that people who have invested a large chunk of their wealth are essentially financially ruined.

In some cases, the scheme may collapse earlier if any of the subjects get suspicious or if changes in the economic situation cause the subjects to want a return of their capital sooner. But in most cases, the schemes go unnoticed for too long and the losses are simply unrecoverable because the money has either been spent or hidden from everyone under several layers of untraceable offshore accounts and shell companies.

Let's get back to the Madoff nightmare. He admitted to having started his massive scheme in the early '90s and pled guilty to charges of eleven federal felonies. It was determined he caused an estimated $18 billion in losses to investors. Many believed that in reality his scheme may have begun as early as the 1970s.[14] On June 29, 2009, Bernard Madoff was sentenced to 150 years in prison. His legacy is one of ruined financial futures, ruined lives, and likely ruined marriages that could not handle the stress of such financial disasters.

It's easy for anyone who was not involved in that mess to look back and say, "I would have totally spotted him a million miles away," but as we know, most investors didn't do this. Why do you think that was? Madoff presented himself exactly as we would expect a Wall Street guru would: He had "sexy" illusion and he offered an undeniably attractive get-rich-quick-no-questions-asked adventure. Everyone was so blown away by the promises of stable, double-digit growth that they didn't bother to stop and question the methods of this "Prince Charming" to ask exactly how he was making these incredible profits. Furthermore, his aloof, I-don't-need your-money attitude only added to his allure.

"O, what a tangled web we weave, when first we practice to deceive!"[15] In his tangled web, Madoff's deceit won him even more followers. Followers in the form of high net-worth investors with many insecurities of their own, who lusted after a sense of belonging and VIP status, followers who allowed Madoff's intriguing attitude of "don't ask" make them increasingly want to be a part of that insider club. They didn't care that the Big Bad Wolf was lurking just inside the door to that club, waiting to get them when they least expected it.

So who is to blame? Madoff? Definitely! The misled investors themselves? To a certain degree, because many of them likely did have an inkling that something was off but chose to turn a blind eye to their instincts. What about the banks and the major players involved—those who suspected he was a crook and yet did nothing to stop him? Why didn't they take action? Maybe because it was more expedient to do nothing and profit from the money he was depositing with them (rather than to take heroic action for so many). Or maybe even they began to doubt their own suspicions and didn't want to challenge Madoff on the off chance that somehow their suspicions were incorrect, and that this guy truly did come up with some amazing system to make money. So in the end, it's no surprise that once this house of straw had been huffed and puffed at and all blown away, there wasn't going to be anyone left who was completely blameless.

You may think that Madoff was a new or rare breed, but that is certainly not the case. There have been many villains hidden away in the dark shadows of the Wall Street towers. Let's go back a little further.

A long, long time ago, there was a land far away where swing-like music was heard in every lounge and women smoking cigarettes made a statement. I'm talking about the Jazz Age, the roaring twenties, the era of change, when women first abandoned the restrictions of fashion and embraced the comfort of trousers or shorts for the first time. Yet the times were not as innocent as they seemed. This was the era of the fraud that first gave rise to the term "Ponzi scheme."

Although there had been a few similar schemes before, the first recognized Ponzi scheme belonged to one Charles Ponzi, an infamous swindler. He promised his investors phenomenal returns: 50 percent in forty-five days. He explained that his method involved buying International Reply Coupons ("IRCs") from overseas countries at cheaper prices and selling them in the US. He recruited investors and sales agents who brought in significant amounts of cash ($250,000 per day at one point), and built an image of himself as a confident and savvy businessman. He then used new investors' money to repay earlier investors and to fund an extravagant lifestyle. His scheme lasted less than a year because people quickly began to suspect that something wasn't right. Ponzi was arrested in August of 1920, owing an estimated seven million dollars to investors. He pled guilty to mail fraud and spent fourteen years in prison. Seven million dollars may not seem like a significant amount, but when adjusted for inflation in today's dollars, it's equivalent to about eighty-two million dollars.

What is especially interesting about Charles Ponzi is that he came to this country with a dream. He said, "I landed in this country with $2.50 in cash and $1 million in hopes, and those hopes never left me." They obviously did not, except that instead of working tirelessly for his good fortune, this young immigrant's confidence and charisma ended up helping him pull off one of the greatest financial swindles of the time.

And he got away with it for a while, but at least not as long as some of the ugly villains who followed him, including Madoff.

By the way, these men are by no means the only two villains out there. The list goes on and on. Many, many people have been defrauded over the last century in countless Ponzi schemes of various sizes. For example, David Dominelli defrauded investors out of $80 million in the 1980s and served over a decade in prison. Reed Slatkin, co-founder of EarthLink, cheated the rich and famous out of almost $600 million by creating fake statements and referencing fake brokerage firms. He was caught in 2000. Michael E. Kelly defrauded thousands of people, many of them seniors, out of half a billion dollars, while using their money to buy properties for himself.

As I've said, the thing all these swindlers had in common was a charming and confident personality, which played a big part in the success of their Ponzi schemes. In the world of investments, there are many villains and they come in many shapes and sizes, and somehow they always seem to find some poor suckers who are ready to jump in with both feet. These villains are like magicians who create an illusion, and many smart people choose to believe that illusion. Maybe it's because of a sense of magic. Maybe it's because people misinterpret the saying "Fortune favors the bold" and believe that the opportunity to reach their dreams is finally here and that they have to take the chance no matter what the warning signs are. Or, as we've noted, maybe the people who fall for these schemes are so insecure that being part of some magical illusion gives them a sense of worth and a sense of belonging. This makes these schemes all the more tragic.

The sad thing is that some fairy tales already have prepared us for dealing with situations like Ponzi schemes. Consider the older version of the infamous Little Red Riding Hood story, where she is in fact eaten by the wolf at the end of the story. The dialogue goes like this:

> **Little Red (to the wolf disguised as her grandmother):** What a deep voice you have.
>
> **The wolf:** The better to greet you with.
>
> **Little Red:** Goodness, what big eyes you have.
>
> **The wolf:** The better to see you with.
>
> **Little Red:** And what big hands you have!
>
> **The wolf:** The better to hug you with.
>
> **Little Red:** What a big mouth you have.
>
> **The wolf:** The better to eat you with!

At which point the wolf jumps out of bed and swallows her up. Then he falls fast asleep.

There are some obvious comparisons between the scene in Red Riding Hood's grandmother's house and the scene that has been repeated so many times between the Ponzi villain and the unfortunate potential investor:

> **The unfortunate potential investor:** What a convoluted investment method you have.

The Ponzi villain: The better return you shall have.

The unfortunate potential investor: Goodness, what big and ever increasing gains you pledge me.

The Ponzi villain: The happier you will be with me.

The unfortunate potential investor: And what big promises you make!

The Ponzi villain: The better off you will be.

This is the point in the story where you need to stop and listen to the alarm bells going off in your head, your built-in early warning system. Remember—when something sounds too good to be true, you need to *stop* and *think*. If you have any doubts, kick the "investment opportunity" to the curb before your life goals are eaten alive like poor Little Red Riding Hood (before the original ending of the story was changed to be more palatable and less frightening). In a fairy tale we may have the luxury of being able to change the ending, but in situations like those with Madoff and Ponzi, we most certainly do not!

This is why it's important to never assume that bad things can't or won't happen to you. And I don't mean just Ponzi schemes: I'm also referring to risky investments where the potential gains are heavily promoted and the possibility of losses is glossed over as being almost nonexistent. Be careful of winks and nods that suggest "it's a sure thing," as if the risks are being disclosed because of regulations but aren't that serious. Remember—if it looks too good to be true, it probably is. We all know that in order for us to have a fairy-tale ending we need to save money, accumulate our wealth, and protect our portfolios from huge losses. And we need to get it into our heads that there will be no Prince Charming riding in on a white horse coming to our rescue.

Trust me—most investors who lose money due to bad or risky investments do not have the Securities and Exchange Commission (SEC) knocking on their door to help. There is no one holding a bouquet of roses waiting to give them a big rescue kiss and return their life savings in the form of a check. Most of the time the SEC doesn't even answer the complaints they get—not because they don't care, but because with their limited resources they can only focus on the truly big villains like Madoff.

So it's up to you, the investor, to protect yourself. And as a woman, you have even more obstacles to watch out for and hurdles to clear.

In the glamorous world of Wall Street, you have to remember that what might be considered hot and sexy is not necessarily a good fit for you. Unlike that new pair of the season's trendiest and hottest Louboutin heels, whose only consequence comes at the end of the night when you have to soak your feet in hot water (or possibly rethink your showy investment), you can't simply toss the wrong investments from your portfolio and purchase some new ones. Sometimes it's too late.

So always make sure that you are educated and that you understand the risks associated with growth. Keep your eyes wide open when it comes to the secrets that Wall Street holds. Then you'll stay safe from the witches' spells, the villains' schemes, and the storms associated with collapse, such as the mortgage meltdown that occurred in the not-too-distant past. The lesson here is that the less you know, the easier it will be for crooks to take advantage of you. Women with money confidence will see through these shiny promises built on lies. And you know what they'll do? You got it: They'll keep on moving!

Think about it carefully. When do you think Wall Street insiders first knew about a serious housing bubble and that they could potentially benefit from it by betting *against* the market? Some figured it out as early as 2004.[16] Remember that you can only make money betting against a bubble as it unravels. As far as Wall Street was concerned, if there was room for the bubble to grow, their overwhelming intention was to keep it going. And, of course, that is when the nightmare began. When they saw that the bubble was about to pop, their intentions and methods changed. By 2006, many on Wall Street started massively betting on its collapse.[17]

As all this was going on, what do you think was happening, or starting to happen, to the new homeowners and all the little people who were not insiders? They were starting to drown financially because they, too, got caught up in the real estate frenzy and bought homes at prices they couldn't afford. And the smaller investors who were trying to take advantage of the mortgage industry paid the price for trying to swim with the big fish.

It is truly sad how many investors were so drastically affected by the credit crunch that grew out of the real estate bubble, and it is even worse when you realize that without a doubt, Wall Street saw it and felt it coming. So the best lesson to learn from this is to forget about the big players, and instead think of *you*, the most important investor. In everything you do, you need to know that you are the only one who can keep your money safe and sound. Listen to your instincts and trust your gut feeling.

And if you happen to be like some of the investors I talk to, who compare themselves to Warren Buffett and say, "I listen to Buffett and he says this and that . . . he does this when the market is down . . . and he does that when the market is up . . . ," well, guess what I say? When you have the big bucks that can get you seats on the boards of directors of the companies you invest in, then, and only then, can you invest the Buffett way. For now, be honest with yourself, realize that you're not a big fish, and please start investing appropriately for the size of fish that you are. Because folks who aren't honest with themselves are taking a real chance of being served up on a plate to the sharks of Wall Street. There's no shame in admitting to yourself that you're a smaller fish. In fact, that will separate you from the average investor and will make you an astute decision maker.

Money Confidence 101: Things to Keep in Mind

- Ask questions—lots of them—and do not let any know-it-all "experts" peer-pressure you.

- Watch out for the typical sex appeal of Wall Street—there's nothing sexy about being broke.

- If you decide to swim with the big fish, be aware that you can end up as dinner.

- Never stop taking notice of your gut feeling. In most cases, all of the victim investors had a bad feeling about the bad investment but decided to ignore their instincts.

- Unlike some government agencies, please try to learn from history's mistakes.

- As I like to say, when you dress your size and invest your size is when you look your best!

Most importantly, remember: In the real kingdom of Wall Street, there are a lot more Gordon Gekkos and a lot fewer Bud Foxes[18] (if in fact there are any at all) who are willing to stand up and say, "No more, speak up, and come clean!"

And why is this?

The answer is relatively simple: because money will *always* win on Wall Street because unfortunately, some of the players don't care who they have to use or abuse to get what they want!

And in this kingdom of not-so-righteousness, it's every player for him- and herself. There are no loyalties and no guarantees; there are no princes and most definitely no heroes. There are only investors—only investors with no one to save them but themselves. So be wise about where you invest your money and be mindful about whom you trust.

Be smart and be savvy! And more importantly, toughen up . . . *especially when it comes to Wall Street!*

PART TWO

DOES THE
GLASS SLIPPER FIT?

Chapter 6

THE TALE OF TIMID-ELLA

"Beware of false knowledge; it is more dangerous than ignorance."
—George Bernard Shaw

I n a faraway land, many years ago, there lived a fair maiden by the name
of . . . let's call her "Timid-Ella." Through a friend, she was introduced
to a financial advisor who she thought was a real Prince Charming.

Now, Timid-Ella was an intelligent woman who had built a successful career and was an otherwise confident, well-rounded person but who
became very, shall we say, timid when it came to insisting on real answers
from her financial advisor/prince. And how could she not feel a bit intimidated? After all, he had everything you could imagine! He had a fantastic
castle (his office), had great servants (his assistants), and he talked the
talk, walked the walk, and constantly showed off all the big portfolios he
was handling. "Oh, yes, Timid-Ella, I'm handling the duke's portfolio,
and I gave the earl a great stock tip, and I even attended a conference
where the keynote speaker was the oracle of the magical lands of Omaha,
by the name of Warren Buffett! I am definitely quite important! Now let's
take a quick look at your portfolio . . . "

This pseudo-prince even repeatedly told Timid-Ella that her
account was way too small. He told her she was not the same caliber as
the people he usually did business with, but that he did business with
her anyway because she was his friend. Poor Timid-Ella felt pretty sad
that her account wasn't large enough; but she always felt gratitude to the
prince because he was taking care of her accounts even though he was of

royalty and she was obviously only a tiny fish in a big pond. *What a nice fellow that prince is,* Timid-Ella would think. *There he is, such an educated, confident man, who knows all about the markets. He doesn't even need my tiny account, yet he's taking time out of his busy day to help me.*

So, understandably, Timid-Ella felt awkward pressing for answers about her investments, because the prince would purposely use unnecessarily sophisticated lingo when explaining them, and she would still be confused afterward. This made her uncomfortable, and she either felt too embarrassed or too frustrated to ask for more clarification. But it wasn't all her fault. When she did ask the prince questions regarding account fees, or how risky her investments might be, or tried to talk about her financial goals to see if her portfolio was on track for *her* future, the prince always did pretty much the same thing: He would look at her with the same comically dismissive smile—the kind usually reserved for silly questions from little children—and would proceed to briefly explain things in general terms. The moment Timid-Ella appeared even slightly confused, he would stop his explanations and say it was his job to manage her money. He told Timid-Ella not to worry and that she should stick to what she was good at. He would then proceed to tell her he had everything under control and would suggest that it was silly for her to ask any more questions about these things, as it would simply confuse her since she wasn't a professional. This would make Timid-Ella feel silly, almost as if she were interfering with a doctor during surgery, so she would tell herself there probably wasn't anything to worry about anyway, because the prince was a professional and she shouldn't meddle so much. Even worse, sometimes she would feel guilty (yes, *guilty!*) and humbled, thinking that because the prince was kind enough to take care of her small nest egg, she should not be questioning him or his methods because he had to have been an expert, at least based on how confident he was.

After some time, Timid-Ella stopped questioning and would leave the prince's castle not understanding what she was planning for her future. Even though that little voice inside her head called *woman's intuition* told her that something didn't feel right, she stayed with the prince for many years, hoping things would somehow work themselves out.

Sadly, many years later, after contributing more and more money into her retirement account, Timid-Ella made a startling discovery. After the markets became highly volatile and after yet another investment bubble, her portfolio experienced a significant decline in value. "How could this have happened?" she exclaimed. "Wasn't the prince looking after my interests?" With huge losses so close to retirement, Timid-Ella grew furious. Finally, after many previously missed opportunities to set things right, she became angry enough with the prince to confront him and obtain real answers—because walking away and hoping for the best was simply no longer an option. After learning all the details, she realized that all this time she had been invested in a way that she never intended to be. The investments in her portfolio were too risky for her age and were significantly beyond her comfort level. Finally, she realized that the prince was never a prince at all. He wasn't even a court jester. He was simply an ugly toad who got along in life through blatant confidence but little actual concern about what his clients wanted.

As she kicked herself for being so complacent about these issues before, she also faced the sad truth that it was now unfortunately too late to fix anything. She was simply too close to retirement, and there was not enough time to wait for a market recovery. Too late for her fairy godmother to save her. Her portfolio had turned into a pumpkin, and there was nothing she could do about it.

Sadly, this fairy tale is based on the true story of a woman I met at one of my seminars. I won't reveal her name, but the moral of this sad tale is that when it comes to your financial security, you simply can't afford to act like a Timid-Ella!

Unfortunately, her situation is a common one, and many women get sucked into a bad relationship with their financial advisors because they don't feel like they can speak up. Either they don't feel confident enough to demand answers or they slowly get bullied into feeling insecure about their decision-making abilities. The consequences to their portfolios can be devastating because their financial plan doesn't match what they wanted for their futures.

The only way to avoid a disaster is to ask questions, lots of questions, when you see your financial advisor. You are smart enough to understand what you are invested in; it may take a little effort, but it's definitely a lot easier than brain surgery—and you won't faint from the sight of blood (unless your portfolio is bleeding losses from an overly risky allocation). When working with a financial advisor, don't blindly invest in things you don't understand. Always ask questions until you are clear about *any* investment features. Building your money confidence will give you the courage to get a second opinion.

It is essential that you form a productive relationship with your advisor so their experience will help you brainstorm ideas for your financial future and take the right steps to get you to your goals.

Chapter 7

WAKE UP, SLEEPING BEAUTY!

"He that is good for making excuses is seldom good for anything else."
—Benjamin Franklin

H ave you ever fallen asleep and dreamt that you were being chased, or in some other scary situation where you're trying to run away or hide, and in the dream you're trying to say something, to scream out for help, but you can't speak? You're trying so hard to say something, but all that comes out is either complete silence or a barely audible whisper. Then you wake up in a cold sweat, trying to make sure it was all a dream, and saying, "Thank goodness" it wasn't real.

It's Time to Wake Up!

These dreams are like situations where someone is in a bad relationship with an advisor but feels powerless to do anything about it. They feel like they can't speak up and can't run fast enough to get away from the nightmare. But in this case, the bad dream isn't a dream at all; it's reality, with genuine feelings of fear and helplessness—fear that comes from having uncertainty about the future, and helplessness that comes from feelings of having no control over your situation. Unfortunately, when people in these situations wake up, the harsh reality does set in, but by then it's a little too late because they have lost their financial security. You see, losing your financial security is not like losing a wallet. A wallet gets lost all at once, in a moment of carelessness. But losing financial security is something that happens over time. A person gets chance after chance after chance to fix the situation and speak up, but for whatever reason they can't bring themselves to take action; their voice is a faint whisper. Eventually, they cross a point in their life when taking action may help somewhat, but if the damage has been done, there will simply be no time to rebuild their finances and recover from mistakes.

Over the years, I've had the opportunity to meet with many women who came from various walks of life and have achieved various degrees of professional and financial success. Some of them were entrepreneurs, some were teachers, nurses, doctors, homemakers, lawyers—you name it (although I've never yet met a woman astronaut). And the one thing I've noticed over and over again is that no matter how successful a woman may be, most of the time it is difficult for her to stay in control of professional relationships that involve her finances. It's quite fascinating, and this trend has baffled me for many years. I could not, for the life of me, wrap my head around how it is that well-rounded and intelligent women, who in some cases have built even better careers than their male partners, can have such a difficult time getting what they want from the people they hire.

The obvious answer is a person's upbringing, the way our society portrays traditional female roles, and the social cues that women get all the time as to what is acceptable or unacceptable for a woman to do. But as I kept meeting more and more women who wanted better control over their finances, I realized that the problem was twofold. Yes, a big part of it is simple lack of self-confidence when it comes to investments because of the traditional male/female roles that have been ingrained in our minds from the time we were young girls, but a big part of it is also because our thought processes and the way we approach relationships is fundamentally different from how men approach an identical situation.

As human beings, we are social, and our lives are built on our interactions with others. We have friendships, romantic partners, our family, our professional relationships, and we spend a large chunk of our day interacting with others in one way or another. And because we deal with different types of relationships all the time, it's sometimes easy to blur the line as to how these relationships *should* work.

Let's look at it this way: There are three basic types of relationships—personal, romantic, and professional. Each one works differently and has its own set of rules. For example, your relationships with your friends are different than the one you have with your husband or boyfriend. Your relationship with your family is different than the one you have with your doctor. But all relationships are founded on the same idea that people end up benefiting more if they are together than if they are on their own. Think about that for a second. The whole point of any relationship is that two people will decide to interact together because they *both* benefit in the end. This can be as simple as enjoying an engaging conversation with a friend (just try having a fun conversation with yourself!) or something as complicated as love, where both people experience that nuanced elation that comes from finding their soul mate.

All relationships work this way because they are founded on a subtle *give-and-take* among all the people involved. You fulfill your friends' emotional needs by being there for them, and they fulfill yours by being there for you. You provide a shoulder to cry on when things are bad for them, and they should do the same for you. The same thing happens in a romantic relationship: You fulfill your partner's needs for stability, family, and the warmth of love, and your partner should (ideally) fulfill your needs in the same way. So the first thing you've got to realize is that relationships are like a delicate barter system, and for a barter system to work, everyone has to play fair. Simply put, the idea is that when everyone *does* play fair, the whole (the relationship itself) becomes much greater than the sum of its parts (the people in it). What we're essentially saying is, "I'll be there for you when you need me if you'll do the same for me, and we'll both be happier by being in each other's lives than we would be on our own."

But here's the thing—in a romantic relationship or a friendship, this exchange of benefits can be subtle and is based largely on emotions and trust. In a *professional* relationship, the barter exchange is different because it's much more straightforward: The professional provides you with a service in return for a fee. They allow you the use of their expertise in order to make your life better. No feelings and no emotions should be involved. Pretty straightforward, right? Well, from what I've routinely observed over the years, the answer to that question depends on whether you are a man or a woman.

For men, this exchange is pretty simple: They are able to compartmentalize their feelings into separate little boxes inside their brains, and if a professional doesn't deliver on their promises, a guy will easily call them on it because the situation is unfair. Men tend not to allow feelings to get in the way of their judgment just because they like the person they are working with, and they will usually have no problem telling a professional if they are unhappy about something.

But for women, professional relationships can sometimes become affected by emotions, feelings of insecurity, and awkward loyalty. Perhaps it's because we are hardwired by nature to be mothers, to be caregivers to our children, and to bring stability to our families. But a woman's desire to avoid commotion for the sake of stability can make its way into other aspects of our lives where being nonconfrontational and forgiving is absolutely the worst strategy. To avoid this behavior, it's important to learn how to control your professional relationships so your financial future can stay on course and not be sidetracked by misunderstandings or simple laziness on the part of your financial advisor.

Your Relationship with Your Advisor Should NOT Work Like a Relationship with Your Family

Because professional relationships are a straightforward exchange system, make sure to ask yourself from time to time if you might be cutting your professional too much slack by treating them like you would a family member who's doing you a favor. A great way to do this is to ask yourself the following questions:

Am I Forgetting to Step Outside the Situation?

Stepping aside and observing what's really going on in your personal relationships can do wonders for your decision making, because it will help you notice things you hadn't before (when emotions tugged at your heartstrings and clouded your judgment). If you think back to your younger and more naive days, you'll probably remember one of those seriously messed-up relationships where one person was clearly taking advantage of the other, but the relationship just wouldn't end! If it wasn't you specifically, you probably know at least one person who was in such a situation. If you think back to a relationship like that, the most interesting thing was that the person who was being taken advantage of was the only one who didn't realize what was going on. They wouldn't listen to anyone and kept playing make-believe, pretending that the bad parts of the relationship didn't exist.

I remember my best friend was going out with this jerk (I'd rather use a different word, but I'll keep it clean), and it was so obvious to all of us that this guy was trouble and up to no good: too many disappearing acts, not showing enough interest in her. He was from Italy, and obviously desperately seeking a quick and convenient marriage to stay in the States. We all saw this. All of us . . . well . . . except my friend. She was the only one who didn't! She was a well-educated, intelligent woman who worked as a CFO at a major corporation and made over $300K a year. But even with all those achievements, she still felt insecure, and this guy would play games with her that kept her constantly confused about the nature of their relationship. Because she was so emotionally involved, she couldn't step outside the situation, so she was oblivious to all the red flags.

Now, she had some good friends who tried to help her (yours truly is one of them), and we did an intervention to get her to see what was going on. Thankfully, she eventually realized it all. The funny thing was that later she said, "What was wrong with me? How did I not see all those things before?"

Like in a bad romantic relationship, feelings of insecurity and self-doubt can make you blind to the fact that you're in a bad professional relationship. So from time to time, especially if you already feel anxiety about your finances, take a moment to step outside the situation and look at it objectively. A good way to do this is to make a list of all the specific things that bother you and then set up a call or a meeting with your advisor to address those specific items. After the call or the meeting, ask yourself if the advisor genuinely addressed your concerns or if you got the runaround and no real answers.

Am I Feeling Guilty for No Reason?

Remember the classic fairy tale "Beauty and the Beast"? Beauty was always the most generous of her family, waking up at the crack of dawn to take care of their country home and asking little from her poor father, even when her sisters kept asking for new wardrobes and accessories. And the poor thing didn't even have a skinny "double caf" latte with extra foam to help her start the day! One day, her father returned home, having had to make a deal with Beast that involved exchanging one of his daughters for his own life. Beauty volunteered to go and live with Beast. She refused to show any sadness because she didn't want to make her father feel worse (this is how the original story went, not the Disney version). Ok, I seriously admire Beauty's dedication to her family, and of course things definitely worked out to her benefit in the end. But seriously, she thought she was heading off to her doom, and to make her dad feel better, she didn't express any of her own feelings. "Umm . . . yeah, I'm going to die a horrible death, Dad. But, you know . . . don't feel bad about it or anything." She even felt guilty for being sad. What kind of life lesson is that? If you're shaking your head at this, as I am, think about all of the times you've done the same thing! We've all felt guilty about stuff that wasn't our fault, and instead of getting pissed off at the situation or the person responsible, we substituted guilt for anger!

If at any point in time you ever find yourself feeling guilty about "bothering" your advisor with phone calls or repeated requests for explanations, then that should be a clear sign that you are behaving in the same way you would with a friend. Whether your advisor made you feel this way or these feelings are driven by a sense of insecurity about your finances doesn't matter, because the end result of this will be the same: Your financial future *will* suffer. Feelings of guilt will prevent you from asking all the questions you'd like to, and that means you won't have all the information you need to make smart decisions for yourself. In a professional relationship, there is absolutely no place for feelings of guilt. So when it comes to your money and asking questions about it, all I have to say is: Ask away!

Am I Just Making Excuses for the Other Person?

One particular situation that drives me up the wall is when it's completely clear to a woman that her advisor is obviously ignoring her. But instead of getting upset, she'll come up with excuses. The advisor was too busy to return her phone calls, or maybe the advisor had already explained the investments to her and now she feels dumb for not understanding. Regardless of how complicated something related to your portfolio is, you have every right to ask as many questions as you need until you do understand what is going on. There is no need to make up excuses for why what you asked for wasn't done.

I remember one of the first times I started paying close attention to how I approached situations, and I realized that I was making excuses for someone else—for no reason at all. I had been working long hours and had started getting bad back pains from sitting in a chair all day. So when one of my coworkers suggested I go to her massage therapist to help loosen up all those stale back muscles, I was more than happy to do it. She told me that her massage therapist was great and that all her clients loved her. Well, great! Relaxation? Tension relief? You don't have to tell me twice! So I made an appointment and couldn't have been happier—until I got the massage.

It's kind of hard to describe what that first massage session was like. Let's see. Imagine that you went into a massage place fully expecting a gentle touch to slowly ease all the tension in your body, but instead, a rhino ran in, tossed you up and down and all over the table, and then stomped on your back. Yes . . . I think that's a pretty accurate description. I didn't feel relaxed at all! But I still paid the therapist and told myself that maybe I didn't complain loudly enough when she was digging in too hard into my fragile muscles or when her fingers felt like daggers in my back. Or maybe I was the one who didn't understand how a real massage should feel, and maybe it takes a day to feel the difference. Making up excuses definitely made me feel better. Instead of feeling like a pretzel that had been untwisted and twisted again, I could calmly tell myself, "No, the massage was completely worth it. I didn't just pay someone to torture me, and it was totally worth the money." That way I didn't have to feel so bad about it anymore.

Well, unfortunately, I did such a great job making up excuses that I went to this masseuse two more times. And every time, I felt the same way: as if the Spanish Inquisition had set up a massage parlor and I was going for torture. No matter what I said to her, no matter how I tried to explain what I liked or didn't like, no matter what cues I gave her with the pained grunts I'd make, she wouldn't listen! And I did the same exact silly thing when I'd get home: I would think that maybe she didn't hear me well. Maybe because English was her second language, she didn't fully understand what I was trying to say. Maybe it's all in my head . . .

Finally, I realized I was making excuses. Before the session started the fourth time, I went in, I told her that I had now asked her several times to do the massage the way I liked it, but she had ignored me. I flat out asked her if there was a miscommunication or any other type of issue.

To my surprise, she apologized. She said she *did* in fact hear me all those times, but she felt she knew how to do a massage correctly because she was a professional. She told me that she'd ignored my requests because she'd been doing massages for many years and all of her clients liked her techniques. I thanked her immediately and said, "Thanks, but no thanks," and I walked out.

All painful and annoying experiences have silver linings, because every bad experience is an opportunity to learn. I was so upset with having spent several hundred dollars on her barbaric services that I couldn't stop dwelling on it. That's when I realized that, yes, the massage therapist was a fool for treating her clients that way, but I was an even bigger fool because I was the one who wasted my own money by making up excuses for her. Had I stopped making excuses and confronted her right away, I wouldn't have wasted all that money!

The moral of the story is if you want to be in control of your future, then you've got to train your mind to catch yourself when you start making excuses for others—*especially* your financial advisor—because your money is on the line. A great technique is to pay attention to how you think throughout the day. The next time you find yourself trying to rationalize your advisor's actions (or anyone else's, for that matter) because they did something that makes you uncomfortable, ask yourself if you might be making excuses for that person. Perhaps it's because you're feeling a little helpless about the situation and the only way to stifle your anger and discomfort is to rationalize the other person's actions. At first, it may take you a little while to get the hang of it, but if you're genuinely honest with yourself, you will find this technique useful in all aspects of your life.

Money Confidence Mentality: Things to Keep in Mind

- Your relationship with your advisor is a professional one, so treat it as such.

- Your advisor's job is to take care of your financial needs—*not* to provide friendly chitchat while giving you no answers. Bedside manners are always good, but only when done in conjunction with good practices—not in place of them.

- Never feel guilty about asking your professional for help or about asking questions, even if you didn't understand the answer the first time.

- Learning to catch yourself when you make excuses for others will help you make better decisions. This skill is absolutely invaluable.

- Don't forget to step outside the situation from time to time and look at your professional relationships objectively.

Chapter 8

WHO IS WORKING FOR WHOM?

"This above all: to thine own self be true."
—William Shakespeare

In the previous chapter, I talked about common mistakes women make when working with their financial advisors, and I gave you some tips for being honest with yourself about the level of service you are getting. In this chapter, I will focus on proactive steps you can take to improve your interaction with your advisor so you can build a long-term professional relationship that truly benefits you.

As I mentioned, the whole point of hiring a professional is to gain the benefit of their education, their training, and their experience over the years to make your life better. It's that simple! You use their experience so you don't have to learn everything yourself, right? You *could* go to medical school and complete residency requirements so you could be your own doctor, but it's easier to hire someone who's already done it: your physician. You *could* take classes on auto repair and learn to fix your car, but it's easier to take it to the mechanic. When you hire a professional, you're paying them because you don't want to invest all the time and energy it would take to become an expert in their fields. You pony up some money, they pony up their expertise, and you're both better off.

The purpose of working with a financial advisor is, first and foremost, to use their knowledge and experience to build a better future for yourself, to use all the experience they've accumulated from seeing thousands of different client situations over the years to help you avoid rookie mistakes. The purpose of hiring an advisor is *not* to have personal, feel-good conversations or to chitchat about the stock market without addressing your specific situation. Even if they happen to be your friend or you develop a friendship with them later, it's important not to blur the line between the relationship so that your finances and your retirement plans don't suffer because of misplaced trust.

Ensuring Your Relationship with Your Advisor Is a Productive One

A big part of your financial success is building a good relationship with your financial advisor, a relationship based on respect and true concern about your financial future. Here are some hands-on tips about working with your advisors and structuring your relationship with them in a way that will help you get the most out of their expertise without feeling pressured or overwhelmed.

Whenever you feel concerned that an advisor may not be addressing your needs or is not being responsive, try these money confidence strategies:

Make It Clear That You Expect to Work as a Team

Working with a financial advisor is a lot like working with an interior designer. They should give you current trends and their opinion. Then you can brainstorm the best design ideas, together. For example, imagine your interior designer said something like, "Umm . . . Darla, I have some new drapes here for you . . . don't worry about what color they are or what the fabric is, I'm the professional. I know what I'm doing, so why don't you just let me handle it from here." Would you let them do as they please? No chance, right? So if your advisor brings an investment proposal to you, keep in mind that you don't have to blindly agree to it or make any decisions right away, especially if you don't fully understand it. Don't be shy about asking questions, even if you think a question is silly.

Whether you are starting out with a new advisor or would like to improve your interaction with your current one, feel free to openly tell them that you expect to work as a team. Let them know that detailed explanations are important to you and that you expect your comments or concerns to be addressed fully. Being direct about this doesn't mean that you're being rude; it means that you're openly sharing something that is a big concern for you. Watch the way they react to you bringing up your desires: It should tell you a lot about how they will react to your concerns in the future.

Email Important Topics Ahead of Meetings or Calls

If you'd like to get the most out of your meetings or calls with an advisor, send them an email ahead of time to let them know specifically what you would like to talk about. This is such an easy and simple practice, but I'm amazed at how many people don't take the time to do it. Sending an email ahead of time helps you in two specific ways: It helps you organize your thoughts and remember detailed questions you might forget, and it helps you make sure you get answers to those questions and that your meeting doesn't go off topic.

Treat Your Advisor the Way You Would Your Hairstylist—Speak Up!

The most important thing to remember is that if you feel something is wrong, you should always feel comfortable speaking up and resolving your concerns. You already do this in your everyday life, and telling your advisor about your concerns isn't all that different from dealing with your hairdresser.

When you go to a hairstylist, you have a certain image in your mind of what you'd like your hair to look like. As your hairdresser is working and you notice that she's doing something you don't like, your first thought will not be, "Well, she's so busy and fit me into her busy schedule, so I'll just stay quiet and let her do things her way." Heck no! Every woman I know and every woman I've ever seen at a salon will *continuously* give feedback about how she wants her hair done, exactly how she wants the highlights and the haircut—down to the style of the blow-dry!

That is how engaged and verbal we are as women. "No, not too short. No, not that dark. No, not that style." So apply that same approach to your money and be that verbal when it comes to your portfolio. "No, not that risky. No, I don't like those fees. Why is this investment better? Is there another similar investment but with fewer fees or less risk? How does this investment match my retirement goals?" You didn't find that great, sassy hairstyle by being silent, did you? You can't build a great portfolio without being assertive and clear about what you want, either. Both should reflect you, your personality, and your goals!

What If You *Are* Friends with Your Advisor?

If you're friends with your advisor, it may sometimes feel a bit awkward to behave extra professionally, because you might worry it could affect your friendship. Most of the time, that fear is misplaced, and you have nothing to worry about. Doing so is totally fine and helps make sure that your advisor is doing their job, that they don't become lazy when it comes to your needs *because* you are friends, and that they're taking care of your financial needs in a real and meaningful way. A businesslike attitude won't only help your professional relationship become stronger but will help keep your friendship intact as well. If your financial advisor is also your friend but is not fulfilling your retirement planning needs or is not addressing your concerns, then your financial future is being jeopardized, which will have real consequences for how you live your life in retirement. And what do you think will happen to your friendship then?

Here's a good example for how to structure your relationship with your advisor if you already are friends or may become friends in the future. One of my closest friends, Bobbie, is also my client. We have a great friendship and a great professional relationship, and we're able to have both of these seemingly opposite relationships without any awkwardness at all. Here are some ground rules that we use to help make sure there aren't any misunderstandings:

Set the Agenda in Advance

Whenever she comes to visit me at the office, we always label it ahead of time as either a personal "meet you for lunch" visit or a professional "I need to look at my finances" visit. This helps both of us get in the right mind-set in advance and prevents any miscommunication. If it's a professional meeting, it also helps us figure out in advance how much time we'll need to set aside to cover all the important items.

During Business Meetings, Keep Personal Conversations to a Minimum

Even when we determine in advance that we are having a professional meeting, there is obviously a desire to chat and catch up, because, yes, we are friends and it's hard to just meet and get right to business. But it doesn't have to be awkward. We'll talk a bit about personal news, but quickly we will—no matter what—turn the personal chatter off and delay it until after the professional meeting. This helps us ensure we have enough time to cover all of her financial business first. Then afterward, when we've covered everything important that pertains to her finances, we can relax and chat about life, the weather, the family, shopping tips, and all the fun stuff.

We Have a Zero-Tolerance Policy for Sugarcoating

The great thing about Bobbie is that she is a strong woman, and she would never hesitate to make sure she gets the answers she needs. But nonetheless, when we started working together, we both openly agreed that if something was bothering either of us on a professional level, we would speak directly and would not try to communicate by using hints or assumptions. So if either of us has a professional concern, we say exactly what's on our mind, without trying to soften the message. Bobbie would have no problem calling me out on something if she felt I wasn't addressing her concerns—and she would say it directly. And if *I* feel that she is slacking on some part of her financial plan, I'd have no problem frankly telling her that she needs to shape up. Neither of us gets offended because it's *her* future and *her* retirement, and the point of our professional relationship is to get her to her goals. This openness and directness helps keep peace and harmony for everyone.

When in Doubt, Imagine Your Portfolio Is an Ailing Puppy

When in doubt as to how you should act, imagine that your nest egg is a cute little puppy by the name of "Retirement Portfolio." And imagine that you took your sweet Retirement Portfolio to a veterinarian because she was sick. Well, if the vet didn't feel like helping her and said, "Oh, you shouldn't worry about her; I'm sure she'll be OK" as your poor little puppy was howling in pain on the floor, you'd have no problem calling the vet's BS (that doesn't stand for Bachelor of Science) for what it is, and you'd immediately confront the situation, right? You would demand immediate attention to your poor little puppy—no question about it! So, if you're not getting the level of service you need to keep your Retirement Portfolio safe, then imagine it as a cute, fluffy puppy, and you'll have no problem demanding answers from your advisor.

Things to Keep in Mind

- Remember that you are paying for your advisor's services, either through fees or commission. So even if you don't pay them out of pocket, it doesn't mean they're doing you a favor—it's their job to make sure all your questions and concerns have been addressed. I will outline things to look for when working with an advisor later in this book.

- Organize your meetings with your advisor beforehand so you stay on track and get the maximum benefit from your conversations.

- Treat your advisor like your hairdresser—speak up anytime you don't like something or simply want to double-check an answer.

- If your advisor is also your friend, there are easy ways to keep your personal and professional relationships separate without any awkwardness.

Chapter 9

MONA AND THE
ENCHANTED SPELL

"Follow your honest convictions and be strong."
—William Makepeace Thackeray

I'd like to share a true story with you about how sometimes things can get really out of control. This doesn't happen often, but once in a while you or one of your friends may encounter a professional who will blatantly try to take advantage of you. Again—this doesn't happen to everyone, but it happens often enough. This is a cautionary tale of a real nightmare experienced by one of my prospective clients.

I met Mona when I was doing a presentation at an event in Los Angeles. Even though I didn't catch on to the situation right away, Mona was in a relationship with a financial professional that was blatantly detrimental to her finances, and frankly, to her emotional health, too. When we first met at the event, we did the typical small talk, exchanged contact information, and went about our day. To my surprise, I got an email from Mona the next day, where she said, "Nice to meet you," but then asked if we could set up a time to go over her portfolio. A week or so later, we met at my office, and that's when I started to notice that something was odd about her situation.

What I found out was that she had already seen at least two other financial advisors who had made great proposals to reallocate her investments to be more in line with her comfort level. So, by the time I met with her, she had already considered changing her investments on more than one occasion and seemed ready to move forward. But for reasons I did not understand at the time, Mona could not take action. So we came up with a plan and decided that we would make changes step by step so it wouldn't be a drastic change for her all at once.

Adjusting Mona into investments to better fit her age and risk tolerance made perfect sense, and she agreed that she was not comfortable with her present investments. As we started making changes to her portfolio based on the plan, she kept getting cold feet and would call me saying that she wasn't sure what she should do. This behavior seemed strange to me because Mona wasn't asking any additional questions or telling me what bothered her; she was simply in limbo and couldn't make up her mind. This alarmed me, because when it comes to financial planning, if clients are hesitant to proceed with something, it's usually because they have valid questions that need to be addressed. They want to understand something better to make sure they are taking the steps that are right for them. But in this case, Mona seemed stuck for no apparent reason at all—or so I thought at the time.

You may have already seen this coming, but it turned out that Mona's previous financial advisor was pulling her puppet strings. Poor Mona had herself a seriously manipulative financial Geppetto, who was telling her that she was making a huge mistake by leaving him, that he had always watched out for her best interests, and that she was now going to lose everything by making this decision to change course. He wasn't giving her any logical reasons why her decision was supposedly incorrect, but was simply building up fear inside this poor woman who was already having a hard time dealing with the transition.

Does this story remind you of anything? If this were a romantic relationship that one of your friends was in, you would probably get furious, because you would see how blatantly obvious the emotional abuse and manipulation were. What makes situations like this difficult is that there is a real gap in knowledge and experience between the client and the financial advisor. In a romantic relationship, at least both people are on somewhat equal footing. If things get really bad, the person who is being abused eventually realizes that the constant put-downs and manipulation have no justifications behind them. But, because Mona thought her previous advisor was smart, and doubted her own know-how, she became overcome with fear at the thought of losing her entire nest egg (a fear that her advisor had instilled in her). She became paralyzed, like a deer in the headlights. She was so scared of making the wrong choice that she simply couldn't make any choice at all.

But she didn't get into her situation overnight. She had been with the advisor for about six years and had allowed herself to become bullied into decisions with which she wasn't comfortable. Remember when I mentioned that you should set the rules about how to work with your advisor? Unfortunately, Mona was a "Timid-Ella" and had allowed the professional relationship to get seriously out of control. But she wasn't entirely to blame. She had grown up being constantly reminded that it wasn't a woman's place to make major decisions, so she didn't learn how to stand up for herself when she felt that something was wrong. Mona never learned that she was fully entitled to ask questions and make her own decisions.

Every time she agreed to make an investment she didn't understand, it became easier and easier for her advisor to pull another string and get her to make more decisions about confusing investments. He became more and more her puppeteer, and she became less and less independent.

Mona's situation had become so obviously unhealthy for her that it was essentially no different from a relationship with a manipulative boyfriend; she became so confused and insecure about her ability to make the right choices that she became stuck and didn't know what to believe. She didn't have a group of friends who were looking out for her and telling her to drop the jerk, because we normally don't talk to our friends about our feelings when it comes to professional relationships. So she stayed in this relationship for almost six years without ever feeling secure or happy. Eventually, just thinking about her finances became uncomfortable and stressful, so she turned a blind eye to her concerns in frustration. At some point, the stress of the situation became so bad that she started having mini breakdowns, because she was feeling so completely lost and didn't know who to trust or what to do.

My advice to her at the time was that she needed to discover what was going on with her, to take a step back and think clearly about her experiences. She had to cut unhealthy ties and feel comfortable and confident in her ability to make decisions that were right for *her*. She needed to feel empowered enough to be able to start thinking clearly about her money—without being bullied—and that meant getting out of the professional relationship she was in. Because her mind was in an erratic state, she felt completely unable to take any steps. I told her to take some time off, stop thinking about the situation, and clear her head. Believe me, I wanted to tell her exactly what I thought of her advisor and what she needed to do. But I couldn't force her to do what I knew was right; it had to be *her* decision. If I forced her to make up her mind, then I would be no different from the bully who was her advisor at the time. Trust me, I would love to have screamed at the top of my lungs, "Toughen up, Mona!" But at this point, she had become a little girl pulling the blanket over her eyes to escape the monsters in her closet. She was no longer a grown woman who could open up the closet door, face the monsters in the closet, and say, "No more!" If you want to empower someone, you have to give them space to learn how to think for themselves.

She listened to me, but honestly, she was so manipulated, confused, and helpless that I wasn't sure if she would follow through with my advice. It was sad to see an otherwise strong woman being derailed by her situation—financially and more importantly, emotionally. I believe, unfortunately, that in her case what will eventually need to happen before she can stand up for herself and make a decision is for something drastic to occur to shake her up! Something drastic in this case will sadly be a huge loss, and maybe then she will have enough courage to make decisions that are right for her. I doubt she will recover from a huge loss, and she will have to readjust her lifestyle to account for it. But sometimes in abusive relationships, no one can help the victim until they decide to help themselves!

Chapter 10

WHEN THE PRINCE
TURNS OUT TO BE A FROG

"Actually, it's not me. It's really you."
—Anonymous

A s young children, we all had those moments when we were fright-
ened of something silly. Maybe you were afraid of the dark. Every
time you heard a creak or some other noise, your ears would prick up, and
you'd lie perfectly still in your bed, thinking you'd heard a ghost walking
around. Maybe you were afraid when your mom or dad would leave the
house. Perhaps you were very attached to them, and you felt anxious
when they were away. Or perhaps when there was a thunderstorm, you
felt so scared you'd run looking for your parents because you didn't want
to be alone. Whatever the case, your fear, like all fears, was based on
feeling weak and vulnerable. You felt you weren't in control and couldn't
protect yourself.

My biggest fear wasn't of the dark or monsters or ghosts—those
things never bothered me. The one thing that absolutely terrified me
growing up was public speaking. Until I was about twelve or thirteen
years old, I absolutely hated going up in front of the class to answer
questions or do presentations. I don't know why people say you get butterflies in your stomach when you're nervous. I definitely felt something,
but it sure as heck wasn't butterflies. The feeling was like my stomach
twisting and turning in every which direction, as if it were trying to

jump out of my body so it wouldn't have to witness my public speaking skills. Every time I had to speak in front of the class, I could feel my face getting red and my temperature rising. And the redder my face got, the more I felt everyone focusing their attention right on me—to the point that I thought I'd throw up right then and there. It was like this terrible cycle that fed on itself and grew bigger and bigger.

Well, I hated that feeling so much, and I became so frustrated, that one day I realized I had to do something about it. The only way to fix the problem was to get control of the situation instead of letting the situation get control of me. I decided to face the very thing that scared me so much, so I joined a drama class and volunteered to help with announcements during assemblies. I figured if I could learn to be comfortable speaking on stage in the auditorium in front of all those people, then doing an assignment presentation in front of my classmates would be a piece of cake. And you know what? After I did a couple of auditorium announcements, I realized it wasn't that scary to speak in front of others. After a few more times, it became quite enjoyable, because now I was in control of the situation, and even though I'd still get nervous, the fear didn't bother me much anymore.

You probably had your own fears about something as you were growing up, and you eventually got over those fears by realizing they were silly things to be afraid of. Or better yet, you confronted them head-on and realized you weren't weak—that you were stronger than the things that scared you. But growing up and letting go of your childhood fears is only half the battle, because even though you're not a little girl anymore, you still have to face fears on a regular basis—except they're a little different now. As an adult, your fears become more complex, and instead of monsters you become afraid of certain kinds of situations and confrontations. The funny thing is that these fears are based on the same feelings of weakness and vulnerability you had as child, except that as an adult, you call them insecurities. So as that monster in your closet goes away, insecurities about your physical appearance might take its place. Or that fear of the dark might be replaced by feelings of not being smart enough or not being strong enough to deal with a bad situation. And like you'd sometimes feel stuck as a kid when you were afraid, you now become stuck in your mind when faced with an uncomfortable situation.

When it comes to your money and your ability to build a good future for yourself, having your insecurities prevent you from making the right decisions can turn into a real-life nightmare. Remember the story of Mona from the previous chapter, who was being manipulated by her advisor? Well, her advisor quickly latched on to her insecurities and manipulated her to the point that she didn't know how to make the right choices for herself anymore. You may find yourself in a bad professional relationship with a financial advisor who is manipulating you. Or perhaps your advisor invested your money without your permission and then told you it was a misunderstanding. You know you're in a bad situation, but your fear of confrontation or your fear of losing your money or your insecurity about your ability to make the right choices can paralyze you. These worries eat away at you and build up to a point that you know you want to make a change. But you don't know how.

If you're stuck in a bad situation, and you realize your financial advisor is hurting your financial future, then it's important that you confront the problem head-on, and either change it or get out of that professional relationship. As uncomfortable as the confrontation may feel, and as worried as you might be that you won't be able to assert yourself to make a clean break, you have to realize that your financial future is at stake. The longer you stay with an advisor who is detrimental to your financial future, the more chances you are taking with your money.

There's no reason to dread this type of confrontation. You're right wanting to do something good for yourself. Confrontations are not a bad thing; they give you the opportunity to correct a situation that otherwise will eat away at your sense of well-being. A confrontation is a way for you to assert yourself and regain the sense of confidence that feelings of doubt and insecurity can sometimes shut off. It's the same exact thing as opening up your closet door and confronting a big scary monster; you realize you are much stronger than you give yourself credit for and that your fears sometimes have absolutely no basis in reality. Remember, the opposite of confidence is insecurity. But if you have clear expectations about your finances and the people you choose to work with, then you are moving toward money confidence. The more you affirm your expectations—both to yourself and to your advisor—you're tapping into the powerful force of money confidence. You won't believe how effective it is until you start using it!

So when, and if, you do conclude that your current financial professional isn't the right person for you and you decide to break things off, here are a couple of points that can make the process a lot easier on you.

This is what I call the three-step, Money Confidence Technique. It can help you walk away with your head held high and feeling completely in control, confident, and empowered!

Step #1—You Don't Need to Say "I'm Sorry"

When I was about eighteen, working as a teller at a major bank, I had a real issue with my then-manager. I felt like she pushed me around a lot and gave me fewer shift hours because I was younger than the other tellers. This was frustrating for me because I had consistently good performance. Even though I did a great job at opening new accounts and was one of the top-performing tellers in the branch, she wouldn't acknowledge my accomplishments. Then I discovered I was not the only one who felt frustrated. Several other tellers had the same issues with her management style. So when an opportunity with a nearby branch opened, the three of us applied for a transfer.

But, it wasn't as easy as we thought it would be. Sure enough, we were confronted by our manager. The other two tellers who had applied for the transfer told her that they were really sorry, that they loved working with her, and that they only did it because the other branch was closer to their homes (without thinking, by the way, that she had their addresses in the employee files, and their lie could be easily revealed!). The two tellers were young women themselves. They were scared, didn't want to upset their manager for fear of retaliation, and didn't know how to have a professional confrontation. Neither did I. But when my turn came and my manager asked, "Let me guess. You want to go because it is more convenient distance-wise for you, too?" I replied, "Actually, no, not really. I am asking for this transfer because I know that I do a great job, and I believe that I deserve more hours, and quite frankly, a promotion. But for whatever reason, you're not noticing my effort, or how hard I am trying, and I want to go somewhere that may give me a better opportunity." I didn't say "sorry," and I didn't try to soften the situation. I stood up for myself, remained professional and respectful, and in a sense, almost demanded that transfer. Well, guess what happened? At the end of the day, I was the only one chosen for the transfer! (And I was promoted within a month at the new branch!)

That was truly a great learning experience for me. It taught me that I should never compliment someone or say nice things if I don't mean it. It also taught me that even in uncomfortable situations, where your instinct may be to try to soften things, sometimes it's better to avoid the sugarcoating for the sake of your own sanity. Most women don't feel comfortable being blunt when dealing with professional relationships, especially when trying to end them. They feel guilty or awkward, so they start apologizing. They try to make the other person feel better and let them know how great they are and that they like them as a friend, but as a professional, they just "want to see other professionals." See, it's just like a real breakup! And like in a real breakup, saying, "I'm sorry, you're such a great person" just confuses things.

Forcing yourself to be nice when you don't actually feel that way makes you feel kind of stupid afterward. Have you ever ended a romantic relationship with a person you didn't like, but you went on and on to them about what a great person they were? How did you feel afterward? I bet it didn't feel all that great, because you just told someone who wasn't right for you that they were a wonderful person and suggested that you're sorry for letting them down. You can't do this in a professional relationship. When you get to a point in a bad professional relationship where you feel the need to leave your advisor, it's pretty clear that they let you down—and it's not your job to apologize for someone else's mistakes. You're not a little girl who didn't let her friend play with her dolls; you don't have to say, "I'm sorry." That's absolutely the worst thing you can do because if you are unhappy, and if your financial advisor has been ignoring your needs, then what the heck are you sorry about? They should be sorry because they were too foolish or too selfish to care about what you needed as a client and didn't take your needs seriously. So no—you're not sorry; you're doing what's right for you and your financial future.

Step #2—You Don't Owe Anyone an Explanation

Remember the fairy tale about Rapunzel? The girl with super long hair who sat in her tower until a prince showed up? Imagine if Rapunzel had explained to the evil witch why she needed to escape and leave the tower—she would have never gotten out and would have been stuck there forever!

So I'd like you to take this point seriously: Once you've made up your mind to do something you feel is right for you, you don't owe anybody an explanation. As you initiate a breakup with a professional who doesn't seem to have your best interests in mind, you don't need to go into too much detail as to why you are leaving. Remember, this is not a romantic relationship, so you don't need to make anyone feel better. This is not the same thing as when you are breaking up with a boyfriend or going through a divorce. In a romantic breakup, when done properly, the talking is important because it gives both people closure, which is essential when genuine feelings and emotions are involved. But in breaking a professional relationship, your professional is not emotionally invested, so there is no need to talk things out. That's why going into detail is absolutely unnecessary—it just makes the process more difficult on you for no reason at all.

Here's why this is important: If you do go into too much detail, then your advisor will try to talk you out of your decision, and this will make you feel insecure and will make you doubt yourself. When you make decisions on a whim, a little self-doubt is healthy because it helps you avoid mistakes. But in a situation where you've already thought carefully about your decision, unsuccessfully tried to fix the problems, and now decided to make the break, you know it's the right step for you. And if someone causes you to second-guess your decision after you've already clearly made up your mind, it will make you feel beyond lost, to the point where you won't know what to do at all. That was exactly Mona's problem; she second-guessed herself into decision paralysis!

I have seen many situations like this. Instead of staying firm, women would fall into the trap of "talking things out" and answering their advisor's questions when they would try to leave. So these poor women would pour their hearts out about what bothered them, only to then be ridiculed about their reasoning for moving on. "Oh, you should have told me sooner." "I had no idea you felt that way about such and such invest-ment." "I never received those voice mails, so that's why I didn't return your calls." The stupidest part about all this is that the ridiculing happens not because these women's reasoning is erroneous (their current advisor *was* being inconsiderate and was *not* focused on their needs), but because in their attempt to sound nice and make the professional feel better, they came up with alternate reasons that sound softer. Because these reasons don't truly come from the heart, they are harder to back up by facts.

If you're trying to leave a bad professional relationship where you have been constantly ignored, and you just want to end it, I've provided an example below to show you how wrong the situation can go and leave you feeling weak and insecure.

> **You** (trying to be nice): Well, you know, I just don't think these investments are the kind I want, and there are other things I'd like to try, because that plan wasn't what I really wanted.
>
> **Financial Professional:** Oh, not a problem. I didn't realize you felt that way. You should have told me earlier. I can definitely fix things for you. Only taking the concerns seriously now because you are leaving.
>
> **You:** Well, I did mention during our meeting that I wasn't really comfortable with the plan, but maybe I didn't explain myself cor-rectly. In any case, I just want to move along in the new direction I found. Still trying to sound nice, and blaming yourself so as not to appear confrontational.
>
> **Financial Professional:** Hmm, well, you did sign the paperwork saying that you understood what the investment was about, and all the risks. I guess I just don't understand why the change of heart, and why you're leaving altogether instead of just asking me to change your allocations. Trying to make you second-guess yourself as to whether the advisor truly was unresponsive when you voiced your concerns, and making you feel like the miscommunication was on your end.
>
> **You** (now flustered and uncomfortable): Yes, but I would like to con-tinue with moving the accounts anyway, because it's just not for me.

Financial Professional (in a confused and indignant tone of voice): I don't understand what you mean by that, but sure . . . I guess . . . I mean it's your money. You can do what you want.

Do you see what can potentially happen next in that conversation? If you try to be nice during a professional breakup by trying to explain things with explanations that aren't what you're truly feeling, the professional will offer solutions and start pointing out why you are incorrect. Because you are trying to be nice and are not explaining the real reason you want to leave, there is absolutely no way they can offer a solution that will make you feel better. In their mind, you're being headstrong, and they'll make you feel as if you're being unreasonable because you're rejecting all the solutions they are offering.

The bottom line is that you should only bring up concerns when you think there is a chance that there may have been some genuine miscommunication or a legitimate misunderstanding, and you believe that once the professional understands your concerns, they will attempt to fully rectify the issue. But once you've made up your mind, there is no point in going into detail—you should no longer care what the professional does with the information you've provided. You have already found a solution that is best for you—and that's the decision to leave.

Even if that advisor is also your friend, they should be able to understand the difference between your professional and your personal connection. They should be able to see that on a professional level, they are simply not satisfying your needs; they should be humble enough to accept your decision and understand that a split on a professional level doesn't mean that your friendship has to end. If they can't see that, and don't want to maintain the friendship after the professional relationship has ended, then they were probably never a real friend to begin with. Seriously—would you want to be friends with someone who has a requirement that you do business with them to remain friends? Of course not! It means that the friendship isn't real.

When in doubt, remember: You don't owe anyone an explanation, except your future self. That's the only person who will have to live with the decisions you make today and who will have to deal with any issues that might come up because you don't have enough money for retirement.

The only thing that separates you from your future self is time. You will have to meet your future self one day, and it's up to you whether that meeting will be a happy one or one filled with regret and self-kicking.

Step #3—It's Not Your Job to Teach Them

When you're breaking up with a financial advisor, one thing they may ask is what they did wrong. They won't make it sound like they want to talk things out, but only as if they want some friendly tips on how they can improve themselves. And like you don't owe them an explanation, you don't owe them free training about how to treat their clients. You want your advisor (like your doctor or lawyer) to be proactive about helping you, not reactive after they know you are leaving. Think about it this way: If someone in your life does something that's detrimental to you—like talking about you behind your back—is it better if they feel guilty and come to you on their own to tell you the truth and apologize, or if they apologize only after you confront them? In both cases, the person might genuinely feel sorry for their actions. But in the first case, where they came to you to apologize first, it's their own conscience that makes them uncomfortable and it's because they truly are thinking about you. They, themselves, feel uncomfortable enough to the point that they need to be proactive and set things right. And that's what you want from your financial advisor and any other professional you hire; you want people whose character drives them to take care of you proactively and to make sure that all your needs are met. You don't need someone who waits for a threat of losing you as a client before they start caring about your needs.

That's why I always say that when you are breaking a bad professional relationship, it is absolutely not your job to teach somebody how to provide better service. They should know how to do their job, and if they have not been able to learn by listening to the questions you have been asking prior to the breakup, then it's not your responsibility to sit down and explain what they can do better. It's not your duty to improve their business or to help them grow, because a person who really does want to learn and grow will do so at their own initiative and for the good of their clients.

Let me give you an example about a problem I had with my previous dentist. I had been going to her for several years but was feeling that she didn't listen to me. I kept complaining about ongoing pain in my teeth, and she would always say, "Oh, you're probably grinding them at night" but would never recommend any solutions. One time, when I visited her office after years of feeling like I had been ignored, I again complained about sensitivity in my teeth because it had become a real problem. Again, she barely examined them and had her assistant take some X-rays. Then, she came back and said, "Oh, it's your fillings. They need to be replaced."

I asked her, "Are you sure?"

She said, "Definitely," and went on to tell me how fillings eventually become loose and cavities continue to form.

I then asked her, "Are you one hundred percent sure those are my X-rays? I just want to make sure before we do any work."

She looked at me with a quizzical expression on her face, and said, "Of course, we just took them!"

This is when I realized this situation was out of control, because as my dentist, she should have known that I had never had any fillings—ever! So why would they need to be replaced? Well, that's when I knew it was time to break up and get a new dentist before my teeth would suffer any drastic consequences.

At that point, I decided that no explanation was needed as to whether she had the wrong X-rays, because she was about to perform unnecessary work on my teeth. It didn't matter what the situation was—honest mistake, incompetence, or laziness. So I said, "Thank you, but I will not be doing that work today, and I will not be coming back, so you can close my patient file." I then paid my co-pay and left. There was no point in explaining to her what the reason was, as it wouldn't have done anything good for me, and wouldn't have solved my problem. Because after all, it was about my well-being—not her feelings.

Things to Keep in Mind

At the end of the day, ending professional relationships that are bad for you and having to confront someone because they're not meeting your needs is never a pleasant experience. There's no way around it. But you know what? Neither is taking your car in for service. Nor is it a pleasant experience to sit down with your checkbook to pay your bills or to do laundry or to go to the dentist to get a root canal. So if you're stuck in a bad professional relationship with your financial advisor and you can't seem to get the attention or the answers you need, then at some point you have to make the decision of what's more important to you—avoiding an uncomfortable situation or protecting your financial future and ultimately your retirement.

If you do end up in a situation where you have to make the break, keep the following points in mind to make it as simple as possible:

- You don't have to apologize. Saying "I'm sorry" won't make you, or them, feel any better, and may make things worse.

- You don't owe anyone an explanation once you've decided to take action that you know is right for you. Talking things out only makes sense if you still want to fix a broken professional relationship.

- It's not your job to teach your advisor how to be a better professional.

- Confrontations, whether with your advisor or another professional in your life, will never be as scary or uncomfortable as you think. And the relief you feel after confronting a problem will make it worthwhile.

PART THREE

THE WOLF THAT STOLE
THE GOLDEN EGG

Chapter 11

THE YELLOW BRICK ROAD
TO INNER PEACE

"Everyone who wills can hear the inner voice. It is within everyone."
—Gandhi

Whether you just got out of a bad relationship with an advisor who wasn't paying attention to your needs or maybe haven't had an advisor for a while, the best thing you can do for yourself before you form another professional relationship is to take a little time and figure out what you want out of life. In your romantic life, one of the best ways to avoid bad relationships is to become comfortable in your own skin. You have to love and respect yourself and feel confident to the point where you don't *need* someone in your life just to feel complete, but *want* someone in your life because they genuinely make you feel better. Getting into a relationship simply because you feel lost when you're alone is when you're likely to let things slide. You're less likely to command respect from your partner because you're afraid that if you assert yourself, they might leave you and you'll once again feel alone and like you're drowning.

When it comes to your finances, it's much the same thing. If you don't feel confident about your understanding of basic financial concepts, and more importantly, if you don't feel in control of your financial situation, then you're likely to end up in another bad professional relationship. Instead of feeling empowered and in control, you will look for a savior, someone who will solve your problems *for* you rather than *with* you. The real danger is that you'll end up in a hopelessly frustrating situation where you will feel weak and lost—and that's something you can't afford to do, emotionally or financially. The only way to avoid a scenario like this is to take steps that will make you feel strong and empowered. Steps that will help you feel in control of your future, and ultimately, in control of your destiny. When you feel confident and strong, you will choose relationships that are right for *you*. That's why it's so important to have at least a basic understanding of financial concepts.

Do keep one thing in mind: Before you decide to drop everything and get a PhD in finance, remember *why* you decided to take action in the first place. Remember why you decided to replace your financial situation with more than just the status quo. And even more important, remember that you didn't set out to learn all there is to know about the world of investing in a couple of weeks—or to try to figure everything out on your own. It's important that you keep this in mind, because nothing can ruin a good nest egg like a newbie investor who is overconfident and knows just enough to do some damage. I've seen this happen, and it's not pretty. It's kind of like using the Internet to diagnose your health problems yourself and then never going to the doctor. Yeah, you'll get *some* useful information, but you won't necessarily have the experience to carefully analyze that information from all angles to come up with a prudent action plan.

Instead, you should first take some time to familiarize yourself with basic financial concepts. It's also of the utmost importance that before rushing into a professional relationship, you spend some time interviewing and getting to know other financial advisors so you can find one who understands your needs and life goals. Remember—the whole point of having a good financial advisor who is right for *you* is knowing that the person you choose will be on your side and genuinely interested in helping you achieve your goals and dreams. It should be someone who acts like a trainer at the gym and uses their experience to help you fine-tune your workout routine to get the most out of it. But just because you have a personal trainer doesn't mean you shouldn't know why it is that you are doing the exercises and whether the exercises are helping you toward your personal goals. We all need professionals in our life to help us with important concerns. Eating healthily and taking vitamins can help prolong your life, but it doesn't mean you don't need a doctor. Brushing your teeth and flossing regularly will give you healthier teeth, but this doesn't mean you don't need a dentist. It's the same thing with your money; you should be the one working diligently to improve your finances, but having an experienced financial professional watching out for you and helping you avoid pitfalls is priceless. It just has to be a person who is right for you.

In the next few chapters, I'll provide you with a basic overview of some of the more common financial concepts with the intent that it will give you a better understanding of investments and budgeting. It will also help you have a more productive conversation with your advisor when you finally find your financial soul mate. Remember, you might not know everything about navigating financial waters, but having a compass and a map is way better than sitting in the boat with a blindfold on. (I have also included additional information and definitions in the appendix section of this book if you would like a more in-depth understanding of certain financial topics.)

There are two big reasons why you should understand at least the basic financial concepts: First, it will help you be more confident when it comes to discussing your retirement, your investments, and your portfolio allocations—which will help prevent you from making rash decisions or decisions based on feelings of insecurity—and second, it will enable you to better interview and select a financial advisor who will meet your needs, because you'll be able to ask more meaningful questions during the interview process. It's important to hire the right person and not try to figure everything out on your own. I've seen many people throughout the years become their own financial advisors, and the problem I see over and over in these situations is that they will get lucky because the market happens to be doing well at the time. Instead of realizing that the stars happened to be aligned in their favor, these folks will start to think they've got the entire stock market figured out. However, most people can't consistently beat the performance of the market, and a novice who gets lucky a couple of times is making a huge mistake when they start thinking that everyone else who is actively investing (at least tens of millions of people over the last few generations) is too foolish to get the magic formula right, but that *they* somehow figured it out based on intuition and by reading obscure online blogs. Even Jack, from the fairy tale "Jack and the Beanstalk," probably thought he was super savvy for getting those magic beans that grew into a giant beanstalk—but he obviously had just gotten lucky.[19]

I want you to take this seriously. If you start managing your own money and see some early success, please don't let it go to your head. Many people make the error of mistaking luck for the ability to beat the markets. There are tons of professional money managers out there who have delivered amazing short-term results but who can't do so regularly, because a lot of short-term investment success is based on timing and luck.[20] Even experts who study and follow the stock market and the economy all day long still can't accurately predict what will happen next. They are definitely not dummies; they're PhDs who devote their lives to studying the markets, statistics, and all that other fun stuff that makes for great party small talk. I once heard a great joke that went something like this: "An economist is someone who can explain to you on Wednesday why the prediction they made on Monday didn't happen on Tuesday." So if they have a hard time beating the markets, what makes you think that you can do better? There have been few investors throughout history who were able to consistently beat the markets, and many of them also incurred disastrous losses. If it were truly easy, we all would be rich, right? Better yet, anyone who could figure out the perfect formula for making money would probably keep it a secret and be the richest, most powerful person in the world! So let's take our naive hats off and put our learning hats on. Consistently predicting the market is an illusion, no matter how luxurious and couture it may feel. Such a notion is simply fake—like most of the Louis Vuitton bags you see teenagers carrying in downtown Los Angeles. So as you learn various financial ideas and concepts, keep reminding yourself *why* you're doing it: to be better equipped to protect your nest egg and keep it on the right path—not to become the next Warren Buffett.

Remember when I said earlier that it's all about the choices we make? There are many intelligent women who are making the wrong choices because of their lack of understanding and their fear of the financial implications of retirement and financial planning. But it doesn't have to be that way. A bit of effort and a desire to be in control can get you a long way toward having a better grip on your financial life. With that in mind and with your learning hat on, sharpen that pencil and get your lunchbox ready, because you're about to learn some fun stuff! Actually, forget the learning hat and the lunchbox—pour yourself a glass of wine, cozy up under a warm blanket, and get ready to learn about your finances. And if you're already thinking, *Ugh. Finances are boring. Why do I have to read about this stuff?* Then I say, you owe it to yourself! I promise it will be fun! There is nothing more fun than being on the right track and in control of your money, and you can only do that with good old-fashioned, solid planning. The only way to plan better is to gain more knowledge and a better understanding of the financial world around you, which will help you make better and wiser decisions.

Chapter 12

401(K)—YOUR NOT-SO-MAGIC BEAN

"Even if you're on the right track, you'll get run over if you just sit there."
—Will Rogers

We have all heard of the fairy tale "Jack and the Beanstalk" and how Jack's wondrous, magic beans grew into a giant beanstalk that gave him access to an enchanted world where he found treasure. Even though we know fairy tales are fiction with no basis in reality, many of us mistakenly believe that our 401(k) is our very own magic bean. And so, we live our lives with the idea that if we plant this magic bean, it will grow all by itself and will eventually become a pile of treasure that will provide for a comfortable retirement. We think that if we work hard and regularly contribute our hard-earned money into our 401(k) accounts, everything will work itself out, and a lifetime of income will magically appear for us. But remember, life is not a fairy tale, you're not Jack (or Jacqueline), and your 401(k) is not a magic bean; a happy outcome is not guaranteed. Just because you're contributing money to your retirement account on a regular basis does not mean you will accumulate wealth.

Let me give you one of the more glaring examples of this lack of attention toward a 401(k) that I encountered in my career. I had a client, Irene, who genuinely believed that because she was contributing money into her 401(k), it meant she would automatically get exactly the amount of income she desired when she retired. She believed that, even though her contributions were less than 10 percent of her salary and her company only matched 5 percent of that amount, her 401(k) would grow large enough to the point where it would generate sufficient income during retirement to cover her rent and all her other expenses. Apparently, she had heard somewhere, probably from someone who was as confused as she, that if she saved with a 401(k) (the magic bean) that it would automatically give her the money she would need in the future. She didn't understand that it wasn't only about contributions, but about how much she contributed, where she allocated her portfolio, and for how long she saved. In her head, the mere fact that she had a 401(k) meant she would be OK. Now, it may be tempting to laugh at her, until you realize that her outlook could have had tragic results, and especially when you realize how many women also have this same outlook. Fortunately for Irene, she still had about nine years until her retirement, and after I explained to her why her assumptions were incorrect, we were able to figure out a plan of action to get her retirement on track. She increased her contributions, cut back on unnecessary spending, and started saving more in her regular savings account. Doing this wasn't super easy, but it helped her avoid the disaster of running out of money during retirement.

But, unfortunately, this story is representative of how most people think about their 401(k) accounts. Their belief is especially dangerous since for most people, their 401(k) is one of the biggest retirement assets they will have when they get to their golden years. Whether you retire with one huge 401(k) account after working at a company for decades or have lots of small Rollover IRAs from your previous jobs, you will likely have saved up a large chunk of your retirement nest egg through the 401(k) program during your working years. Because of this, it is important to take good care of your 401(k) in a way that will get you to your retirement goals. Growing your retirement plan contributions into a mini-fortune that can sustain you throughout your retirement requires more than simply stuffing contributions into your account. It requires your time and attention, like a real beanstalk or any other plant. You have to water it regularly, make sure it has enough sunlight, and check the leaves regularly to make sure your plant is healthy and there aren't any bug problems. You should tend to your 401(k) account on a regular basis and constantly check to make sure there aren't any small issues that can eventually become big problems and prevent you from enjoying your retirement.

Mistake #1—Thinking That Someone Else Cares about Your 401(k)

Let's break it down, shall we? First and foremost, it is essential for you to realize that your 401(k) is not a magical solution whose sole purpose is to look after you in your retirement. It is not! Your next wake-up call is to grasp that your 401(k) is not being managed specifically for you. The company you work for is not watching your portfolio's investments carefully to ensure you avoid any risky situations should the stock market collapse. Trust me, Joe Schmo from Human Resources is not sitting there watching *your* account and thinking about *your* retirement and lifestyle goals.

When I talk to most people about their 401(k) accounts, I love it when they say, "Oh, my job has people for that. I don't need to worry about it—it's all taken care of." Umm . . . NEWSFLASH: it is not! No one at your job has "people" looking over your account, and *nothing* is being taken care of the way you think it is! What your company has are several general staff members who handle general account tasks (you know . . . the really important things, like printing statements and sending you reports), and that is all! All accounts are treated the same regardless of your personal circumstances. Whether you're twenty or fifty, single or married, have children or not—nobody gives a hoot. They have zero idea about what your retirement goals are, what kind of lifestyle you would like, or when to warn you that your allocations are too risky for your age. Your 401(k) account is one of many, and as such, it is treated with the same lack of interest as everyone else's. So if you want your 401(k) to work for you, you've got to accept the fact that making sure that it is on track is all up to YOU! *You* need to watch your magic bean, nurture it, and protect it from the ogre; you need to watch it like a hawk (a ninja hawk who's been trained in martial arts!) and question its allocation and growth; you need to find out whether you are contributing the right amount and whether that amount is being invested appropriately for your circumstances. Only your actions can make a difference, and the sooner you start taking steps to keep your financial future on track, the sooner you will be in control of your retirement.

I remember when I first met Irene, one of the first things she told me was that there was no reason to review her 401(k) because the "people" at her work were taking care of it. I had, of course, heard these kinds of comments before, so I wasn't surprised at what she said. I explained to her that there was no one at her job who was specifically dedicated to monitoring how her 401(k) was doing, and I helped her figure out how to read her statements. When we sat down to go over her paperwork, what we realized was that she was only contributing 7 percent of her salary, and she was shocked! Yes, shocked! Until that day, she was always under the impression that as she was getting closer to retirement, which was now only about nine years away, that the "401(k) watcher" was automatically increasing her contributions every year! That someone was sitting in the back office at corporate and saying, "Hmm . . . looks like Irene's account isn't high enough and she's getting close to retirement—we've got to increase her contributions! Stat!" What was even worse was that because her contributions were invested in a mutual fund that had the word "growth" in its name, she thought everything was fine. In reality, she was still invested in the original, aggressive, mostly small-cap stock fund that she selected when she set up her 401(k) in her late thirties. Yes, she was less than a decade from retirement, taking the same risks with her money as if she were in her late thirties. This was a huge wake-up call, or what I refer to as a Rude Awakening. Irene made this mistake and will have to work an extra four and a half years to make her nest egg large enough to retire comfortably. And when you think about it, only a couple of hours a month spent on reviewing her 401(k) would have saved her four and a half years of work. Don't let this happen to you.

Mistake #2—Confusing Accumulation with Growth

It is imperative that you learn how to read your 401(k) statements. I am not just talking about gazing nonchalantly at the numbers and thinking, *Wow! They look good—I'm sure they've increased since the last statement* . . . I'm talking about reading and understanding the *growth* (the return on your investments) and being able to differentiate it from a simple increase in your account balance.

Think about it this way: Your 401(k) can grow in only two ways: from your contributions (and your employer's matching, if you're lucky!) and from the growth in the value of the investments in your portfolio over time. There isn't any magic to it at all. Now, out of these two things that affect your accumulation of wealth, you can only directly control the first one—the amount of your contributions. The second force, growth, is only partially controlled by you, and like a moody boyfriend, it can be unpredictable at times. So when you're looking over your 401(k) statement and you see that your account balance has increased from the last time you checked, it's incredibly important to understand how much of that increase came from your contributions and how much of that increase came from your investments growing in value. If you don't take the time to review your statement carefully, you might not even realize that your 401(k) has become a giant black hole that sucks in your hard-earned dollars, never to be seen again.

When you look at your 401(k) statement, you should expect the account balance to be higher than the previous statement because you've been contributing money into it on a regular basis. But what you need to understand and focus on is the actual capital growth on your hard-earned principal investment (i.e., how much your investments have increased in value). You need to look at the growth on the contributions, and don't forget to subtract any fees you may be paying. Sometimes it is not obvious that you're losing money, because the contributions made by you and your employer are masking a drop in value of your investments—the account balance will increase even though there is zero or even negative capital growth. This means you don't necessarily notice the big drops in value as much as you should, because at first glance, your account balance is up.

This is why watching your 401(k), your magic retirement bean, and understanding your 401(k) statement is really important. Remember, no one else is watching it like you thought they were! And furthermore, no one cares about it as much as you. By reading your statements correctly, you will be able to find out what you are truly earning on your investments and where you are heading when it comes to your retirement target.

Mistake #3—Not Taking the Time to Understand the Risks in Your 401(k)

Let's go back to the beginning. Once upon a time you started a great new job somewhere; you were excited, filled out the new-hire paperwork, and by the time you got to the benefits applications, the process probably went something like this:

> **Human Resources Representative:** So, welcome aboard. Just a few more forms to fill out—here is your 401(k) paperwork. The company matches up to 3 percent of your contributions, if you'd like to take advantage of that. You just need to put down how much you'd like to contribute from each paycheck and select your investment allocations.

The new hire then looks over the paperwork and thinks about how much money she can "afford" to set aside; and I use quotations because I want to tear my hair out when people say, "I can't afford to set that much money aside." Then, after devoting about three minutes to reviewing her options, which is probably less time than you spend on choosing what to order at a restaurant, she selects a few mutual funds from the incredibly limited number of investment options offered by the company. The thought process is pretty much something like this (and you *know* it's true):

> *Hmm . . . This fund has "growth" in its name, and I do want my port-folio to grow, so let me put some money here. Oh . . . and this one says "value" . . . I definitely want value because value is better than no value, so let me put a few percent here. Hmm . . . who could help me with this . . . maybe I should call my friend. She has a son who is majoring in business, so he must know about this stuff . . . yeah, that should get me to a good retirement . . .*

Ok, maybe the example above is a bit exaggerated, but you get the point. Most women make their 401(k) retirement portfolio selection without taking the time to understand what it is they are investing their money in. Most men do the same thing for that matter, even though they won't admit it—because they're great at faking confidence. You know, it's like when you hear something like, "Don't worry, honey, I can totally fix the roof myself without falling off and breaking my legs in the process. Trust me, I know what I'm doing." A few of us will try to read the investment prospectuses, the long-winded documents full of legal language describing the funds—which are also a great cure for insomnia. A cup of hot cocoa, a mutual fund prospectus, and you'll pass out in no time! Even fewer will try to understand what these funds invest in or the risks involved. Think about the implications; the funds you choose will directly impact two things about your portfolio: growth, or how quickly your investments could appreciate, and risk, or the possibility that your investments will lose money at some point, which could be a lot, as we saw with the meltdown of 2008. And because most women don't know much about the funds they're putting their hard-earned contributions in, or the risks associated with those funds' strategies, they throw a Hail Mary and pray for the best.

Remember when I mentioned that you can only increase your 401(k) through your contributions and the growth of your investments? Well, most people leave the growth portion of their wealth-building strategy completely to chance. If you planned a cross-country road trip from Los Angeles to New York without a map or GPS, and decided to drive down any random road, do you think that might be a risky thing to do? *Oh, Mulholland Drive—that sounds like a good street name. I think I'll take it! Why? I don't know. But it sounds nice! I'm sure it will take me where I need to go!* Well, when you're selecting random funds for your 401(k) without understanding where those funds invest, that's exactly what you are doing: driving down a random road that will get you *somewhere*, but likely not where you want to go!

And to be clear, this is your *retirement* portfolio we are talking about! This is not a lottery that you hope to win or a game of bingo, but money you will need during your retirement. These are your hopes and dreams, and the way you allocate your money will directly affect how those retirement hopes and dreams turn out. This is your future! Remember, life isn't like a fairy tale, and taking the time to understand your portfolio may be annoying and sometimes downright frustrating, but if you approach your retirement planning with an I'm-sure-it-will-all-work-out attitude, then you're leaving your future completely to chance.

Mistake #4—Setting Your 401(k) on Autopilot

Now this part is what really gets me: After setting up their 401(k) account, some women will set it on autopilot and won't bother to adjust their contributions or investments as time passes. Think about how silly that is. As you move along in your career, you probably received a promotion or a raise or moved to a better-paying job, and of course you increased your 401(k) contributions in line with your increase in pay, didn't you? Well, if you're smart, you will always deposit the maximum amount possible; but if you have more of a "set and forget" mentality, then your contributions to your 401(k) account are probably not the highest priority in your life. And what happens to things that aren't a priority? Well, the same thing that happens to your plants when they're not a priority and you forget to water them. Irene learned that lesson the hard way, and it cost her dearly, but she was still one of the lucky ones, because she had at least some time to fix her situation. Had she found out about her problems on the day of her retirement party, her story would have had a much sadder ending.

If you haven't looked over your 401(k) recently or haven't increased your contributions in years, ask yourself, "Why not?" Perhaps you forgot to increase your contributions or maybe you decided to buy a brand-new car, upgrade your kitchen, or take an exotic vacation instead. For most people, their contributions usually remain the same as they were when they first started working. Since no one ever comes along to take your hand and let you know that you should be investing more money and investing it into different allocations, you remain blissfully unaware that you may be aimlessly adding your contributions to a black hole.

Whatever your point of view when you started cultivating this 401(k) bean, you were certainly younger and less concerned about funding your retirement. As you get older, it's important to make sure that you're making the necessary changes to avoid major mistakes. Think about it: You wouldn't wear a short miniskirt in your mid-sixties, would you? Of course not! As the years have gone by, you have updated your fashion, you have changed your style, your hair color, maybe even your taste in music to match your sophisticated age. So why are your 401(k) contributions and investment allocations stuck in the late 1980s, wearing power shoulder pads and huge, poufy hair?

There isn't any magic to selecting a proper 401(k) strategy; the simple truth is that the long-term growth of your account and the risks associated with your investments are intertwined. Like Jekyll and Hyde, they are the flip sides of the same coin. One has the potential to bring you positive returns in the form of growth, while the other has the potential of causing your 401(k) value to drop. These two will always go hand in hand: The bigger the possibility for growth, the more risk you are likely taking. At the same time, the less risk you would like to take, the less growth you are likely to see (you will read about risk in more detail in chapter 16). It's kind of like watching movie stars on the red carpet: The more attention they want to get, the more ridiculous their outfits will be. But when they do decide to wear something that stands out too much, they're also taking a risk that the attention they get will not be the attention they want. So when you are accumulating your wealth, you have to watch your magic bean like a hawk and make sure that the amount of risk you are taking is appropriate for your age.

The further away you are from retirement, the more risk you can take. As you get older (in age only, because we're all eighteen forever at heart), it is important to start reducing the amount of risk you are taking because you have fewer working years left and less time for your portfolio to recover from potential losses.

Generally speaking, on the topic of allocations, when you are between the ages of thirty and fifty, your focus should be on accumulation, which is more of an aggressive growth allocation that accepts more risk for a higher potential return. You can afford to be more aggressive when you are younger, because you have the luxury of time on your side to be able to deal with any potential hiccups along the way. Then, between the ages of fifty and sixty-five, your focus should be on preservation, which is a conservative growth allocation that reduces the overall risk, as well as potential returns. It's important to exercise more caution as you get older to make sure you don't lose any of your principal. I can't stress this enough: Making sure that your portfolio is properly allocated to match your age is one of the most useful things you can do for yourself. Finally, after age sixty-five, your focus should be on distribution, since by this age you are retired and most likely will have to use your retirement accounts as supplemental income.

Now, let's consider what would happen if you left your allocations the same as they were when you were in your thirties and forties and never made any changes as you got older. If the market crashed, you would stand to lose way more than you could afford to without having the time available to recoup your losses. How fun do you think your retirement would be then?

Mistake #5—Not Contributing the Maximum Amount

When it comes to investing for retirement, time is your biggest ally. The more time you have until retirement, the better chance you have to reach your goals. Remember when I said there is no magic to growing your 401(k) portfolio? Well, there is a little magic, or something close to it, and it's called *compounding*. It is a magical little tool that requires you to do little but works hard on your behalf and goes a long way to help you achieve your goals. It's almost like the ultimate magic bean: It helps your money grow faster and bigger, like a magic growth potion.

Now, this is *very* important: Compounding is the concept of earning returns on top of returns. In the simplest of terms, I can explain compounding this way: A dollar contributed to your 401(k) account twenty years before retirement is worth much more than a dollar contributed five years before retirement, and this is all because of compounding. For example, if you invested $10,000 into your 401(k) in Year 1, and earned a 5 percent annual return, you would have $10,500 by the end of the year, or a net gain of $500 ($10,000 x 5% = $500).

If in Year 2 your investments earned another 5 percent, you would have $11,025 at the end of the year, or a net gain of $525 ($10,500 x 5% = $525). Notice that in Year 2 you've earned twenty-five more dollars than in Year 1, because you had an extra $500 (your growth from Year 1) sitting in the account at the beginning of Year 2. And here's the awesome part: You didn't have to do anything extra for your portfolio to earn this extra twenty-five dollars. What you are doing is putting time on your side, and letting the investments in your portfolio work for you over a longer period of time, which lets you earn more growth on top of the returns that your portfolio generates.

Now, of course, the example in the previous paragraph doesn't do much justice for the true benefits of compounding. After all, what can you buy with twenty-five dollars? Two movie tickets maybe—not even enough to include popcorn. But over long periods of time, and with regular contributions, compounding can help generate stunningly better returns on your investment, because again, you're making time work for your benefit.

Take a look at the chart on the effect of compounding interest. If we take a hypothetical investment of $10,000 that pays 7 percent on an annual basis, then after thirty years it would have grown to over $70,000. But the important thing is to pay attention to how much of that return came from compounded interest, which is interest earned on top of interest. In this scenario, over half of the total return comes from compounding! When it comes to making your 401(k) work for you, time is one of your biggest allies. That's why contributing as much as possible, as early as possible, can go a long way toward building your retirement nest egg.

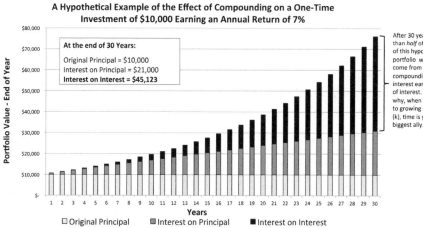

A Hypothetical Example of the Effect of Compounding on a One-Time Investment of $10,000 Earning an Annual Return of 7%

At the end of 30 Years:
Original Principal = $10,000
Interest on Principal = $21,000
Interest on Interest = $45,123

After 30 years, more than *half* of the value of this hypothetical portfolio would come from compounding, or interest earned on top of interest. This is why, when it comes to growing your 401 (k), time is your biggest ally.

Mistake #6—Leaving Your 401(k) Behind

Now that we have covered 401(k) contributions, allocations, and not confusing account increases with growth, let's talk about what you should do with any previous 401(k) accounts.

For those of you who may not have rolled over your previous 401(k) account from a previous employer into an Individual Retirement Account (IRA), find a mirror and shake a finger at yourself in an admonishing way! Look at it like this: When you change jobs, you wouldn't leave your personal belongings like the pictures on your desk behind, would you? So why would you *ever* think of leaving your most precious belonging behind—your nest egg for retirement? I mean, it is a no-brainer, right? Wrong! You'd be surprised how many people do this regularly and leave their 401(k) accounts behind after changing jobs.

So what should you do with a previous 401(k) account? Some people choose to roll it over into their current 401(k) account at their new job. You can do that, but in my opinion it makes more sense to roll it over into an IRA outside of the confines of an employer. Why? Because by doing so you will have more investment options to choose from than what most 401(k) plans offer. By moving your funds into an IRA in a brokerage firm outside of your work, you can have your choice of different stocks, mutual funds, ETFs, etc.; you are not restricted to the limited options of an employer-provided 401(k).

But whatever you do, don't simply cash out your 401(k) unless you have no other options and unless you've spoken to your tax preparer or a CPA ahead of time. Cashing out your 401(k) early can result in higher taxes as well as penalties. So the vast majority of the time, it's better to roll it over into an IRA and allow your nest egg to continue growing.

Let me tell you about a client of mine, Anna. I met her about five years ago, around the time she had just retired. She was so happy to finally be done with work and that she could now spend time on herself and her family. We reallocated her IRA into several funds that made more sense for her age and the stage of her life. As part of the process, she also asked me to help her locate an old 401(k) from one of her previous jobs so she could roll it over, since she wasn't working there anymore.

Well, as it turned out, she had left that account with her previous company when she left thirteen years ago! I was shocked! I couldn't understand how she was so comfortable with that fact, and I was even more concerned when she couldn't show me a recent statement for that account. I remember specifically the conversation I had with her, because of what she said to me. It was right around the Thanksgiving holidays, and I remember asking her if she could give me copies of her statements, and she replied with something like, "Hmm, I can't do it until after the long weekend." And then she jokingly followed it up with a phrase that would make her cringe a few weeks later. She said, "Uh, the money's been there forever. I'm sure it can wait another week or two." After the holidays, I met with Anna, and she showed me her documents, but all she had was an old 401(k) statement dated from about eight years prior, which showed that just under 85% of the portfolio was invested in company stock and as of the date of that statement, it was worth about half a million dollars.

Without naming the major hotel where she had previously worked, and where she left that 401(k), when we tried to find out why she was not receiving her statements and where the account was being held, we learned that the hotel chain had filed for bankruptcy years ago! That hotel was then bought out by another major hospitality brand, and all of that company's stock, where most of her portfolio was allocated, was now valued at less than $20k, because it became valued at pennies on the dollar after all the bankruptcy proceedings were finished. So instead of having a value of about half a million dollars, her portfolio was now a pittance in comparison. Anna was devastated and shocked. And by the way, so was I. Witnessing someone think that they have hundreds of thousands of dollars in an account, and helping them track down the information only to find out that it had pretty much become worthless, was an emotionally wrecking experience, because there was nothing I could do to help her recover any of that money. It was gone! Anna couldn't believe this had happened. It never occurred to her that something like this *could* happen. She didn't break down or cry; she just had this lost look of disbelief about her when we found out.

Her unfortunate mistakes were leaving her account at her last job, and setting her account on autopilot and completely forgetting to check in on it from time to time. The other problem is that she was a product of her environment, and like so many other people I've met over the years, she simply believed that *someone* was watching over her money and would alert her if there was a problem. But no one was watching, and no alert ever came. So I hope you learn from Anna's tragic story, and if you even *think* of leaving your 401(k) behind, understand that you can lose all of it.

The problem with leaving your account at an old job is that you simply don't know what's going on with your previous company. At least the present employees will know something is up and can get out of the company stock when they feel trouble brewing. But how could Anna have done that when she was no longer working there and had no contact with previous coworkers? Her false sense of security unfortunately cost her close to half a million dollars.

If Anna had possessed the attitude of that brave lady at the beginning of the book who protected her precious purse by yelling, "Give me back my purse! I'm not giving you my money!" Anna would have had her retirement intact. By leaving her money behind, she subconsciously told the universe, "I don't really care what happens to my money. Go ahead, take it away from me. See if I care." Of course, she didn't actually say that, but that's certainly the attitude she projected out into the world.

If you don't believe in the power of intention and the messages you put out by your actions, then I suggest reading books about the many success stories that started out by someone simply setting forth the right mind-set and intentions. Keep reading and you will get to a great success story in chapter 18 about an experience of a client of mine that at first glance would appear hopeless. But you'll learn how she changed the course of her life significantly by using the right thought process of intention, followed by meaningful actions.

Mistake #7—Treating Your 401(k) as Your Emergency Fund

It is important for you to understand that your 401(k) is your *retirement savings*, not your emergency savings! I know this may sound elementary, but to many people, these two concepts often mean one and the same thing. Over the years, I have met many clients whose thinking I've had to shift to ensure that they understood the concept that their 401(k) is their funding for retirement, not a contingency fund for emergencies. I completely understand that sometimes dipping into your 401(k) may be the only choice open to you, but if you plan ahead and build up an emergency fund in a savings account, then you may be able to avoid taking money from your 401(k). Your 401(k) is meant to supplement your income during retirement, because, trust me, Social Security alone won't be enough, unless you love an all ramen noodle diet—yum! But it's definitely *not* there to help you deal with the challenges you may encounter along the way.

So touching your retirement money should be reserved only for true emergencies, where you simply have no other options. Because every time you dip into your 401(k) before retirement, you are putting yourself a step behind.

Now let's assume that there is an absolute emergency and you have to decide whether it is better to borrow from your account or to take a distribution. Notwithstanding special circumstances, if you're under age 59½ and you take a distribution from your 401(k), you will be penalized by the IRS. There may also be other tax consequences. So in this case, borrowing would likely make more sense. Most 401(k) plans have an easy way to pay yourself back, and you're not paying interest because you borrowed from yourself. Borrowing is sometimes even better even when you are over 59½, as long as you are still working. Again, the first preference would be that you do not dip in your 401(k) at all and that you treat it the same way you would treat a soufflé while it is baking in the oven: Don't open the oven door until it's fully baked or it will collapse! But if you absolutely had to, then you need to ensure that you discuss the situation with your tax preparer before you do anything, and seriously consider any tax consequences and any penalties that may be involved.

Things to Keep in Mind

I hope this has helped to shed some light on how to treat your 401(k). Remember, if you love your 401(k) and treat it well, it will love you right back and will be there for you during retirement. The bottom line is that understanding how your 401(k) works and how the choices you make *now* will affect your lifestyle *later* doesn't require a high IQ or some secret, magical knowledge—just a little common sense and a desire to be in control of your own future. In fact, the concept is similar to learning how to read a map before going on a road trip; you can make all the right and left turns you want, but if you don't know how to read the map, or at least buy a GPS, you'll never get to your destination, and you might drive off a cliff! And no, it won't be in the cool *Thelma-and-Louise* style.

The effects of risk, growth, and contributions can mean the difference between a good retirement and one where you have to make heart-rending decisions about whether to pay the electric bill or to purchase medication. It can mean the difference between staying independent and making your own decisions for many more decades, or becoming dependent on your children and having to ask for help all the time. Sure, you raised your kids, and they definitely owe you for all your hard work and patience, but if you think that after awhile, asking them for help won't become humiliating, then you're in for a rude awakening.

Remember, your 401(k) is not like a magic bean; it won't grow exponentially by itself. It's more like an ordinary bean that requires a certain level of care and attention, as well as some understanding of proper cultivation techniques, to ensure that it grows into the tall, healthy beanstalk you need it to be.

Chapter 13

THE "B-WORD"

"I hear and I forget. I see and I remember. I do and I understand."
—Confucius

B udget. I know that most people don't like to talk about the "B-word." But if you're looking to be successful in your financial planning and to move forward to a happy and healthy financial life, there's no better sidekick than your trusty budget. When you think about it, all a budget really means is that you have taken control of your finances. A woman who can skillfully steer her financial ship is a woman with the foundation of money confidence. You're not simply hoping you have enough money, but you're carefully figuring out what you have, what you need, and what you can spend.

Knowing how much money you spend and what you spend it on is one of the most critical pieces of information you can have. Being in the know about your spending habits and understanding how your money flows through your hands is what lets you have a clear picture of your financial situation. Even more importantly, understanding your cash flow is the first step to understanding how much money you will need during retirement. And if you know how much money you'll need, then you'll be able to prepare for your golden years, or what I refer to as your Life Vacation, in a much more meaningful way.

In the tale of "Rumpelstiltskin," a greedy king believes that a young woman can spin straw into gold, because her father told him she could in a mind-boggling attempt to impress the king. Most dads brag about a daughter's grades or fabulous soccer-playing skills, but I've always been a bit confused about the miller's choice to tell the king that his daughter had supernatural powers of alchemy. I mean, what did he think was going to happen? That the king would just take him at his word and forget about it? Well, the king was a greedy guy, so he decided to swallow his morals and kidnap this beautiful girl so she could fill his treasury with lots of glittering gold. Threatened with all manner of danger and destruction if she didn't come through for him, the young girl is locked in a dungeon and is desperate. Of course, she jumps at the chance to take the help of a slightly maniacal elf-like creature named Rumpelstiltskin who agrees to perform the impossible task in return for payment in the form of things precious to the young woman—a necklace, a ring, and, finally, her firstborn child. Wow—Rumpelstiltskin was quite the negotiator!

However reprehensible he may have been, Rumpelstiltskin did have an amazing skill: He could make money out of basically nothing! Sometimes I think we all wish we had a magical imp in the basement who could take our yard clippings and turn them into gold. And sometimes, many of us act like we do! We'll spend our money on completely frivolous stuff or we won't plan ahead as if somehow, magically, there will always be enough money in our checking accounts to cover it all. We'll log on and check our balance on the bank website, and eyeball it to see if we can reasonably assume that we can afford some purchase, but this process is rarely methodical for most women.

In many ways, we tend to think about the way our money works as this magical straw-into-gold formula. While we may understand some fundamental basics about what's going on with our money, a lot of the time we act as if there's some unknown magic that is the reason why our account balance either grows or it doesn't. And at the end of the month—or sometimes in the middle—we are often totally confused about why we have the amount we do in our bank account. Instead of trying to understand it better, we seek out our own Rumpelstiltskin. We try to make money out of nothing by purchasing lottery tickets, going to Vegas to play roulette, searching the couch cushions for money, or looking around our homes and attics for some long-forgotten antique worth thousands. I don't know about you, but I've never seen anyone have much luck in these attempts to turn nothing much into something substantial. Usually, they are just out more time, effort, and money. I've never been into gambling or buying lottery tickets, because although it may be fun, I could never see how counting on pure luck makes any sense. I'd rather make my own luck by effort. And effort requires knowledge—and more than anything else, persistence.

One of the most important things you can do when it comes to your personal wealth is to understand your expenses, because your expenses are the key to accurately understanding your income needs—now and in the future. If you want a genuinely solid foundation for your financial plan, you absolutely have to start with understanding how, where, and on what you spend your money. By doing that, you will begin to see how much money you will need in retirement to maintain the kind of lifestyle you want. No one wants to get to retirement and be unhappily surprised, so this element of your financial planning could not be more important. Being able to effectively plan a budget and work that plan is crucial to your financial happiness. It's absolutely vital to take this step seriously.

I've always been bothered by the fact that the financial industry still fails to recognize that their clients' spending habits and lifestyle are a major part of their retirement. It's not simply about investing money somewhere and hoping it will grow over time. Why are you buying an investment in the first place? Just so it grows and you have more money? By that rationale, you should also go to the gym and aimlessly do exercises without any plan at all. Do some squats here and some yoga there, and maybe it will eventually address the reason you went to the gym in the first place. But if you go to your workout with a plan to improve your health in a specific way, like to get some cardio or build up strength or maybe make those love handles less handle-ey (yes, I made up that word), then you'll do exercises that are meant to address those specific goals. Planning for your retirement income needs is much the same. You need to look at your future work pension, if you've got one. Then estimate Social Security benefits, and compare your total estimated income in retirement to how much money you will need to cover your living expenses. And only after that will you be able to make a genuinely smart decision about how to invest your nest egg.

With that same idea, you can't plan what investments are most suited to you if you don't know exactly what your future expenses will be and how much income you will need during retirement. We are living longer and healthier lives, and planning for lifetime income is essential for everyone. The most important step to a good plan is understanding your expenses now and in the future. So this is one area where you have to hop in the driver's seat and figure things out.

Budgeting—The Poor, Ugly Duckling

In a lot of ways, budgeting is like the ugly duckling—seriously misunderstood and neglected. If you are like most people, you probably look at budget planning like you looked at eating your Brussels sprouts when you were eight. Yes, you know you have to, but it's no fun at all! However, budgets unfairly get a bad reputation because most people incorrectly believe that budgets are a source of deprivation rather than a source of wealth. A budget has somehow become synonymous with the idea that you absolutely cannot have everything you want, when in reality the opposite is true! It's a way to have more of what you *do* want by eliminating the spending on things that don't mean much to you and which you only buy impulsively. Strategic budget planning is the key to success for companies and individuals who understand how to grow their money.

Take Google, for example. By anyone's definition, Google is a hugely successful company (just "Google" it) that recently overtook Microsoft in market value. This was a huge feat since Microsoft had a twenty-year head start.[21] In order to become an industry leader, Google certainly had to strategically plan its expenditures. But imagine for a moment that they didn't. For the next three, six, or even twelve months, Google just did whatever Google executives wanted to do in the moment. They tossed their budget plan out of the high-rise window, so to speak, and operated the business based on whim and guesswork. Revenue projections were suddenly a thing of the past. Checks were written whenever someone requested one—perhaps all at one time—regardless of when revenue had been received. If this strategically brilliant technology giant operated like this, do you think the company would be able to keep its doors open? Do you think Google would be as successful as it is today? Of course not! It would be shuttered before we knew it, having wasted away its opportunities because it failed to plan a budget. Well, you're a successful person, an individual Google so to speak, so why should your financial activities be any different? Unless you have an elf spinning straw into an everlasting slush fund of gold in your basement, you should be mindfully planning your budget the same way.

Much as you may wish it to be true, your financial life is not a fairy tale. The only person with the capacity to increase your wealth is *you*, and you are entirely capable of doing it. Furthermore, you have some tools at your disposal that will help you increase your net worth with a little effort. Even Rumpelstiltskin had to put his shoulder to the wheel all night long—and it's important that you, too, put in the effort to make your money work for you. Understanding your finances in detail will help you take that step toward a more lucrative outcome for your financial future.

Money Comes In, Money Goes Out

The first and most important part of budget planning is to understand what money is coming in, what money is going out, and what that money is earmarked for. First, let's talk a bit about the types of expenses you encounter each month. Fixed expenses are what they sound like—bills you are responsible for that, for the most part, are a fixed amount each month. These expenses might include things like your mortgage or rent, your car payment, your phone bill, or your utility bills. Again, I'm not talking about credit card bills that may radically change from month to month, but the things that change little from one month to the next. Of course, inflation rate changes may cause some of these charges to fluctuate over time, but for the most part, you can count on fixed expenses to be about the same, most of the time. Most people tend to have a good grasp on these bills, because these are usually *needs*—the things you know you always have to plan for and pay. Because they are fixed expenses, these might also be the bills that you have automatically debited from your account, simply because they are so regular you can anticipate them with confidence.

The flexible expenses are an area where most people tend to go a bit off the budgetary rails. That's totally normal, because these are the hard-to-pin-down expenses like entertainment, eating out, and shopping. If you're like most people, you don't sit down on the first day of the month and say, "This month, I am going to purchase three pencil skirts and a fabulous bag, for a total of $300." Of course not! You saw that beautiful purse in the store window or you signed up for that new set of dance classes on a whim! Sometimes we can get a bit carried away with our flexible spending habits, much like that storybook emperor who wanted some new clothes but ended up strolling around naked.[22] We hear some buzz about a new play, or a designer with amazing handbags, and decide that we *have* to check them out. We want it. We deserve it. So, darn it, we're getting it! Because flexible expenses are *wants* and aren't planned for, we tend to behave like the emperor with no clothes did—we pretend that everything is ok, even if we are suspicious that maybe that purchase wasn't the smartest financial decision we've ever made.

Where Did It All Go?

The only way to truly understand the state of your finances is to start tracking your expenses as you pay for things—there's no way around it. If you're already a list-maker, and many of us are, this won't be too much of a challenge for you. If you aren't, this process may feel a bit uncomfortable at first, but it's definitely not brain surgery. Nevertheless, it's important for you to make a list of your fixed expenses and track your flexible expenses in order to get an accurate picture of your financial life. Once you do, you will have a much better understanding of how your money is currently working, and even more importantly, where you could cut impulsive spending on things you don't really care about so you have more money for the things you do want.

Keeping track of your finances is as eye-opening as tracking your calorie intake. A few years ago, I had gained twenty pounds—like overnight. Ha! Well, that's how it felt, anyway—as if it happened within a day! When I had a hard time figuring out why this had happened, my trainer gave me a food diary and committed me to writing down everything I was eating. All of a sudden, my morning latte was not just a daily dose of caffeine—it was 480 calories! Going directly to my thighs! I suddenly realized that even a simple cup of delicious coffee in the morning could have a substantial impact on my goals. It was almost a third of the daily calories I was allowed under my workout plan. It was no wonder that I was gaining weight. I was going merrily through my day, not realizing the large amount of calories I was consuming, thinking everything was fine. Only when I started writing things down did I realize my mistakes. Imagine, a latte here and there, then a protein bar (or a chocolate, depending on my mood for the day), then dinner, maybe a glass of wine . . . maybe two . . . and now, my "nothing" calories were really like 2,000—or even more many other days! Well, no wonder I was gaining!

Your spending habits work the same way! When you take the time to write down what you are spending your hard-earned money on each month, you will see your finances in a completely new light. Physically keeping track of your expenses each day, writing them down in one place, is eye-opening. Some people prefer to use an app on a smartphone or an Excel spreadsheet; whatever you want to use, the most important thing is to be consistent. However, I strongly suggest to my clients that, in the beginning, they write it down on paper. Remember your time in school—if you needed to remember something, you took notes. You highlighted the textbook and wrote in the margins. You probably do the same thing now when you are sitting in a meeting or a seminar. It's human nature, because when you write, you learn. Our brain registers the information differently than if we type it or swipe it into an app or program.

Since this is definitely a learning process, and I want my clients to learn in the most effective way possible, I created a tool I call Your Personal Money Diary because so many of my clients needed a tool where they could organize their spending notes. You'll catch your mistakes faster, and nothing prevents you from translating those handwritten notes into software or an Excel spreadsheet later on. But whatever system or software you decide to use, make it work for you. I guarantee you will love the result even more than the Tory Burch wallet you just bought, because now you can get the matching purse—since you have more cash flow because you are spending more wisely!

At the end of each day, take a few minutes to write down what you've spent, keeping track of the expenses as either fixed or flexible. If you wrote a check to pay the mortgage, that goes in fixed expenses. If you went to

Starbucks and bought a scone, or found a pair of shoes you loved at the mall, those purchases should go under flexible expenses. It doesn't matter what you've spent or how you spent it—just record it. No judgment; just accountability—to no one other than yourself. I promise, no one will steal your notes and expose them to the world.

Seeing your strengths and weaknesses in black and white each day as you record your spending may jar you in the same way that my epiphany about the latte did for me. Suddenly, your successes—and the failures you have been blind to until that moment—are staring at you in all their glaring truth. It's not always easy to come to terms with your spending habits and realize you've been throwing your money away on things you didn't need. You may even feel a bit like the emperor after the little boy told him the truth no one else had the courage to tell—naked, silly, and a bit foolish for not seeing it all along. Well, don't! Instead, be grateful you had the courage to start the process and face any previous mistakes. Those failures will soon turn into opportunities for wealth-building and budgetary success in no time. The first step is to start so you can make smarter, better decisions with more information.

Planning a budget, even if it's not 100 percent complete, will help you see and make better spending choices in the future. If you need help, you can take this new information to a financial advisor to fine-tune your budget planning. But I can tell you this, though: Most of my clients who commit to recording their expenses in this way end up making all of the changes I would have advised them to make on their own—they simply learned what they needed to learn through the process. You will too!

I'm including a few sample worksheets from the Money Diary at the end of this chapter to help you get started. Grab a pencil and start filling them out. You'll quickly notice that simply organizing your thoughts about your finances and your expenditures can make a huge difference.

	EXAMPLE 1	EXAMPLE 2
WHAT YOU OWN		
VALUE OF HOME	$450,000	$200,000
VALUE OF CAR	$50,000	$10,000
401(K)	$100,000	$-
SAVINGS ACCOUNT	$-	$2,000
TOTAL YOU OWN	$600,000	$212,000
WHAT YOU OWE		
MORTGAGE ON HOME	$340,000	$185,000
CAR LOAN	$40,000	$9,000
CREDIT CARDS	$20,000	$25,000
TOTAL YOU OWE	$400,000	$219,000
NET WORTH:	$200,000	$(7,000)

Woof, Woof—What You're Really Worth

Once you have a handle on how much money you have coming in and the money you've been spending, the next step is calculating your net worth. Normally, companies are judged based on their net worth, or the assets of the company (the things in their possession) minus the debts of the company (everything they owe). If you are evaluating your own finances, you should do the same calculation to see how much you have once you subtract everything you owe, all your loans, credit card balances, and any other debts.

Though it might be confusing at first, the definition of net worth is pretty simple when you break it down. Net worth is what you own minus what you owe. For example, if you have a $450,000 home, a $50,000 vehicle, and a 401(k) with $100,000 in it, but owe $340,000 on your mortgage, $40,000 on your vehicle, and have $20,000 in consumer debt, then your net worth would be $600,000 of assets minus $400,000 of debts, or a total of $200,000. Your numbers may be much smaller and more complicated or larger and less complicated, but the equation is always the same (Net Worth = What You Own – What You Owe). You always, obviously, want your net worth to be large and positive, but in certain periods of your life, you may not find that to be the case. In some cases, you may have a $200,000 home, a $10,000 vehicle, a savings account with $2,000, and a mortgage of $185,000, a car loan for $9,000, and consumer debt in the amount of $25,000. When you were first starting out, a scenario like that might have been the case. In this second scenario, your net worth would still be calculated by taking the assets of $212,000 and subtracting the debt of $219,000, for a total net worth of negative $7,000—meaning that if you sold all of your possessions, you would still owe $7,000. In this situation, someone is praying either for a magical goose to wander into the backyard where it can start laying golden eggs, or for a handful of magic beans with a rich, sleepy giant at the top to sprout in the garden—anything to catch a financial break. But if you find yourself in a situation like this, don't despair. With careful budgeting and a desire to improve your situation, you'll be amazed at how much you can achieve.

Sometimes, like in the second scenario, you might wonder why you even need to know your net worth. Although it can sometimes be disheartening to see your current situation, you can't start making adjustments or strategic plans about how to do better if you're not even sure where the problems are. It's like walking up to the mirror in the morning (not a magic, ego-stroking mirror, but a real one) and realizing that maybe it's time to hit the treadmill—a budgeting treadmill that helps you pay down your loans and lose some debt.

The truth will always set you free and help you make better decisions. During my continuous battle with dieting, my mom told me something I will never forget: "Honey, you only have two best friends who will always be true to you in this area: the mirror and the scale. They will never, ever lie to you." And you know what, she was right! Unlike my actual friends who kept telling me that I looked great, the mirror and the scale were never going to feel bad for me and lie to make me feel better. The mirror and the scale weren't going to say, "Don't worry, you don't look like you gained that much weight" or "You are skinnier than you think!" Well, I realized that what my mom said was so similar to what I tell my clients about their net worth. Your Money Diary and bank accounts are never going to lie to you. They will show you exactly what you need to see so you can make the necessary changes to be more successful.

As you are looking at your expense sheet in combination with your net worth calculations, you can decide where to shift your money so you can make strides toward financial freedom. Perhaps you'll decide that you want to focus on paying off your mortgage faster or that you want to build up your 401(k) more quickly. Something about consciously knowing your net worth, in combination with tracking your expenses, will help you begin to make better, wiser financial choices for yourself. And that "something" is nothing more than seeing the truth about your financial situation. The thing is, most people already know the right decisions they need to make, but it can be difficult to make the right choices if the uncomfortable truth is not staring you right in the face.

Get on the Money Fast!

Once you have begun tracking your fixed and flexible expenses, and you have created an accurate picture of your net worth, you can begin to improve your buying behavior in order to make smarter money decisions. If you have looked at your net worth and your expenses and have decided that you want to save more each month, you'll likely find room to do so in your flexible expenses category, and you can start by money fasting today. I know everyone is doing all kinds of fasting diets these days and starving themselves to lose weight. The strategy I teach my clients is the 30-Day Money Fast, which will open your eyes about whether you are buying the things you want because they are important to you, or if you are buying them impulsively without thinking through the decisions on how to spend your hard-earned money. But I promise, the Money Fast is much easier than saying no to a delicious midnight snack that is reaching out to you with its sweet carbohydrate arms, saying, "Just one bite . . . no one will ever know . . . it will be our little secret." The Money Fast will leave you feeling fulfilled.

The 30-Day Money Fast is pretty straightforward. Instead of buying something right away, start window-shopping. Make a list of the things you see and like and would normally purchase right away—but don't buy them. Make your list, perhaps on the same piece of paper where you are tracking your expenses. Include dates on the list, and tell yourself that after thirty days you can buy the items on it; but until then, they are off-limits! You are not depriving yourself. You are simply waiting to see if an item is as important to you as building your net worth or paying off some of your debt. Once the thirty days are up, you can go back to the Apple Store to buy the latest release, or back to the mall to buy those Jimmy Choos or whatever new gadget you can't live without—if you are still dreaming about it. But only after the 30-day Money Fasting period is over!

I will promise you this: Two-thirds of what you write down in your 30-Day Money Fast list will stop being important to you pretty quickly. Sometimes we buy things we don't need or even truly want, simply because we are caught up in the moment. By taking the time to evaluate your true desires, by giving yourself some time, you will make sure you are only spending your money on the things you truly want. Again and again, this strategy has worked brilliantly for my clients who have tried it, and they are always astonished by the results. Each and every one of them who tried this while in the store thought they wanted some item; thirty days later, their true desires became much clearer and, as a result, they were able to make better and wiser money decisions, rather than impulsively throwing money in the trash.

Another step I encourage my clients to take in order to feel empowered in their financial lives and build that money confidence muscle is education. As I mentioned earlier, many women, because of cultural messages and habits, simply don't take control of their finances. They feel it's not their place or that they are not capable of managing their money effectively. I hope, by this point, you realize that's absolutely not true. Educating yourself about areas of financial planning and management that still feel like personal weaknesses is one way to truly ensure you have all the tools you need to take control of your financial future. Look for interesting workshops in your area, podcasts that you can listen to at the gym or in your car during your commute, instructional courses, books—all of these can help you proactively plan for your own financial happily-ever-after.

Keeping a good habit, whether it's eating healthy, spending wisely, or playing volleyball to stay in shape, takes determination and continuous, positive reinforcement. You can't forget that. Creating a budget to keep track of your expenditures is not a one-time thing. It requires your regular attention and effort. Look at Maria Sharapova. She's an amazing tennis player. Don't you think this is because she is always practicing her skills and trying to get better? What would happen if she practiced a bit here and there and then stopped? Do you think she could win a competition again?

Investing IN Your Money

When Snow White's stepmother stepped in front of that devoted magical mirror every morning, she didn't say, "Mirror, mirror on the wall, who's the most hateful, horribly ugly, woefully ignorant stepmother-with-bad fashion-sense of them all?" No. She stepped up with swagger and confidence and said, "Who's the fairest of them all?"—and believed, without a shadow of a doubt, that the answer would and should be her. While I don't think the Evil Queen should be our model for healthy, productive relationships or moral judgment, I think—at least in this particular area—she got something right. She put out into the world what she expected to get. Her confidence and her ridiculously huge sense of self-worth were infectious.

If you're hesitant to get behind the Evil Queen's confidence model, ask yourself if you've heard people joke about their financial future in negative ways. "Oh, I'll just end up eating cat food when I'm eighty" or "I'd better get used to this shopping cart, because this will be my home when I retire." Maybe you laughed at the time, because the person seemed as if they were joking as well. I wish you wouldn't, and if these were your jokes, I'd like you to stop.

Think about what you are telling yourself, subconsciously, about your future every time you say negative things like that, or even think them. You're not suggesting wealth or privilege, certainly, and it's fine if that's not your ultimate goal. But you're not even suggesting that you will be comfortable or have sufficient money for your needs. You are telling yourself that you will be impoverished, and if we tell ourselves enough times that we will be something, then we shouldn't be surprised when that's exactly what happens. Of course, this isn't what you intend, but our lives are the result of our attitude and words. So—create a self-fulfilling prophecy that works for you rather than one that works against you by wholeheartedly believing you will have an amazing retirement, and this simple attitude change will drive you to take steps that will get you there!

Imagine if you behaved this way in any of the other relationships in your life—in your marriage, with your children, or with your colleagues. If you consistently showed no real interest in what was happening, put no thought into the future, didn't invest in that relationship, or spoke negatively about the future constantly, the relationship would likely not last. Nobody wants to be in a relationship with Sleepy or Dopey or Grumpy for long. Whether you have thought about it in these terms or not, you do have a relationship with your money. If you keep telling yourself you don't care about where your money comes from or where your money goes, then you won't have a healthy relationship with it. Money will stay and work for you so long as you work to create an environment where it is appreciated (pun intended). It may sound silly, but what does it hurt to try? Working to be more focused on positive, constructive actions and attitudes about your financial future can change your entire outlook on what is possible, and it will help you take more positive steps to get there. You might be really surprised: Treat your money with respect, and it will respect you by sticking around longer. You can start by listening to financial inspiration CDs or reading positive books about money. Change your negative and frustrated thoughts about money, and start thinking of money as a loving life partner who only wants to make you happy. This way, money will be your loyal companion for the rest of your life!

When you start the budget planning process, you may feel a bit like the girl in the dungeon in the Rumpelstiltskin story. Desperate for success, you may feel that by tracking your expenses and limiting yourself on the 30-Day Money Fast, you are signing away your firstborn child for something that may not even be successful. The reality is the opposite. Unlike that miller's daughter, you'll be entirely in control of your future. You won't have to depend on an ugly elf-like creature—a creature who will force you to give away the things most precious to you to be able to pay the bills after retirement—for your survival. Instead, you'll be the one creating your success and building your wealth, one little step at a time!

Money Confidence through Budgeting: Things to Keep in Mind

- Realize that budgeting is an important foundation of your financial future.

- Recognize that budget planning *makes* you money—not takes it away.

- Know the difference between your fixed and flexible expenses so you can better estimate your income needs.

- Track all of your expenses by writing them down every day so you can get an accurate snapshot of how your money is currently working for you.

- Calculate your net worth and ask yourself if it's where you want it to be.

- Take steps toward making wiser financial decisions, like participating in the 30-Day Money Fast and any educational opportunities that will help you be more in control of your cash.

- Think positively about your financial future! Create a successful, positive self-fulfilling prophecy.

Making and working a budget plan is like spinning straw into gold—with a bit of effort, you get a big return on not much at all. And the best part? *You* will have done it—no magic required—and the amazing returns will help you be much further along in your plan for a financial happily-ever-after.

MY NET WORTH

ASSETS	AMOUNT	LIABILITIES	AMOUNT
CASH		**LOAN**	
Savings Account		House	
Checking Account		Investment Property	
Business Account		Car	
Money Market Account		Education	
Foreign Currency		Credit Cards	
Other		Tax	
INVESTMENTS		**CURRENT BILLS**	
Government Bonds			
Other Bonds			
International Investments			
Stocks (Domestics/Foreign)			
CDs			
REAL ESTATE		**TAXES**	
Domestic			
International			
MISC			
Vehicles			
Precious Metals			
Luxury Collectibles		**MISC**	
Furniture			
Electronics			
Tools/Machinery			
Insurance			
Cash Settlements			
TOTAL:		**TOTAL:**	

TOTAL ASSETS – TOTAL LIABILITIES = NET WORTH

The following pages are from Your Personal Money Diary. If you want to download the usable lite version, go to:

http://CrystalOculee.com/money-diary-lite

MY APPROXIMATE FIXED & FLEXIBLE EXPENSES

EXPENSES	MONTHLY	YEARLY
HOUSING		
Rent/Mortgage (principal, interest, taxes)		
Home Association Fees		
Parking Garage or Space Rentals		
Electricity		
Gas		
Home Telephone		
Mobile Telephone		
Internet		
Home Improvement		
Utilities (water/sewer/trash)		
Other		
TRANSPORTATION		
Car Payment(s)		
Car Registration(s)		
Gas/Fuel		
Maintenance (Regular Oil Change/Service)		
Repairs		
Public Transportation		
Other		
DAILY LIVING		
Groceries		
Dining/Eating Out		
Clothing/Shoes		
Cleaning Services (Dry Cleaning)		
Housekeeping		
Salon/Barber		
Other		

EXPENSES	MONTHLY	YEARLY
INSURANCE		
Life Insurance		
Health Insurance		
Dental Insurance		
Car Insurance		
Home Insurance		
MISC.		
HEALTH		
Emergency		
Medicine/Drugs		
Other		
EDUCATION		
Tuition Fees		
Books		
School Supplies		
Lunch		
Clothing/Uniforms		
After-School Care		
Other Specialty Courses		
Other		
SAVINGS		
Emergency Fund		
Savings Account		
Retirement (401k, IRA)		
College Fund		
Investments		
Other		
CHARITY/GIFTS		
Religious Donations		
Medical Donations		
School Donations		
Charitable Donations		
Other		

EXPENSES	MONTHLY	YEARLY
DEBITS		
Alimony/Child Support		
Student Loan		
Bank Loan(s)		
Credit Card 1		
Credit Card 2		
Federal Taxes		
State Taxes		
Other		
ENTERTAINMENT		
DVD/CD		
Movies/Theaters		
Rentals		
Concerts/Plays		
Toys/Video Games		
Electronics		
Books		
Film/Photos		
Sporting Events		
Outdoor Recreation		
Other		
Other		
BUSINESS		
Office Supplies		
Office Equipment		
Restaurants		
Travel		
Gas/Fuel		
Mileage		
Other		
VACATION		
Travel		
Rental		
Lodging		
Food/Dining Out		
Entertainment		
Fun Activities		
Gifts		
Other		

EXPENSES	MONTHLY	YEARLY
HOBBY		
Supplies		
Collectible Objects		
Tools/Equipment		
Other		
Other		
SUBSCRIPTIONS		
Magazines		
Newspapers		
Internet		
TV/Cable/Satellite		
Gym/Health Club		
Other		
MISC.		
TOTAL:		

Chapter 14

THE GOLDILOCKS METHOD

"At the center of your being you have the answer;
you know who you are and you know what you want."
—Lao Tzu

D o you remember the story of Goldilocks? She was the girl who went into the forest, stumbled upon a cabin, and decided to make herself at home while the inhabitants, three bears, were away. While she was inside their house, Goldilocks helped herself to their food and took a nice, relaxing nap in their beds. Then she came up to the table where three bowls of porridge sat. Instead of having just one bowl, she tried all three to find one that was exactly the right temperature. Then, instead of simply sitting down and eating, she sat on all the chairs in the house until she found one that was just the right height for her. And after her meal, she felt sleepy, but instead of lying down in any bed to take a nap, she tried all three beds until she found one that wasn't too hard, wasn't too soft, but was "just right."

Although in the fairy tale, Goldilocks is made out to be a completely inconsiderate girl who helped herself to others' stuff (she *was* kind of rude!), there *is* one thing about this girl that is commendable: She didn't like to settle for things if they weren't to her satisfaction. When you decide to set out on your quest to find a financial advisor who will listen to your needs, will answer your questions, and will take your future seriously, you can greatly improve your chances of a successful match by using what I call the Goldilocks Method. Now, when I talk about the Goldilocks Method,

I'm definitely *not* saying you should start breaking into people's homes and eating their food. Although it might initially seem like a great strategy for saving money toward your retirement, you will eventually get in trouble. I also don't suggest trying to steal food from actual bears, as they tend to get cranky when you do that. What I *am* talking about is searching for a financial advisor with the same pickiness that Goldilocks used for food or a bed. She didn't settle for the first thing she saw! No. She knew what she liked and wouldn't accept anything less.

To be successful in your search, it's key to figure out what qualities you are looking for in an advisor and what questions to ask as you interview potential advisors to ensure you can find the right fit for you and your financial needs. Yes—I said *interview*, because you are hiring this person to help you care for your finances. When my dentist moved and I was looking for another one, I literally went to three different dentists before I chose one. I went to what they thought was a standard dental checkup with my list of questions and, through X-rays and discussions about flossing, I interviewed them to see if they were the right match for me. I was looking to find the dentist with the right personality and a methodology/approach that made sense for me. I am picky about who I have in my life—professional or personal. So whether it's a doctor, a lawyer, a massage therapist, or even a friend, I always make sure they have the qualities I am looking for before I commit to a relationship.

You likely feel the same way about the important things in your life. You certainly wouldn't hire a nanny without thoroughly checking references and making sure the person was a good fit for you and your family. You wouldn't hire a contractor without seeing their work and speaking with other customers. So there's absolutely no reason to act any differently with your financial advisor! In all these cases, you are hiring a professional charged with maintaining the safety and security of the things most precious to you: your family, your home, and your future. Your investments and portfolio are more than just dollars and cents: They are the key to achieving your dreams and turning your vision of a happy retirement into reality.

Deciding What You Need in a Financial Advisor

So it's time to strategize and create a plan of action. There are lots of financial advisors out there. You have to find one who's right for *you*, who fits well with your personality, and takes your future as seriously as you do. That's why one of your first steps in this process should be deciding on the qualities you would like your financial advisor to have. The best way to go about this is to write those qualities out on a piece of paper. So dig out that dusty notepad where you used to make your shopping lists before they became digital. You're going to make a list of qualities you hope to find in your new financial advisor. If this process is feeling familiar, it's probably because you already do this kind of comparison list-making for many important decisions you make in your life. Think back to when you bought your home—before you were wooed by the beautiful marble in the kitchen or the incredible closet space. You probably sat down with your family and decided what you loved about your prior home and what features were important to have in the new one. That way, you could keep those things in mind as you shopped around. When you write it down, that list becomes a concrete, unemotional compass to keep you on the right path.

If this process isn't feeling familiar or maybe even feels silly to you, don't worry. No one is looking over your shoulder, and no one else needs to see this piece of paper. So simply write without thinking about right or wrong answers. In this situation, there aren't any. What you like and don't like is as personal and unique to you as your fingerprint or taste in shoes; no one can replicate it, even if they try! You can go back and reword your descriptions later, if you want to. Right now, simply commit to writing what comes to mind.

Your Mission Statement

When you begin at the top of the page, write a few short sentences about what you want your relationship with your financial advisor to accomplish. Think about goals and objectives, but also think bigger! Think about this statement as your mission statement for this new financial planning relationship. A series of questions might help you take these thoughts and turn them into a clear statement of objectives:

- What do you want your financial advisor to do for you?
- How would you like to be treated?
- What would you like to understand better about your finances?
- What financial goals do you have that you'd like your financial advisor to be working toward?
- What would you like your relationship to be like? (Think of specific, descriptive words here.)

Your statement should be two or three sentences long, and might look something like this:

I want my new financial advisor to explain investment strategies to me.

I'd like to know my risk tolerance as well as my worst-case scenario.

I want to be able to be comfortable during retirement.

I want to be able to have an efficient, professional, and friendly relationship with my financial advisor.

You can see here that, as you write down this statement, what you want in a new relationship becomes clearer and clearer. The more specific you are, the clearer the vision of what you want will become; you should be as clear about this list as Goldilocks was about the height of the chair she wanted and the ideal temperature of her porridge. This is not being demanding or unrealistic; this is simply being clear about what you want your advisor to do, what you'd like to understand, what goals you have for your future, and the kind of interaction you want to have with your financial professional. Remember what we talked about earlier—having true money confidence means defining your expectations and affirming them to yourself and the people you work with. If you don't respect or care about your finances—why should anyone else?

This is why it's so important to be specific. When you find the person who meets your expectations, you will recognize him or her right away. Goldilocks knew immediately when something didn't fit her criteria, and she dismissed it without another thought. You want to be able to do the same thing, quickly and without worry that you're making the wrong decision. Think about how helpful that clarity will be when you are interviewing potential candidates!

List of Qualities

If you had an amazing opportunity to have a world-class fashion designer create a one-of-a-kind outfit just for you, and that designer asked you for your input, would you sit there and say nothing? Of course not! You would be a fountain of helpful and thorough suggestions, based on your personality and your vision for yourself. You might suggest what silhouettes you thought looked best on you, and other details you liked and wanted to have on the outfit. You'd probably be as specific as possible, because that specificity would mean the difference between a classic outfit you could keep forever and a piece that might be better suited for a garage sale because it didn't work for you at all. To put this in perspective, that's just a dress! Something you wear a few times a year at the most! When we're talking about choosing the right financial advisor, we're talking about ensuring the possibility of buying *every* dress you will need during your retirement, taking *every* vacation your heart desires, sleeping easily *every* night, and being certain that you are well taken care of *tomorrow* because you chose so wisely *today*.

Like with the designer dress input, you must be specific about what you need and want in a financial advisor. Figuring out exactly what you need can be tough, but I suggest you make a list that looks at your past and at your future. It should look something like the following three-columned list that focuses on what you liked and didn't like about your old financial advisor and what you believe you want in your new one. Being super specific matters here too—you're trying to find the financial advisor who will fit your financial goals in the same way that a great dress should fit you.

Jot down the ideas as they come to you, and don't worry about putting them in any sort of order or how many qualities you come up with in each column. Keep going until you feel like it's a complete list, because that's all that matters. As you're reading this, you might be making the list in your mind already. Go write it down!

THE GOLDILOCKS METHOD

WHAT I DIDN'T LIKE ABOUT MY OLD FINANCIAL ADVISOR	WHAT I DID LIKE ABOUT MY OLD FINANCIAL ADVISOR	WHAT I WANT IN MY NEW FINANCIAL ADVISOR
1. Didn't return my calls	1. Was friendly & upbeat	1. Faster communication
2. Was never on time	2. Brought me chocolates!	2. Prompt meetings
3. Didn't have an assistant to help me	3. Was willing to meet at my house—I didn't have to drive!	3. Would like him/her to have a team/assistant
4. Didn't answer questions clearly	4. I was used to him/her and felt comfortable asking questions	4. Want clearer/better explanations

When you have written down all of the qualities you can think of, top to bottom, highlight the ones that are most important to you. These are the crucial ones that will make a difference in your financial life, so only highlight the must-haves—not the ones that are irrelevant to your main financial goal. Then, cross off the rest. Here's an example of how your list might look:

THE GOLDILOCKS METHOD

WHAT I DIDN'T LIKE ABOUT MY OLD FINANCIAL ADVISOR	WHAT I DID LIKE ABOUT MY OLD FINANCIAL ADVISOR	WHAT I WANT IN MY NEW FINANCIAL ADVISOR
1. Didn't return my calls	1. Was friendly & upbeat	1. Faster communication
2. Was never on time	2. Brought me chocolates!	2. Prompt meetings
3. Didn't have an assistant to help me	3. Was willing to meet at my house—I didn't have to drive!	3. Would like him/her to have a team/assistant
4. Didn't answer questions clearly	4. I was used to him/her and felt comfortable asking questions	4. Want clearer/better explanations

What you're doing here is working on identifying the essentials. You don't have to forget the nonessential stuff, but think of the nonessentials as extra perks. Even if you loved the little gifts your financial advisor got you—the box of chocolates for the holidays or the gift certificate to the spa every year on your birthday—you'd probably agree that these things are not essential to your overall financial goals. Instead, when you're making a list of what you need and want in a financial advisor, the focus should be on what will help you accomplish those goals.

Take a look at your new, refined list—these are your personal criteria for your new financial advisor, based on what is most important to you. Your list is as unique as you are. And with this list, you'll be able to start your search for someone who truly is the right fit for your goals. Here are some additional important criteria you may want to consider:

Money Confidence Checklist: The Top Ten Must-Haves for My Financial Advisor

These ten qualities are the things I think every financial advisor must have if he or she is going to help you accomplish your long-term financial goals. Some of these you may already have on your list, perhaps phrased differently, and some may be entirely new to you. Regardless, these are qualities to which you should give careful consideration as you are interviewing potential financial professionals.

1. Your Advisor Should Be Passionate about Their Job

For the right financial professional, advising clients about their investments and helping them plan their retirement should be a career. It shouldn't be a side job or a hobby, something that he or she dabbles in with some spare time for extra money. No. It is what they should breathe and eat, every single day. For example, you may think it's fine to have an accountant who does financial advising on the side. It seems to work, on the surface, since both occupations focus on finances. But trust me—that person is bad at one of those jobs, and it's likely the one that's the side gig. If I asked you if you'd like to go to a cardiologist who is also a gynecologist, would you feel comfortable doing that, or would you hesitate because you'd feel like they're probably average, or below average, in one of those fields? It all comes down to experience, and if your advisor is also your CPA, then he or she is not spending enough time gaining experience in either field. Because of that, one area will definitely suffer. So beware if you gravitate to the jack-of-all-trades types, thinking you'll get more for your money. Remember the end of the saying, "Jack-of-all-trades and master of none." You deserve better.

2. Your Advisor Needs to Have the Proper Licenses to Conduct Transactions and Needs to Be Listed with FINRA

Here's some technical information you may not have known about financial professionals. FINRA (or the Financial Industry Regulatory Authority) is the agency that helps the financial industry self-regulate. In addition to conducting audits and other oversight activities, FINRA provides licenses to financial professionals that allow them to conduct specific transactions for their clients. Depending on what investments your advisor wants to work with, that advisor must pass a series of tests and be licensed to help you with those investments. You need to know what licenses your advisor has and his or her standing with FINRA. Don't end up with a financial advisor who seems great on the outside but ends up being exactly the opposite—like that Dolce bag you thought you got for a steal from a friend but were shocked to find it was actually a "Dolce & Gabbana" that she picked up on Canal Street, along with that Rolex that upon closer inspection turned out to be a "Folex." Nobody likes a counterfeit of any kind.

3. Your Advisor Should Have Been with Their Current Firm for at Least Five Years

You want to build a long-term professional relationship with your advisor. If you discover that the professional you are considering has frequently hopped firms, you should view that behavior as a major red flag and a sign of a lack of commitment. What you want is the little black dress equivalent in your financial advisor—someone you can be confident will stick around for years, someone who is dependable and always comes through when you need them to. A financial advisor who has roots demonstrates credibility and strength of character. The last thing you want is someone who cannot survive more than a few seasons.

4. Your Advisor Should Have at Least Five Years of Experience in the Financial Field

It's great if you find an advisor with whom you really click, but if they're new to the business, chances are they're not the best fit for you. When it comes to your money, like when hiring a doctor, experience is important. You need someone who can call on experiences at his or her fingertips and has seen enough real-life scenarios to be able to use them to help you. Even if this new financial advisor has been working under someone's supervision, perhaps a senior financial planner or someone who has a solid, time-tested record of successful investments, their supervisor's experience is not their own. Look for a track record. You don't want a rookie practicing with your hard-earned money.

5. Your Advisor Should Have Good Communication Skills

Anyone who tells you that communication skills are not necessary in the financial world is telling you the worst kind of lie! Finding out about your investments should not be a guessing game with huge consequences. Instead, you want a financial advisor with the qualities of a good teacher: one who uses clear explanations, has patience, and is not easily frustrated by questions. Your financial advisor should answer your questions courteously and in a timely fashion, and should make you feel better for having asked them.

6. The Office Should Always Return Your Call within Twenty-four Hours

Emergencies and weekends notwithstanding, your financial advisor or a member of his or her team should get back to you quickly—every single time. You need to be able to count on their accessibility. Imagine you are purchasing or refinancing a home. If your financial advisor's office makes you wait days and days for a response to every question or request for information from the mortgage company, you may not only be looking at frustration—you may be looking at an increased interest rate or a lost opportunity for a great deal because your financial advisor failed to return your phone calls.

I have one other note on this: When you do find an advisor who is responsive and returns your calls the same day or within twenty-four hours, you will likely feel happy and grateful for the attention and service you're getting. But honestly, you shouldn't—because prompt replies to communication from you should be the industry norm. It isn't yet. But seriously—when an advisor is handling *your* money, expecting a callback within twenty-four hours should feel as natural as knowing that the sun will rise in the morning.

7. Your Advisor Should Have at Least One Assistant or Team Member as Support Staff

One person simply can't do it all. When your financial professional is a one-man or one-woman show, your needs may not always be met if he or she is out of town or unreachable during an emergency. If that person has an assistant or a team member who is working to help serve clients, you will always have a point person available. Remember the fairy tale about the shoemaker who worked tirelessly to make all of those shoes but couldn't quite do it, despite his best efforts? He had a magical elfin entourage that worked all night to finish the work. That's what you want—your financial professional should have a back-up system in place so when he or she is busy and can't quite finish everything, nothing that's important to you slips through the cracks.

8. Your Financial Advisor Should Have a Clean Record

When you're looking for a financial advisor, it's important to investigate their background. Any professional might have a few random complaints, because just as there are bad financial advisors out there, there are also bad consumers. But if you do find out there is a record of consistent complaints against or issues with consumers and regulators concerning the advisor you are considering, then you should see the red flags flying high. You can look up background information in several ways. One way is through the Central Registration Depository (CRD), which is a computerized database containing information about individual financial professionals and the firms where they work. You can get the information from the CRD from your state securities regulator or from FINRA's BrokerCheck website. The same reason you shouldn't let a plumber into your house unless he is bonded and certified is why you don't want to let a financial advisor near your money without taking the time to make sure they don't have major complaints against them.

9. Your Advisor Should Be Able to Give You at Least a Couple of References upon Request

In this industry, advisors cannot have testimonials. It's a rule that was created to protect potential clients from being misled about an advisor's abilities. But you can get references upon request. When you are about to upgrade the appliances in your kitchen, you do the research, read the reviews, and decide which models are best for you. You consider energy efficiency, think about whether you want stainless steel or standard white, decide whether the whisper-soft feature of the dishwasher is worth the extra money—and then you talk to people who purchased the appliances. But all of those descriptions can't tell you as much as the day-to-day experiences of someone who actually has them. You should be doing the same sort of investigation when you are choosing your financial advisor. He or she should have a long list of satisfied clients, and if they can't come up with a few that will talk to you, that ought to tell you a lot.

10. It's a Good Idea to Work with an Advisor Who's at an Appropriate Age for Your Retirement Needs

You want your financial professional to be available for you at least during the first decade of your retirement, so it's important for you to be aware of their age. You don't have the magical ability to stop the aging process—and if you do, I doubt you'll have any trouble with retirement funds because you'll be a perpetual money machine, the modern-day goose that laid the golden egg! But since you don't, you need to make sure that the timing of your advisor's retirement won't create unnecessary headaches for you. You don't want someone who is so young that they only realize the mistakes they made with your portfolio when you are already retired, or someone who won't even be in business by the time you begin your retirement because they retired ten or fifteen years before you, or retire at the same time as you.

Add these ten qualities and characteristics to the list you already created, and you'll have a dynamic, comprehensive list to use as you are choosing a financial advisor who is a good fit for you. With these elements in mind, you are sure to choose the person who's absolutely right for you.

Asking the Right Questions

Once you've decided what you're looking for in a financial professional, it's time to start the interview process. As I mentioned earlier, this is the person who will help you make major decisions about your finances, so you want to ensure you are getting everything you need from them.

The interview process can be incredibly insightful—you can find out a lot if you go in with the right questions. Imagine the difference in the outcome of the story if the first two piggies from "The Three Little Pigs" had chosen a reputable, licensed contractor with whom they had an honest conversation about their building needs. "Well, you see, we occasionally have visits from this wolf, who likes to try and blow our house down. What can you do for us?" Or perhaps the emperor who was tricked into believing that he was wearing elaborate clothes should have done some interviewing of his own. Rather than taking the rumor mill at its word about the fashionable nature of those new "clothes" he was ordering, how different would the fairy tale be if he had a conversation with the designers: "Now, what fabric will you be using? How will the design flatter my body type? How will I care for it?" Now, it's possible that mistakes might still have been made, and the two piggies' houses might still have been blown down, and the emperor might still have strutted naked down the street. But even a wise pig or a fictional, insecure emperor would be able to see some warning signs of bad professional behavior if the experts they were interviewing couldn't answer their basic questions clearly.

Because you are creating a list of questions that will help you find the right financial advisor for you, you want to take your list of must-have qualities and translate that list into a set of questions. You might start with the sample questions below as a guide, and add more to them based on your individual needs. Though it may take time and a few initial meetings, these questions will help you assess how well each financial advisor meets the top ten criteria I described above. Remember: Take your questions to your first meeting!

Questions to Ask

- "How long have you worked as a financial advisor?"

  Remember the five-year rule: You want someone who has enough relevant experience so they can use that experience to help you—not learn with your money.

- "How long have you been with your current company, and where did you work before you started with this firm?"

  You don't want someone who jumps jobs all the time, so get a clear sense of your financial advisor's past job history.

- "Why did you leave your previous firm?"

  Don't be satisfied with vague answers. If you get the feeling that they are avoiding the question, you should definitely do your homework. Listen to your intuition!

- "What made you get into this line of work?"

  Look for the passion that you hope your financial professional will have. You should hear the enthusiasm in their answer.

- "Where are you hoping to be in five or ten years?"

  You're looking to develop a long-term professional relationship, so if your potential financial advisor is hoping to move across the country next year, you may want to find someone with stronger and more permanent roots in your community.

- "What are the most important goals for you, as a financial advisor, to achieve for your clients?"

  As you listen to their answer, think about whether these goals fit with your own. Your advisor should share your philosophy about your investments or, at the very least, respect your goals and risk tolerance enough to follow your direction, and bring ideas to you that match your overall comfort level.

- "What is the most important goal for you to accomplish within the next decade?"

  This question can provide an interesting insight into the financial advisor on a professional and personal level. See if the answer resonates with you—if it does, you may have found a person who you can work with effectively.

- "Tell me a little about yourself on a personal level."

  Ask the advisor a bit about his or her personal life so you can get to know them better. Understanding personality traits is important in determining if that person is someone you want to work with. Professional relationships always have a slight personal element, so you need to be able to trust and rely on this individual.

- "Do you have a team that you work with?"

  You want to know that your advisor has a support system in place so your needs can always be met by the professional you choose.

Sometimes, people feel uncomfortable asking too many questions when they begin working with a financial advisor, or any other professional for that matter. It's completely fine to ask these questions and you're not stepping over any boundaries. Remember, you are interviewing them because they will be handling an incredibly important part of your life. You may even feel like you are kissing a whole lot of frogs in the hopes of finding that one prince or princess (please don't actually try to kiss any advisors you are interviewing!), but these questions should help you know which candidate is the perfect one for you.

This Is a Marriage, Not a Date

When you think you've found the right financial professional, realize that this is a long-term professional relationship, not a casual fling. I often see women making a huge mistake when they are in the process of choosing a new professional. They think, "I'll just develop an investment portfolio with this advisor and see how it goes." They plan to wait a little while, reevaluate, and keep changing advisors and portfolios until they find the right person.

Look, I totally understand the logic behind that way of thinking, but this is not like trying different hairdressers until you find the right one. Unless you walk in as Rapunzel and walk out with a pixie cut, it won't take too long for your hair to bounce all the way back from a bad hairstylist. But when it comes to your finances, you're dealing with much more substantial consequences for this kind of error in judgment. Your portfolio may not be able to bounce back from all the mistakes and changes that can come during years of trying to find the right advisor through a "wait and see" philosophy. Think about Goldilocks: What if she tried the first bowl of porridge and said, "Hmm . . . I'm not sure about this one. It's kind of cold . . . there are other bowls of porridge here that might be a better temperature, but I guess I'll just keep eating this one in front of me . . . maybe it will somehow warm up all on its own, eventually." Nope! She knew what she wanted, and she knew she had options. When she didn't like her first choice, she continued looking for exactly the right fit.

From the beginning, you need to think about this choice seriously and commit to finding the ideal financial professional for yourself. The goal is to work with one person until, and even through, your retirement. While it may not always turn out that way in the end, if you go into the relationship with that kind of commitment, you will invest in the relationship much differently in the beginning. Doing this will encourage you to do your due diligence. Think about it this way: When you know you are looking for a pair of shoes that will last, will work with many outfits, and will feel fantastic, you're willing to spend a little more time in the search and a little more money on them. You'll probably end up choosing a pair that's made of quality materials, rather than being tempted to buy a pair on the sale rack. The initial time investment is worth it because the return is so attractive.

When you create a long-term relationship with your professional, it works to your benefit. The bond grows stronger and stronger over time, and that allows the financial professional to find better solutions to your retirement needs. As they get to know you and your needs, you'll see that same kind of return on your time investment with your doctor. The longer you see the same doctor, the better your doctor will know your health history. Illnesses will be easier to diagnose, and treatments will be quicker. Potential problems will be addressed early on because your doctor will know you. Think about that pair of quality shoes. After you've worn them enough to ensure that they are broken in, they feel fantastic. We've all had shoes like that—they feel like they were made just for you! No matter how many hours you spend on your feet, you never have to worry about those shoes hurting you, because they are dependable and the perfect fit. While I doubt your doctor, lawyer, or financial professional want to be compared to shoes, the similarity is there. The longer you work with your advisor, the better they can cater to your individual needs and have the perfect professional fit for you. But that process takes time.

For example, when I'm working with a client, and I know other advisors who feel the same way, it takes me a good year to get to know her personality and potential problem areas. After the second and third year, I feel like I know her so well that I can begin to see a pattern about what's working and not working in her financial life. I can then help her, whether it's budget planning, adding more to her income planning, or adapting her portfolio so her investments match her true lifestyle better. But I can only do that once I know her well, and this is what helps give my client much more freedom in retirement. With continuous planning comes more income, and that leads to a better lifestyle during the retirement years. You don't get this when you are working with someone in the short term or are constantly switching advisors. It's one thing to set a skeleton plan to fit someone's retirement objectives. It's an entirely different thing to keep clients motivated and encouraged to stay on the right track so they can save more and contribute more to their retirement nest egg. Remember, it's not only about the investments you have; it's about following a budget that's right for your situation so you can reach your retirement goals and make that dream a reality! Spend the time and effort initially and invest in the relationship with your advisor. When you do, you'll reap tremendous financial and personal rewards.

Tomorrow Will Be a Direct Reflection of Today

After you've invested the time and energy to find the right professional fit, your work isn't done. You need to make sure your professional is not only helping you plan for your future but is also managing your finances right now. What this means is that you can't have your eye squarely set on the future alone. Your current spending habits, income projections—every element of your financial life—should be a part of the conversations you're having with your financial professional. Developing a long-term relationship with this in mind helps you both. It helps you, because you have a professional who is watching your habits and giving you advice on how to make your money work for you, and it helps the professional, who can adjust and readjust your portfolio based on your short- and long-term needs.

You want to make sure that your financial advisor is not investing without clear aim. I wholeheartedly believe that when you are planning your retirement needs, you need to understand your expenses today so you can better predict your income needs in later years. Believe it or not, many people are not 100 percent clear on what their needs will be later on! So their goal becomes to save up as much as they can and hope it will be enough to meet their monthly expenses when they retire. Worse yet, sometimes people think they can live on less money than they are currently making, simply because they are retired. It's unrealistic to assume that your tastes and needs will suddenly change just because you are no longer working. You don't want to be in a situation where you are limited in your opportunities for retirement activities—travel with family, hobbies, even shopping and entertainment—because you didn't carefully project your income needs today.

Having worked with many clients over the years, I can tell you that it takes extensive questioning and discussion to come up with an accurate projection of possible income needs and, as the years go by, to make sure the projection is set properly to reflect inflation. An advisor has to do more than just keep up with what the client is communicating; the advisor has to keep up with what that client is doing. I have to take into account all expenses, even something as simple as that weekly manicure or their frequent trips to Nordstrom. All of it goes into the final calculations to make the investment plan better tailored to the real-life situation of each individual. When I'm running numbers, I also like to base those numbers on the most modest projected investment growth performance—even as low as 3 percent sometimes—and to review worst-case scenarios. Many financial professionals will run scenarios that include a high percentage of growth paired with low expenses—of course, that looks good on paper, but those scenarios are likely not going to happen in reality. Remember the old saying that you should hope for the best and plan for the worst? Make sure your financial professional is not going to be more interested in looking good than in protecting your future by being honest, because this occurs routinely in the financial industry, and I hear about it all the time. This is why it is important that you choose a financial advisor who doesn't just think the way you do because they want to make you feel good, but one who can also be direct and honest about the worst-case scenarios you may face.

Most good financial advisors who are properly educated in retirement planning will help you plan for your income and expense needs now *and* during your retirement years, because that's what an advisor who is serious about their profession does. These financial professionals will either do the budget planning themselves or have someone on their team do it for you.

Remember, investing is not only about buying stocks, mutual funds, bonds, or annuities. It's about making sure you are allocating your portfolio in a way that will help you cover your projected future income needs. If you do this, you will be prepared for retirement in advance and won't have to hope for a fairy godmother or a Rumpelstiltskin to magically improve your financial situation.

The Importance of Your Choice

You can see why finding the right financial professional can make a big difference between a comfortable, secure retirement or a haphazardly planned, fingers-crossed, hope-it-all-works-out-in-the-end retirement.

Unfortunately, people often retire blindly and hope the money will last for as long as they live. Don't be one of those people! Remember that the most important thing during the interview process is: "Ask away and get your answers!"

Money Confidence Interview Checklist: Things to Keep in Mind

- Create a mission statement for what you want in your relationship with your new financial advisor.

- Identify what qualities you liked in your previous advisor and the qualities you hope to find in your new one.

- Highlight the qualities that are essential to you in meeting your financial goals.

- Consider the top ten qualities your financial professional should have, and add those to your list.

- Interview financial advisors who match your list of qualities.

- Ask a series of probing questions in your first meeting to get a clear sense of how you will work with this professional.

- Choose an advisor based on who best suits your needs and financial goals.

- Work together to create a future financial plan based on your current spending habits and income.

- Remember that your investment planning benefits from a long-term relationship with the right professional.

PART FOUR

THE MAGIC
WALL STREET GENIE

Chapter 15

THE GRAND BAZAAR

"Do not seek to follow in the footsteps of the men of old;
seek what they sought."
—Bashō

S o now that you understand the basics of budgeting and its importance to your financial planning, let's take a look at the Grand
Bazaar, more commonly referred to as the stock market, so you can have
a basic understanding of how it works. This way, the next time you have
someone (a friend, a colleague at the water cooler, or the nail salon mani-
curist) telling you their opinion of what stocks you should be purchasing,
you will have a better idea of how to look at the situation. And let's face
it, everyone and their grandmother recommends a stock nowadays. I am
not kidding you! My last summer vacation I was at the Grand Wailea in
Maui, Hawaii, and I was at the stand by the beach getting shaved ice (I
love shaved ice in Hawaii), and I overheard a surfer who was paying for
his order in front of me, talking to the cashier about some stock he really
liked. This is how the conversation went:

> **The surfer:** Aloha, my friend, aloha! I meant to tell you last week—
> you should really look into that company I was telling you about
> because they're doing an IPO soon. The more I've been checking
> it out, the more I love their ideas. I heard they produced new tank
> tops that are going to totally change the surfing industry, and I'm
> going to get in on this thing.

The merchant: Really? What are they for, the tank tops?

The surfer: Well, they are supposed to help the water slide off of the surfer easier. I was watching Warren Buffett the other day, and he was saying that new technology stocks could bring a lot of money, if you look at the company right.

The merchant: Akamai, what a great idea. Thanks for telling me. I'll check it out!

Akamai (pronounced AH-kah-mah-ee) means to be smart, intelligent, very sharp.

Really, though, this is not a joke; they were discussing something they had no understanding of, and by pulling Warren Buffett's name into it, they tried to make themselves feel like what they were thinking was comparable to his investment skills. I'm not sure if the cashier took the suggestions seriously or if he was simply being nice to his regular customer. I hope that in reality he was just trying to be nice and never invested in something simply because he heard it was a good idea.

In another situation, I had a client tell me that when she was working at a major hospital, she fell for the typical "I know a secret" advice from a coworker about a medicine that would completely revolutionize the treatment of the common cold. Based on that simple conversation, she invested $30,000 into that company's stock without doing any of her own research. Unfortunately, she ended up losing most of her money, because the company was not successful. The odd thing was that she was an intelligent woman who was educated and pretty savvy. She became so excited by the idea of making huge returns, she ignored the little voice in her head that was probably pointing out some of the pitfalls in her strategy. What she thought of as "sexy" and being "in the know," and probably plain old greed, got the best of her.

The Grand Bazaar

Oh, the magical land of the stock market, with its wild up and down roller-coaster swings. All this action can certainly make your head spin. There's always something going on, the news almost never stops, and there's no shortage of guys and gals on TV trying to predict what will happen next. But a basic understanding of how the market really works should help you stay level-headed and not get caught up in all the hoopla that makes its way onto the daily news. Remember, you are equipped with an amazing superpower: money confidence. With this power you can step back from the drama and assess each situation logically. Prepare a list of questions: How will this affect your investments? What is the real story behind the sensational headlines? Should I make any changes?

When you boil it down to its most bare-bones concept, investing in stocks is a way to easily purchase part ownership in a company. The stock market is like a giant farmer's market, but instead of trading fruits and veggies, this market trades in ownership. When you go to this market and buy a stock, what you are doing is buying a tiny slice of *ownership* of a company—which is represented by the stock itself—and you are sharing in ownership with other people.

The stock market has three important purposes: 1) It allows companies to go public and raise additional money by selling their previously privately owned shares on the open market (these are the Initial Public Offerings, or IPOs, you've probably heard so much about); 2) It offers you, and any investors, the opportunity to become a part-owner of companies (and, hopefully, share in the earnings and success of these firms); and 3) It provides liquidity, or the ability for investors to quickly sell their stocks. Imagine how difficult it would be to convert your investments into cash if there were no readily available market to buy and sell stocks, and if you had to find a buyer yourself whenever you wanted to sell your shares.

Let's take a look at how this works. An enterprising young woman named Little Red Riding Hood decided to open her own company, Red Wolf Coats, Inc. Her business makes coats out of wolf fur (after all, she wanted to finally put all those wolves in the forest to a better use so they would stop scaring little girls). People absolutely love these coats, and Little Red decides she needs to expand her business. After thinking about it carefully, she decides the best way to raise money is not to borrow, but to go public. By going public, Little Red will sell some of her ownership (up until now, she owned 100 percent of her factory) in exchange for money she can use to expand the business. This process is called an IPO. So, after all the attorneys and the brokers hash out all the magical legalities, they set the IPO date and decide to divide the company into 100 equal pieces, or shares. When the IPO date finally arrives, all the forest's critters, elves, gargoyles, toads, and beautiful chupacabras decide to get in on the action, and they, too, buy some ownership of Red Wolf Coats, Inc.

Whenever one of these magical creatures buys one out of the 100 shares of this stock, what they are really doing is buying 1/100th of the company, because the ownership was divided into 100 pieces and they each just bought one of them. Some critters may have bought just one share, which equals 1 percent of ownership in this case (1/100); others bought ten shares (which happens to be 10 percent of ownership in this case, or 10/100), and some may have purchased even more. Now, this doesn't necessarily mean that the critters were paying a fair price when buying or getting a fair price when selling the shares; it simply means they can buy and sell those shares with relative ease because there is a market where everyone who wants to buy is matched with everyone who wants to sell. And, of course, this example is simplified. Publicly traded companies will usually issue millions and sometimes billions of shares. So it's difficult for the average investor to own even 1 percent of a publicly traded company, but the idea of ownership is much the same as with Red Wolf Coats; it's just that the percentage of ownership that an average investor can buy in the real world is much smaller. This is also referred to as having equity in the company; however, it does not give you any right to make any management decisions; you simply get to participate in the upside if the company does well.

The Stock Market Roller Coaster

So if buying a stock means buying a small piece of ownership, why do stock market prices sometimes move about so much? Can the values of companies, and what it costs to buy ownership in them, really change that much in a day? Well, here's the thing: If purchasing a stock means you're purchasing part ownership in a company, then in an ideal world, it should mean that the price of the stock should be based on how much money the company is expected to make in the future. For example, if you wanted to invest your money in a business and decided to buy a beauty salon, you would most likely try to first figure out how much that salon can make in profits. And then, based on how profitable you think it would be, you would figure out the kind of price you're willing to pay to buy it. If you thought it could make $10,000 a year in profit, you might be willing to pay $50,000 for the business—or whatever price you thought was fair. If it were going to generate $100,000 a year in profit, then it obviously would be worth a lot more. And in an ideal stock market, it's supposed to work the same way; investors are supposed to look at a company and buy shares (i.e., become part owners) when they believe it is a good deal based on the potential future earnings of the company. But even though most people and money managers don't have pointy ears or fluffy tails, they sometimes behave in even stranger ways than their make-believe counterparts.

As I've mentioned before, the stock market appears to have a serious mood disorder, and sometimes I honestly think it's on drugs. You know . . . erratic behavior, unexplained actions. Everyone acquainted with it seems to be concerned with its well-being. Hey, from time to time Congress even tries to hold an intervention, but nothing seems to help.

Here's the deal: The stock market provides liquidity and makes it super easy to trade stocks, which means that people can buy and sell on a whim. And because of that, especially in the short term, stock prices often move up and down based on what buyers and sellers are feeling and thinking. So, in the short term, the stock market can almost become more of a psychological barometer rather than a logical market that has anything to do with the actual value of the companies being traded. Think about it: Would it make sense if you went to the farmer's market and the price of tomatoes kept going up and down while you were standing in line? Of course not, because a tomato is a tomato and nothing is going to change much about it! But the stock market is a different story because professional and individual investors keep changing their estimates about how profitable a company is going to be based on every latest bit of news that comes out about the economy and politics in general. And so, as they keep changing their points of view about the potential profitability, they keep buying and selling stocks at different prices. In that sense, the market is like an immediate barometer of people's fear and greed. Stock prices can move up and down simply based on people's feelings (with no basis on a company's future earning ability) or on an incredibly misinterpreted view of what those earnings might be.

In the farmer's market example, imagine if a farmer who was selling grapes kept looking at the line of customers while holding a few grapes out in his hand and had people guess what they think they should pay. What if he raised or lowered the price according to the length of the line? Can you imagine the chaos that would ensue? People would be guessing whether there were twenty pounds or one pound of grapes left; if the farmer would be able to grow more or if there was going to be a grape shortage; if there would be better and more plentiful grapes tomorrow; or how the European debt crisis would affect the grapes. This emotional guessing could go on and on! You think this sounds outrageous? Well, guess what? This is what happens in the stock market a lot of the time. Obviously, it's more complicated than guessing the price of grapes, but it's the same idea.

A lot of the time, it's not even people that are trying to guess. It's computer algorithms trying to make stock market predictions. Sometimes they're very wrong. A great example occurred on April 23, 2013, when the market dropped about 1 percent and no one could understand why. Then they realized that some private stock-trading computer programs created a mini stock crash after automatically reading a fake tweet from an Associated Press Twitter account that had been hacked.[23] So when the average investor is trying to figure out what's going on inside the company they are holding stocks in, and whether it's a good time to buy or sell, a lot of the time it unfortunately becomes almost a guessing game—an emotional guessing game! If you want to play emotional games, go to Vegas. I promise it will be more fun, and at least you'll get free cocktails!

When the market began its meltdown in 2008, it created a chaotic scene for investors. Everyone had an opinion, and everyone had an explanation or prediction about what was going to happen. In hindsight, it's pretty easy to see that the disaster didn't happen overnight but had been brewing for several years, and some would argue that the meltdown had its real beginnings over a decade earlier.[24] But that's hindsight. If you pay close attention to various stock market gurus and "experts," you'll notice that tons of them are great at explaining what happened, but none of them are great at predicting the future—even when it comes to huge drops, like that of 2008, which seemed to catch everyone by surprise. When it comes to building a long-term nest egg, you also don't have the benefit of hindsight. This makes it all the more important to keep reminding yourself that in the short term, the markets can swing wildly and be all over the place—mostly due to investor psychology. If you are a long-term-minded person who is twenty or thirty years away from retirement, the fact that the Dow dropped 200 points, and Joe Schmo on television is saying that the country is at the brink of default, is no reason to start selling your holdings. I also don't believe it's time to buy just because Josephine Schmo is saying that the market will rally. Reacting to *any* major news in this way without doing your own research is likely a bad idea. I believe a better approach is one that proactively diversifies and allocates your investments in a way that makes sense for your specific situation, your risk tolerance, and your time horizon until retirement, and that looks at your overall picture without trying too hard to jump in and out of the market based on what other people are saying or doing.

A Monogamous Relationship with an Individual Stock—"I Do" or "I Don't"?

As I mentioned, the stock market is literally like a huge marketplace where large and small investors alike can buy and sell small pieces of companies. When you are buying or selling a stock, you are really trading a small portion of a company. It's important that you keep this idea in mind so you logically think about buying stocks as becoming a part owner in a company, rather than looking at it as some kind of confusing lottery.

I strongly believe that, under normal circumstances, it is dangerous to allocate more than a small portion of your portfolio into individual stocks. I cannot stress this enough. I say this because to make money by investing in individual stocks, a person has to be great at analyzing them. Analyzing stocks takes a lot of time and a lot of experience to do well, and even with all that knowledge and experience, it's still easy to make huge mistakes. You would need to spend many hours every day following the markets and reading company annual reports. (You think budgeting is boring? Try analyzing corporate balance sheets on a daily basis!) And even if you knew how to analyze them, it still wouldn't guarantee that you could do better than average. So for that reason, for most people, investing into specific individual stocks simply increases their risk in exchange for little additional reward. When you're making a bet on individual stocks, you're losing the benefits of diversification (more on diversification in chapter 17 and the appendix) and are hoping that your analysis is good enough not only to offset the higher risks of not being diversified, but that on top of that, you will also earn a much better return. (Are you *that* good?) Most people don't think about it this way, but I urge you to keep this in mind before you venture into individual stocks. There's just too much to consider not to.

However, if you can't help yourself and absolutely must try your luck, I strongly suggest you only use a small portion of your portfolio. That way, if you make the wrong decision on an individual stock and its value goes down instead of up, you will lose no more than the amount you have invested. A good way to figure out if you should be choosing your own stocks is to look at the worst-case scenario (losing the entire amount you invested) and decide if you could live with that risk.

Many people are confused about stocks, mutual funds, and bonds. The appendix section of this book has more information on these topics and will help you gain a better understanding of how they fit into the context of investments.

Money Confidence Tips and Tricks— Smell Their Deceits!

Over the last several decades, many books have been written about how to choose stocks and make millions of dollars. Of those thousands of books out there, they all have some sort of system. If you've ever stayed up late, at some point in time you've probably seen infomercials for stock market systems where grinning testimonial-giving people are gushing about all the money they made from whichever system is being sold.

I want you to please, please, please keep this particular point in mind any time your advisor or broker or in-law or whoever tells you that one stock or another is a great bet: There are no sure things in life. And because the stock market is part of life, there are no sure things in the market, either. No one has a magical system for making money—no one. There have been millions, if not tens of millions of investors over the last one hundred years who didn't just passively invest in the stock market. They thought they could pick investments in a way that would let them beat the overall stock market returns. Some spent time devising their systems and were moderately successful, but not many have been able to consistently outperform the market over the long term. And regarding those who did outperform, you have to ask yourself whether it was because of their system or was due to plain old luck. Even in a lottery, someone eventually wins the prize. But no one can consistently be Number 1, no matter how great their "system" is. Even in fairy-tale lands it's not possible. Rumpelstiltskin always had some magical solution that was to solve someone's problem, whether it was love, money, or power, but there was a price for the magic that was given. Rumpelstiltskin never helped the poor souls; rather they helped him with his agenda. And the same goes for the so-called we-got-it-figured-out get-rich-quick systems.

So whenever someone comes to you with a "great tip" or system, it is important that you are skeptical and that you thoroughly investigate it and its source before taking any action. This is the basis of money confidence. You *know*—not think or believe, but actually *know* that if something seems too good to be true—like a sure thing in the stock market, then it probably is!

These tips and systems usually stem from someone who thinks they are smarter than everyone else and that they are able to see something in the stock that no one else can see. With millions of investors trading in the market on a daily basis, you have to ask yourself, "What are the chances that this particular person I know happened to understand this particular stock better than everyone else on Wall Street?"

Likewise, if someone comes to you with a great system for selecting stocks (that is, if you're willing to make ten easy payments of $39.99), you have to ask yourself, "What are the chances this system works, and why is this company selling their system if it's so amazing? Why won't they just use their system to make money for themselves instead?" Think about it: Remember those late-night infomercials I mentioned earlier, where the people in testimonials say how they doubled their money in a week? Most people see that and think, "Whoa! I can make *that* much money. Amazing!" But not you, because you are a savvy, confident woman who does not need to jump on every opportunity she hears about. So stop and do the math on this one, and this is what you'll figure out: If you can double your money in a week with this system, and you start with $100, then after twenty weeks you would have over $100 million. And when you see these numbers, you then ask yourself if it is realistic. If someone has a system that could create such amazing returns, why would these people give away their amazing system for just a few easy payments of whatever random dollar amount? I'm sure that by this point, your answer to this "opportunity" is a resounding, "No thank you!" and "Give me back my purse! I'm not giving you my money!"

So no matter what system or great investment tip is being thrown your way, you can weed out most of the poisoned apples by simply thinking logically about the situation and asking yourself a few common-sense questions. Most of the time, you don't need much investment knowledge to avoid making foolish decisions—just a little common sense and the ability to think before you act.

Things to Keep in Mind

- Stocks represent ownership in a company. Buying them means that, in the simplest terms, you become a part owner.

- Even though stock prices are ideally supposed to be related to the earnings ability of a company, in many cases they are not. Especially in the short term.

- Stock tips and investment systems are not a valid investment strategy! Always do your own research.

Chapter 16

THE ART OF RISK

"Strategy without tactics is the slowest route to victory.
Tactics without strategy is the noise before defeat."
—Sun Tzu

R isk is always a chance we take. Whether it's good or bad depends on what it is we are risking. I remember once when I was going to a charity benefit, I decided I would risk wearing a pair of brand-new, red suede pumps I had just bought. They looked ah-maz-ing! But their great looks didn't match how they felt on my feet. They were super high and really uncomfortable. But, because they looked gorgeous, I felt wearing them was a risk I was willing to take. I thought, "What if I can't walk in them for too long? What if they hurt too much? Can I keep a straight face while being so uncomfortable?" Well, I weighed all the options and decided that how I would look in them was well worth the risk. After all, they were Ferragamo Fabulous. So the good news was that everyone loved them, and I got lots of compliments. The bad news was that I broke my little toe! The damage wasn't too bad, and I recovered from the pain within a couple of weeks. And even though that outcome was not the one I planned for, my decision to wear the pumps was, nonetheless, a calculated risk that made sense at the time. Now what if I had been going to a dance party instead of a benefit? Then maybe wearing those pumps would not have been a risk I would have been willing to take! There are numerous factors that need to be considered when we are thinking about taking a risk.

Asking the Right Questions

Most women don't ask the right questions when making investment decisions, especially when it comes to understanding the risks involved. I think this is mostly because the idea of how risk affects our lives is misunderstood and has an undeservedly bad reputation. Most people either look at risk as something inherently bad that should be avoided at all costs, or they completely ignore that it exists. The key to becoming a better decision maker and to being smarter about the risks you take is:

1. Never ignore risk.

2. Realize that risk is not necessarily a bad thing.

3. Train yourself to ask the right questions.

Taking risks is what moves our lives forward and helps us achieve our goals and dreams, but risk becomes dangerous when you ignore it and don't devote the time and effort to try to manage it in your favor.

Here's what you need to remember: We are surrounded by risk. Every day, pretty much with every decision you make, there is always a chance that something could go wrong. You could say that our entire life is one humongous risk! You decide to wear bright red lipstick to a job interview; you're taking a risk. You change your highlights into low-lights; you're taking a risk. You ask your boyfriend if that dress makes you look fat . . . well, you're also taking a risk—a risk that he will soon be single if he dares to say anything other than, "Of course not, honey! You look amazing! As always—my beautiful princess." And like there are two sides to every story, there are both good aspects and bad aspects about risk.

For example, imagine you are planning this year's holiday dinner. You decide to try a brand-new approach: You are going "turkey chic," and by that I mean you are abandoning the turkey altogether, because you're going to cook stuffed quail! That's right—it's the new hot thing on the Food Network, and you want to shine in front of your entire family as an amazing cook. You're giddy with anticipation about everyone's reaction, all the compliments you're going to get, and all the questions you'll answer about this yummy dish you will so expertly prepare. You even have pictures cut out from magazines showing the best ways to present the dish, and you're hoping this holiday dinner will be a smash! Oh, how all your friends and family will be jealous! They will bow to your feet at the sight of your dinner table and will all chant, "We're not worthy! We're not worthy!" And the party poopers who dare complain, "Umm . . . where is the turkey and the stuffing? I don't like trying new, exciting things because I'm boring." Well, they'll just have to sit there hungry and bitter while everyone else partakes in this amazing feast.

But here's the thing. Although you don't know until the actual dinner party if this new feast will make you look good, you also understand that if you're not willing to take the risk of trying a new, modern extravaganza, then you'll never know for sure. So as you sit at your kitchen table glancing through the food magazines and the quail recipe books, you wonder to yourself if taking this risk is a good or bad thing. Well, unfortunately you won't be able to answer that question because it all depends on what happens at the dinner. You might have a breathtaking holiday party and get many genuine compliments, or you might look like a wolf that stole the golden turkey, and everyone will point their fingers and accuse you of ruining the holiday. Ok, maybe that's not going to happen, but at least that's how you'll feel if you don't get the reaction you want—like you ruined things for everyone.

Taking a risk with your holiday dinner is so much easier than figuring out the riskiness of an investment and whether it's a good fit for your portfolio, right? Wrong! You'd be surprised how much your everyday decisions have already prepared you for making smart investment choices, because the underlying thought process is the same for almost all the decisions you make. Let's look at your decision-making process by continuing with that holiday dinner example in more detail.

From the moment you got the idea of attempting the new recipe to the moment you try it out in the kitchen the morning of the feast, you've already asked yourself all the important decision-making questions. You likely did this intuitively without fully realizing it. You subconsciously analyzed all the aspects of the situation, looked at the pros and cons, considered the costs, and then made your decision.

The key to making better investment decisions is to take your usual daily decision-making process, break it down into its individual parts, and then apply it to evaluating your portfolio. You've already had lots of practice making everyday decisions, so you don't need to think about your decision-making process too much—you're already a pro. But you probably haven't practiced analyzing potential investments all that much, so you'll definitely want to approach them with a much more structured thought process. Let's take a look at some of the most common points to consider when you're thinking about any kinds of investments and the risks that come with them.

Upside, Downside (Risk/Reward)

As you pondered if you should try to replace the traditional turkey with the new exotic stuffed quail dish, one of the first things you probably did was think about how much of an impression it would make on everyone. This is really nothing more than considering the potential upside of trying quail instead of turkey. Quail is a bird like a turkey. It has wings, and even though it's smaller than a turkey, it's somehow even bigger in your mind because of the potential upside. You saw different recipes in magazines or on TV, imagined how delicious it would taste, and thought about how great it would make you feel to get all those compliments from your loved ones. But you didn't stop there and hop in your car to go to the grocery store, right? Instead, you must have considered the risk that something could go wrong, or the potential downside of your decision. What if you burn it or don't get the recipe down in time? What if it doesn't fit with your family's image of what a holiday dinner should be? What if you mess the whole thing up, ruin the holiday, and no one ever comes to your house again? Well, maybe not that extreme, but you get the point, right?

When presented with an investment decision, you should think about it in the same way. Consider the potential upside and the potential downside. First, you need to have at least some understanding of how much an investment can realistically generate in growth—your upside. Why invest any money if you have zero idea about how much you *could* earn on it? One way to do this is to look at how much growth this type of investment provided in the past, on average. Think of it this way: There isn't any logical reason to believe that an investment can somehow magically give you a return significantly higher than what it consistently did in the past. While past performance is never, ever a guarantee of how much you will make in the future, it can be a good way to approximate the *maximum* you could hope to earn, on average. For example, if an investment provided 5% average growth per year for the last fifty years, it is unlikely that it would suddenly provide 40% per year for the next fifty years, unless there were some huge change in the market and the economy. Not to say that this isn't possible; it's just unlikely.

So one of the first things you need to do when you're considering any kind of investment is to look at the potential gains and the potential losses you could experience—your reward and your risk. These are questions you should ask your financial advisor, and try to focus on getting concrete answers. If you do this enough times, what you will notice is that, usually, investments with higher potential returns will have higher potential losses. And investments with lower risk of loss will provide you with a lower return, on average.

Probability of Making Money

Once you've taken a look at the potential rewards and risks associated with an investment, the next step is to figure out what the probability is that the investment will turn out in your favor. Let's go back to the quail example: This won't happen often, but what if the recipe you wanted to make was so complicated and required such an incredible amount of skill that only a highly trained chef with decades of experience could pull it off? Maybe it requires a special kind of cooking technique or a special exotic spice or a sauce that had to be made in just the right way. In any of those cases, you might wonder if you could pull it off, and you would ask yourself, *What are the chances I can make this amazing new dish?*

Think about the lottery. You only need a dollar to buy a ticket, and you could potentially win hundreds of millions of dollars! How great is that? But the reason you haven't cashed out your 401(k) to buy thousands of tickets is because you clearly understand that the probability of winning the jackpot is very low. Sure, your downside isn't all that high—just a buck—and your upside is amazing (shopping spree! a Cartier watch, anyone?). But the chances you will ever win big are close to zero. When you're considering a possible investment and you've thought about the possible reward and the possible risk, the next step is to figure out the probability you will make money, or at least will not lose money. For example, if your neighbor's daughter offered you a chance to invest in her start-up social networking company that's operating out of her garage, you could potentially make lots of money, but what's the probability you will? In the same way, if you're considering investing in a couple of stocks your advisor suggested, what are the chances these companies will give you high returns?

These questions are always difficult to answer. Figuring out the probabilities of these things occurring has been kind of like the holy grail of finance—people try hard to figure it out, but no one has been able to find the exact, 100 percent correct approach, and I believe no one ever will. There are too many uncertainties to account for. But you don't need to know the exact formulas—you can often get by on a little common sense. If your advisor is suggesting that you buy stock in a print newspaper company and tells you that print newspapers are going to overtake the Internet, your common sense would tell you that the probability of that happening is questionable, because newspaper subscriptions have been experiencing declines. It *could* happen, but how probable is it?

Again, this question is meant to be almost rhetorical because it will be difficult to answer completely. But keep asking it every time you're thinking about an investment, and try at the very least to make a list of the reasons why an investment may go bad. Doing this will put you in the right frame of mind and will train you to continually ask questions when it comes to your investments. It will get you to think more critically about the opportunities you come across, and will begin to change your way of thinking.

Balance between Risk and Reward

In addition to looking at the risks and the potential rewards, it's also important to see if the two are well matched. Is there too much risk for little potential reward? Now don't get me wrong—the entire topic of measuring the balance between potential returns and potential losses can take up volumes upon volumes of books. It's a subject with many different moving parts and many theories, some of which are still debatable.

But you don't need a PhD in economics to understand the basic idea. The act of asking yourself whether the balance between the risk of loss and the potential reward makes sense can help you see if something about an investment doesn't seem right.

Think about it this way: You've probably heard that old saying "There is no such thing as a free lunch." It means that something can't be created out of nothing. In other words, if you are sitting down to have lunch, *someone* is paying for it. Either you are, or your friends are, or that handsome prince who asked you on a date is (or if you had a coupon for a free lunch, then the restaurant is absorbing that cost). But the idea is that whenever there is a benefit (the lunch) there is also a cost (the payment), no matter who it is who actually pays.

A good way to look at the risk of losing money is to see the risk itself as a sort of payment for the *possibility* of making money. Even though you are not opening your wallet and paying anyone, the simple fact that you are agreeing to the possibility of losing money is a sort of payment. Whenever you are making any type of investment, the potential return on that investment is the benefit you get (your lunch), and taking the risk of losing some money is how you pay for that lunch.

Why is this so important? Because if taking on risk is a way to pay for a possibility of earning a return, then the bigger the return you would like to earn, the more risk you would normally need to take—if you want more, you have to pay more. For example, if you put your money in your savings account, you might get 0.10% in annual interest (one tenth of one percent), which is basically . . . nothing. But the reason for such a small return is because the risk of loss is almost nonexistent! On the other hand, if you decided to invest in a pharmaceutical company that had an untested drug that could potentially cure the common cold 100 percent of the time, you could end up being a rich woman if that drug eventually proved to be all that it promised. But the risk of failure would also be high. The company could fail miserably since their drug hasn't been tested yet. You could lose your entire investment if their new drug never ends up working. With any investment opportunity, this will always be true: The bigger the potential return, the bigger the risk. And the smaller the risk, the lower the potential return.

In other words, you will almost never encounter a situation where you can make a lot of money with little risk of losing, and most of the time when the situation appears to be too much in your favor, it is probably because you're not seeing all the negative aspects of the investment.

Other People's Abilities

Whenever you make an investment, I want you to completely understand that other people's abilities will play a big part in determining whether your investment is successful or not. Let's go back to the holiday dinner example. Before you decide to finally go through with the new cooking plan, you probably thought about your past dishes and whether (based on your previous experience) you could cook a brand-new dish and not turn it into a complete mess. And you decided that, yes, you do think you can pull it off. But since quail isn't a common item you can buy at your local supermarket, you realize that you'll probably have to order it online. Since the dinner is just a few days away, you think, *Will the shipping service deliver them on time? Will they be fresh and not spoil on the way here? What if they're delivered a day late and I can't cook the meal at all—no turkey, no quail, no nothing!* Maybe you look for a specialty food store and find one that's quite a drive away. *Is it worth the drive? Will they have good quality meat there?* And you go through all the possible scenarios to figure out if someone else in the chain could end up letting you down and messing up the entire plan.

These are the same types of concerns that should be on your mind when you are considering an investment. If your advisor suggests a mutual fund for you, you might want to look into how successful the fund managers have historically been. One way to do this is to look at the mutual fund's returns over a long period of time and compare them to the overall performance for that specific investment type. For example, if you are going to buy a mutual fund that invests only in stocks, then it's a good idea to compare how well that fund did over the last few years compared with how the overall stock market did. After all, if a mutual fund is supposed to give you more value by selecting better-performing stocks, then it should give you a better return than the stock market would. Now, good historical returns don't ever guarantee good future results, and you should never, ever invest in something simply because it did well in the past. But on the flip side, is it sensible to buy a mutual fund that consistently performs worse than other similar funds?

These are the questions you need to ask your financial advisor. Make sure to get concrete answers. Whether you're investing in mutual funds, individual stocks, or your friend's new bakery, you have to ask yourself whether the person running the show (mutual fund manager, CEO of the company whose stock you want to buy, or your friend) has enough experience to make the investment a success.

Considering Costs

As you were thinking about changing up your typical holiday dishes, you probably also thought about how much it would cost to make your new recipes look like what Cat Cora or Bobby Flay create when they whip something up on *Iron Chef America* in an hour.

Quail is more expensive than turkey, and if you have a big family, it might end up costing you quite a bit more. One huge turkey will work for everyone, but since quails are so much smaller, you would have to make at least one for every single person attending! The more people attending, the more money you'll have to spend. And what about all the side dishes? Will you have enough time to make mashed potatoes or gravy? Or will you have to spend more money to buy them ready-made because you've run out of time because you're stuck in the kitchen making fifteen quails? What about other side dishes? Will you have to make them yourself or will you have to buy those as well? And after figuring out what all this would cost, you might realize it's probably quite a bit more expensive than a simple turkey dinner.

Well, you guessed it. Whenever you're making an investment, you also have to figure out what it will cost you, like you figured out the costs when planning your holiday dinner. There are fees associated with many types of investments, and they can add up to a nice chunk of money over time. Mutual funds, for example, can charge you various types of fees—when you make the initial purchase, when you sell your holdings, some annual management fees, or trading commissions. You need to be aware ahead of time of what you're going to be paying (refer to the appendix for more details on mutual fund fees). Whatever investment you are considering, you should make sure to check the fund prospectus or ask your advisor what the charges are. With a better understanding of the investment, you can make a truly educated decision and not simply hope your advisor will make the best decision for you.

Lock-Up Periods

We all know that trying new things, especially at holiday time, can turn into a longer than expected ordeal. Depending on what you are preparing, and all the things that need to be done ahead of time, what starts out as "just a couple of hours" can eat up your entire day. You wonder, *Do I really have the time to cook for that long in the kitchen? Is it worth the time to try this new dish?* When you're thinking about an investment, you have to find out how long your money becomes "locked up."

You won't see this with too many regular investments: With stocks, you can buy and sell pretty much anytime you want. But with other investments, like REITs and similar funds, you may have to commit to keeping your money in an investment for a certain period of time. Some mutual funds charge a fee if you sell your holdings before a certain number of years have passed, and you're locked into that investment if you don't want to pay the fees. Mutual funds do this to encourage people to hold on to their accounts longer and to trade the fund less. As an investor, you need to understand these time periods. If you know you will need to withdraw your money after three years, and the fund eliminates the selling fee only after five years, you might want to consider a different fund.

Understanding what the minimum holding period is (if your investment has one) is important. If you have an emergency or decide you hate the investment, you may be forced to pay penalties to take your money out early; or you might not be able to take it out early at all. Imagine how long it takes to prepare fifteen individual quails. What would happen if you had to leave in the middle of the whole thing? It would be a horrible, terrible mess of a dinner. Your portfolio will look like that horrible disaster of a dinner if some of your investments require a lock-up period and you need to take your money out earlier.

Risk Tolerance

Cinderella's mean stepsisters tried hard to make their huge feet look like they could fit into the glass slipper. But no matter how hard they tried, reality would not let it happen. The glass slipper simply was not the right option for them. And just as people have different shoe sizes and can't shrink their feet on command, people have different comfort levels when it comes to taking risk. They can't force themselves to simply change those levels on command. That's why knowing your own comfort level is essential, and it will go a long way toward making you a savvy decision maker. After all, it's not just about how much your portfolio earns over the years; it's also about your own quality of life and your ability to sleep well at night.

There are people who are completely fine with ups and downs in their portfolio, and don't fret much about the risks they're taking. They have no problem plunking down a large chunk of their portfolio into a few mutual funds (or even a few individual stocks). They don't worry about what the investment is doing over the next few years, until they need or want to take the money out.

Then there are people who hate seeing any drops in value, no matter how small. It doesn't matter to them that their retirement is thirty years away. What matters to them is being able to look at their latest account statement and not cringe at the sight of any losses. You'd be surprised, but there are folks with millions of dollars in the bank who feel extremely uncomfortable when they see their investments decrease even $5,000 or $10,000 in value. They have millions, but a loss of just a few thousand dollars (less than half a percent of their portfolio) makes them cringe. Because even though it's such a small proportion of their overall wealth and they are financially secure, they simply hate to experience any kinds of losses. That's just how they feel about it—and who's to say they should feel otherwise?

The reason people have different risk tolerances is because we all have different personalities. We each see the world a little differently, we come from different backgrounds, and we all have preconceived notions of what may or may not happen in the future. All of these things mesh together to create our comfort level when it comes to risk, and there's not much we can do about it—after all, we can't tell ourselves how to *feel*, right? Knowing your risk tolerance and having a genuine understanding of what you are comfortable with is important in making you a confident decision maker. I can't stress enough that it's all about knowing *your* risk tolerance—*not* your advisor's risk tolerance! Many people assume that as long as their advisor is comfortable with the risk level of a particular investment, it somehow means that it is a safe investment for them. Nothing is further from the truth, and this way of thinking has gotten many people into big trouble.

Some people are perfectly comfortable trying new investments, just like some people are perfectly comfortable with unusual dishes like oxtail or *uni* (sea urchin). Others would never even consider eating such food because they would feel too uncomfortable. You don't even need a logical reason to feel uncomfortable; you just know that you would never eat certain foods because they're too far outside your comfort zone. It's the same way with your investments. If you don't feel comfortable with a specific investment, then there is no reason to jump into it. If you don't understand the investment, you might want to take the time to learn more about it; but no matter what your reasons are, you should only stick with investments with risks low enough to allow you to sleep well at night. Here's my test method of measuring risk comfort: If you hear on the news that the stock market is crashing, can you sleep comfortably that night or are you up tossing and turning? If the answer is you can sleep, then you are where you should be. And if not, then you better reconsider your portfolio allocations while you still have your sanity!

If you make your decisions by weighing the pros and cons of investment opportunities, and also by carefully considering the level of risk you are about to take, then you will allow yourself to remain calm and to feel in control of your retirement, rather than fretting every day about what the future holds. This is money confidence in action. The whole world can be in chaos—your financial advisor is telling you one thing, the news is telling you another, and all of your friends have opinions on what you should do—but still you remain in control. Being calm and reasonable will prevent you from making the rash, emotional decisions that people often make when they are invested beyond their comfort level.

Don't assume your advisor knows what your risk tolerance is or that they have studied your situation so closely that they know exactly what is best for you. Cinderella's stepmother thought she knew what was best for her, too. Had Cinderella listened to her, she would have missed the biggest ball of them all, and she and the prince would have never lived happily ever after. But all fairy tales aside, you need to take this point seriously. No one knows you better than you or cares about you more than you care about yourself!

Is This Investment Right for Me?

After you've done all your homework on an investment, ask yourself the most important question of all: Is this investment the right choice for my particular situation?

Asking questions about the various attributes of an investment and understanding your risk tolerance helps you get a general understanding of how the investment works and how it fits within your portfolio. But the most important step is to combine all this information and ask whether a particular investment makes sense for where you are in your life right now. It's important to remember that you are not asking whether the investment itself is good or not (that part you do when you're considering the risks, rewards, and the probability of making money), but in this final step you are asking if the investment makes sense for you in particular, based on your goals in life and your ability to tolerate risk.

Think of it this way: Every year around the holidays, tens of thousands of women will think of trying some new, unusual recipe for their holiday dinner. Some will even consider the same recipe you had in mind—especially if you watch the same cooking shows—but not everyone will actually try to do it (even if they all thought they could pull it off and wanted to). This is because everyone's situation is different, and even if something is a great idea in and of itself, it doesn't mean that it's a great idea for everyone in the same way. You may choose to try this new recipe because you feel it's worth a try in your specific situation, and you have the time and the extra money to go for it. Someone else might not have the time or the money or they might spend the money on new lotion or bath bubbles or whatever it might be instead—simply because that's what they would prefer to do with their money. Why? Because it's all a matter of what's right specifically for them—and *you*.

This way of thinking is something you already do every day, with every decision you ever make, and it's a matter of applying the same approach to your investment process. Try it: The next time you're at a store and decide to buy something, stop for a moment and trace your thoughts backward. You'll realize that with any personal decision you make, you think about the upside and the downside, and then you ask yourself if it is the best decision for *you*. So you might see that delicious cupcake, consider the upside of eating something yummy versus the downside of not being able to fit into your clothes, and you'll ask yourself if buying and eating that cupcake is the best thing for your specific situation. If you work out three hours a day, seven days a week, well then it's probably not a big deal; but if you're always busy and have little time to get any exercise, you'll probably think long and hard about whether eating that cupcake is worth the trouble. Most of the time these thoughts happen in the background as your mind subconsciously thinks about all the pros and cons, and then all of a sudden you've decided what you want to do.

Remember, you get lots of practice doing this with your everyday decisions. From the time you're a little girl to the time you grow up into a strong and confident woman, you're practicing this decision making over and over again. Remember when you first started wearing makeup? You probably didn't do so well in the beginning. You either had way too much foundation and your face looked a different color than your neck, or the combination of eye shadow, lipstick, and blush made you look, well, a bit clownish (hey, in the beginning it happened to most of us—just check your yearbook pictures!). The reason you ended up with those ridiculous looks was because you didn't have enough practice with making the decisions about how to apply your makeup. You considered the pros and cons of the different makeup styles, you considered your own abilities, and you decided to take a risk because you thought it was worth it. Sometimes it turned out much worse than you expected. With time, as you practiced more and more, you found the look that made sense for you, and learned what looks good on you. In the same way you developed your style and makeup abilities, with practice, you will also develop your money confidence. The more you practice money confidence, the easier it will get—like applying eyeliner. Decisions that felt clumsy at first will be effortless in no time. Before you know it, it will just be part of who you are.

You will be able to understand what works better for your specific personality. And most importantly, you'll learn how to think critically about every opportunity that comes your way. It may be difficult at first, but worthwhile things are rarely easy.

Here's a fun quiz to help you understand good risk versus bad risk.

Personal Risk Quiz

Personal Risk Quiz Questions—answer yes or no.

1. Would you wear bright red lipstick for the first time to a family gathering?

2. Would you try a brand new sunscreen lotion on your Hawaiian vacation?

3. Would you eat Indian food for the first time on a first date?

4. Would you wear a super short, sexy dress at the company holiday party?

5. Would you go on a blind date that your coworker set up?

Personal Risk Quiz Answers—if you answered yes, see whether you're taking a good or bad risk below.

1. Good risk. Even if you don't look as good as you thought you would, you are only exposed to your family. They are forgiving and won't blackmail you with pictures.

2. Bad risk. You never want to try anything new that you could have an allergic reaction to on your vacation. It could totally ruin your vacation.

3. Bad risk. Can you imagine how that date will go if the Indian food doesn't agree with your stomach? Your date might leave by the time you come back from your third trip to the ladies room.

4. Bad risk. Can you imagine the comments the next day back at the office?

5. Good risk. Hey, sometimes your coworkers may know you even better than you know yourself. After all, you do spend half of your life at work. It's worth the try!

Investment Risk Quiz

Investment Risk Quiz Questions—answer yes or no.

1. Would you try a new investment that you heard about at the water cooler?

2. Would you invest all your money into one technology stock IPO when you are sixty-one?

3. Would you invest your entire nest egg into the stock of the company you work for when you're fifty-five?

4. Would you invest a small portion of your portfolio in a technology stock when you're forty?

5. Would you invest a small part of your portfolio into a stock you think is undervalued?

Investment Risk Quiz Answers—if you answered yes, see whether you're taking a good or bad risk below.

1. Probably a bad risk. The hot tip could possibly pay off, but the chances your coworkers know the secret to making bundles of money is pretty slim. Stick to only restaurant tips at the water cooler.

2. Probably a bad risk. If you are close to retirement, you absolutely do not have the time to recoup your losses should this hot new stock fizzle out. If your entire portfolio, or a significant portion of it, is in a highly risky investment right when you're about to retire, you're taking a huge risk that your retirement could be ruined.

3. Probably a bad risk. Sure, the company where you work could end up being the next big thing and your shares could make you a millionaire. But if that doesn't happen, there are two problems with having all your money in company stock. First, putting all your retirement money into only one stock is a bad idea—it's like betting all your money on one number at the roulette table; it may pay off, but most likely the house will win. What happens if the company

you work for hits hard times? You'll lose your job. Your entire life savings will be in jeopardy because if they're laying you off, they're probably having profitability issues, and that will affect the stock price. So your livelihood (your paycheck) *and* your retirement are depending on the future of just one company.

4. Probably a good risk. As long as you're not putting all your eggs in one basket, your portfolio has the time to recuperate should an investment go south. This is contingent upon the fact that you have invested only a small portion of your portfolio into something so risky, have done your research, and you clearly understand that you could lose the entire amount. Betting your entire retirement savings on one thing is never a good idea.

5. Probably a good risk. You can always take a bit of your portfolio and take advantage of a stock that may be undervalued as long as it is not going to harm your retirement plans if it completely loses its worth. However, identifying undervalued stocks takes lots of practice, so simply because you think it's undervalued, doesn't mean that it is.

When it comes to risk, the most important thing to remember is how much you are willing to pay. Picture opening your purse and literally handing money out if things don't go your way.

Chapter 17

THE GOLDEN RULE

"The cautious seldom err."
—Confucius

When it comes to their retirement portfolios, most people already understand that investments can be risky and that they can lose money. With all the hype about the stock market on the news, it's easy to forget that the stock market is not the only risk out there.

One of my clients told me about an experience she had concerning her plans to purchase a retirement home some twenty years ago. She wanted to live in Big Bear when she retired, and her plan was to buy a house and rent it out until she was ready to move in. But as often happens, life got in the way. She got busy with work and family and kept putting off the purchase until she just stopped thinking about it. It was still one of her retirement goals, but every time she thought about it, she put off taking action until the next month or the next year. By the time she was telling me about it, the kind of home she wanted was worth four times the original price and she could not afford it.

She had missed out on the opportunity to have the kind of retirement home she wanted, because her salary and ability to afford the home certainly did not quadruple in that amount of time. Buying it would put too much of a strain on her budget. On top of that, she had unfortunately kept most of her 401(k) in stock funds when the 2008 meltdown happened, so she lost a big chunk of her nest egg (over 40 percent). The worst part was that she was about six years away from retirement.

Let's take a look at some of the other common risks that may not be directly related to your investment performance but which can eat away at your portfolio nonetheless. Remember—it may seem daunting at first, especially if you haven't paid much attention to the details of your portfolio before, but you will get the hang of identifying risks and asking the right questions as you get more practice. There are quite a few common risks out there, and I will touch on some of the more prominent ones here. As you read about them, make a mental list for yourself of any other risks you can think of, or that you unintentionally may have exposed your portfolio to.

Inflation

Most people know about inflation and understand the basic idea that our money becomes devalued over time. As prices rise over time, our money loses purchasing power, and we can't buy as much with it. What has always surprised me is that although most people understand that inflation is a bad thing, they don't look at it as an actual risk. Let's take a quick step back: If risk is the possibility of you losing money in an investment, and inflation is one of the ways you lose money over time (because money loses purchasing power), then when you make an investment, inflation will definitely affect your return at the end of the day— any losses that you may experience will be made even worse by inflation, and any gains you may make will be diminished by inflation.

When you make an investment, you are taking a chance that it may not even give you a strong enough return to keep up with inflation. For example, if you decided to keep all your money in a savings account, you might not lose actual dollars but would lose money anyway, because inflation would eat into your purchasing power. We haven't experienced strong inflation in the US in several decades, and we've become somewhat spoiled because of that. However, there will eventually come a time when the rates of inflation will start to rise again. When they do, you will need to find ways to battle this particular risk by finding investments that can help your purchasing power stay intact. It's important to keep inflation in mind, because it will always be there and can hurt you significantly even if you're not making any risky investments.

Fraud and Pyramid Schemes: If It Sounds Too Good to Be True, It Definitely Is

Ok, maybe once in a great while you will have an opportunity to make an investment that will provide you with amazing returns without much risk. Such opportunities do happen once in a blue moon. But it's usually in unique situations where you are able to buy something at a huge discount because it is more important for the seller to get rid of the item than to get a fair price. Think of a moving garage sale. Someone will pretty much take any offer for their big-screen TV because they're leaving that evening and can't fit the TV in their truck. Their only option is to either sell it for the best price they can get right now or leave it on the side of the street and get no money at all. Such situations are rare in life, and never happen in the financial markets. No one will give you some valuable item (an investment) at a significant discount just because. So when you hear of amazing investment opportunities, you need to be aware that most of the time one of two things is happening: You are not seeing or understanding all the risks, or someone is trying to cheat you out of your money.

Let me give you a recent example where a client of mine came across an opportunity that ended up being a pyramid scheme. This particular woman came across a penny auction website that sold everyday items at deeply discounted prices. But on top of that, it touted itself as a website that was a completely new and amazing business model. It also did one funny little thing: If people wanted to, they could become members of this website by "investing" some money, and if they promoted the website a certain number of times per day, they could receive as much as 1.5% return on their money *daily*. Now, I want you to think about this: If you became a member of this website, handed over $10,000, and then posted free ads on message boards, you would earn 1.5% daily on that $10,000 of yours. A great investment, right? Well, that's what my client thought when she told me about it. The moment I looked at it, it was pretty obvious that it was a scam. I arrived at that conclusion by simply looking at the situation from the Risk/Reward Balance perspective that I described in the previous chapter.

I tried to explain to her that this opportunity was not real.

"Why would anyone pay you 1.5% daily interest on your money to spend twenty minutes a day promoting their website? Really think hard about what they're offering you—1.5% daily on a $10,000 'investment' is $150 *per day*," I said.

So I reasoned with her and pointed out that if she invested $10,000 with this firm, they were promising to essentially pay her $150 *daily* for twenty minutes of work.

"Why would they do that?" I asked, "when they could just hire someone for minimum wage and pay them eight dollars for an hour's worth of work and save the other $142?" But that didn't convince her either.

"If they needed money to expand, why would they not just borrow money from the bank, and maybe pay 10% interest for the *entire year*, rather than pay you 1.5% *daily* to use your money?" I continued.

That reasoning didn't convince her either. So finally, I ran some numbers for her in an Excel spreadsheet, which showed that if she invested $10,000, based on what that company promised, after two years she would have about $3 million, and I asked her, "Does this seem realistic to you? Do you believe that someone will seriously pay you $3 million two years from now? Do you really believe if you give them $10,000 and post message board advertisements for twenty minutes a day for the next two years that you will receive a check in the mail for $3 million?"

Still she oscillated for a while, because she had already put in a few hundred dollars before running the idea by me, and she didn't want to believe that she had made such a silly blunder. But I could see that the reality of the situation was slowly starting to make sense to her. She had a difficult time letting go of the idea because in her mind, it was a solution to all her problems. Her mind had been put at ease because she thought she'd stumbled on a gold mine of an opportunity and that she'd finally have the kind of life she wanted. She thought that everyone else was too foolish to understand what an opportunity she had found. But eventually, she realized that indeed no one was going to give her $3 million for doing little work with no risk. She finally understood the basic tenet of investments and the basic idea behind sound decision making. It finally became clear to her that no one was stupid enough to offer huge returns for no risk, and that this had to be a scam.

Sure enough, less than a year later, the Securities and Exchange Commission shut down the website that offered this "opportunity," labeled it as a Ponzi scheme, and froze the company's assets. Thankfully, my client did not "invest" any more money and listened to reason. But you will undoubtedly come across such "opportunities" at one point or another, because people will never stop trying to cheat other people out of money. Every time you do come across these magical investments that promise amazing returns, ask yourself if the potential reward matches the risk you are being shown. If the scale is skewed too much into the reward aspect (like getting $3 million on a $10,000 investment) and you are being presented with a no-lose scenario, then chances are you're being scammed. If you can't quite tell right away, another trick to use is to role-play, and ask yourself, "If I were in this person's shoes, would I offer this investment with such favorable terms? Would I give away all these potential returns to people for basically no risk to them at all? If yes, then *why* would I do that?" And if you think about the situation logically from all angles and don't allow yourself to be blinded by the promise of amazing returns, then it's pretty easy to spot when people are trying to cheat you. Go back to the money confidence basics: Ask questions, get clear answers, and keep moving when someone is making pie-in-the-sky promises that won't come true.

The Ostrich Risk (Keeping Your Head in the Sand)

Nearly every time you go to the grocery store, the mall, or even a car wash, you get a detailed receipt showing exactly what items you purchased. This itemized list is the proof of exactly where and how you have spent your money. And the reason you always want to check your receipt is to make sure you're not being overcharged. Imagine if you left the store one day and the cashier said, "Don't worry about the final amount, ma'am. Just check your credit card statement and you'll know exactly what you were charged." Now obviously, you'd never go to that store again. After all, if you are paying money to someone, then you have every right to know what the amount is and what specific items you are paying for. But people fail to do this with their investments because figuring out what their portfolio is costing them can seem like a daunting chore.

For example, if you are invested in mutual funds, then you need to figure out how much you're paying in fees. All mutual funds have fees associated with them, and they can vary widely. There are annual management fees, for example, that can range from half a percent per year to as much as 1.5% per year or even more. Or there may be 12b-1 fees, which are a way for mutual fund managers to offset their marketing costs. And let's not forget the loads, which are fees that can be charged when you buy or sell a mutual fund.

Why does all of this matter? Because you need to know when someone is taking money out of your account, because it's *your* money, and you need to be sure these fees make sense for your situation and are worth the additional services or earning potential. Don't assume you're not paying too much. (For more details on mutual fund fees, please refer to pages 216-218 in the appendix.)

Let's say there is a fund in your portfolio that consistently gives you a worse return than the overall stock market (it goes up less than the market during a market upswing, and it drops more than the market during a downturn). On top of that, you pay 2 percent every year in management fees. Does it make sense for you to keep your money invested in that fund? Because, if this is the case, you are paying someone to give you below-average results. It's like paying full price for a purse only to realize that it's a designer knock-off! And the only way to catch these types of situations is to carefully review your account statements and get a good understanding of how your investments perform and how much you pay in fees. Even though it's not always easy (because these fees aren't always clearly broken out on account statements), with a little time, effort, and research, you can get the answers you need. It's easier than you might initially think—you just have to keep asking questions until you get an answer and not let any frustration or confusion stop you. You can get this information from your advisor, or you can call the mutual fund company directly. You can also find this information online by looking up the funds on the finance pages of websites like Google.

You'd be surprised how many people pay lots of money on a regular basis on their investment accounts, without even realizing how much they are being charged or what they're paying for! Many people take this approach when it comes to their retirement accounts. They simply take their statement out of the envelope every three months, take a quick look at it, and that's it. They don't try to figure out how much they've paid in fees for the period, and they don't try to figure out what their actual returns were for that period. Instead, they take a quick look at the numbers and think, *Umm, I think this looks all right. I'm sure nothing is wrong.*

Let me give you an example from many years ago. I first became exposed to the world of finance when I was still in high school. It was in my economics class, where our teacher teamed us up with a partner and we used Monopoly money to pretend to purchase stocks. We had to research all the investments and various companies and pretended to buy our favorite stocks. After the research, we followed the stocks we chose every day, and after about a month we had to report our losses and earnings. We could buy and sell like you would in the market; we just had to do it on the tracking board, and the only money exchanging hands was our Monopoly money.

Even if I didn't fully appreciate it at the time, this was a valuable experience that affected my way of thinking and my outlook on the real world. Suddenly, the movie *Wall Street* wasn't so glamorous. I saw most of my classmates lose their paper money and realized that it could have very well been real money. I'm glad this experience happened while I was still a teenager because it opened my eyes early about investments. And it taught me the importance of good research and pushing for meaningful answers, even when they were hard to obtain. What was also great was that my teacher didn't favor the boys over the girls simply because it was an economics class. He encouraged the girls to be equally involved and not to sit the exercise out.

Our teacher asked us to research brokerage companies and brokerage fees because he wanted us to have a realistic experience. We didn't only get to experience the fun aspect of researching stocks, but we gained an understanding of how to open accounts and how everything worked. At first, I thought it was one of the most boring things in the world. I even asked my dad to help me figure it all out, but he said I had to learn it on my own. The Internet was in its infancy back then, and most companies didn't even have websites. So without much help, my team and I had to do our research the old-fashioned way—the Yellow Pages! But as tedious as this little project was, it was also extremely eye-opening. Here's why: Almost every broker I called could not give me a straight answer as to what commissions they charged. Mind you, this was before cheap online trades were available, and you could only trade by calling your order in.

I would ask, "So, what kind of commissions would I pay to buy some stock?"

And the answer I would get was something like, "Well . . . it really depends. I mean, there's usually a base amount, and then there are extra fees depending on the volume being traded."

I'm sure that hearing a teenage girl on the other end of the phone didn't help the situation much, but I would press forward. "Ok, what is usually the base, and how do you calculate the volume-based charge?"

And the answer I would get was, "Well . . . you know . . . we'd have to see what your account balance is first, and then we'd have to figure out the tier where you'd fit in." By the way, at this time, most financial advisors were still being referred to as brokers.

Long story short—no matter how much I would press with my questions, I was never able to get a clear answer, and I could see that the brokers I spoke to were trying to be as ambiguous as possible. Our teacher made us call the brokerage companies back, again and again, until we were finally able to get solid answers. At the time, I was annoyed with the assignment and even more with our teacher. I couldn't understand how it would help me—a teenage girl—to complete what I thought was such a pointless project. After all, didn't he already know the information and couldn't he just tell us about it? It wasn't until a few years later that I realized what he was trying to do. He was helping us learn how to be self-sufficient and to solve frustrating real-world situations (thanks, Mr. H). He gets an A+ in Money Confidence 101.

Don't Be a Guinea Pig!

As I mentioned earlier, looks can be deceiving. Just as a beautiful, red apple deceived Snow White, in real life, danger to your financial future can come in many forms.

Unfortunately, many people think that the larger, well-known financial firms will have the best financial advisors; that the name and reputation of the firm automatically makes the advisor knowledgeable; and that the advisor will ultimately protect them and get them the highest returns on their investments. But advisors are just people, and people tend to make mistakes, especially if they are inexperienced at what they are doing. If you happen to be blindly trusting someone because they have the name of a big financial firm on their business card, you're making the same mistake that Snow White did when she bit into that apple. You're not taking steps to check if that apple is what it seems to be.

Keep in mind at all times that just because a financial advisor happens to be from a large, reputable firm, it does not mean that he or she is experienced in advising clients. It also doesn't mean that their management is carefully watching over their every decision to make sure they don't make any mistakes on your behalf. What you may not realize is that many firms specifically hire advisors with *no experience* so they can train them from the ground up.

You're expecting an experienced financial advisor because you're meeting with someone from a reputable firm. But you might be getting a recent college graduate who hasn't done much in terms of managing people's money. This grad, therefore, hasn't seen enough situations that would prepare him or her for effectively advising clients. Previous experience is essential. Without it, an advisor won't be able to caution you about pitfalls and won't be able to guide you in your thought process as you make your retirement plan and try to align your portfolio with what your retirement plans are. Even someone who graduated from an Ivy League university needs experience. Most people don't realize that an education from a four-year university is quite different from having the tools and experience needed to excel within the financial field. It's the same thing as going to an inexperienced tax preparer at a major accounting company. Sure, they may be intelligent and they may be trying hard, but unless they have done a certain number of tax returns, there's no way they can be as effective as someone who has done a thousand tax returns. No matter how big the firm is, that big, reputable name doesn't translate into actual experience for that person, no matter how hard they try.

Of course, everyone was a novice at some point. I was a novice as well, but I was lucky enough to be extensively mentored by a senior advisor for several years before I handled my own clients. So, if you have a choice between an experienced advisor and a novice at a big firm, always go for experience. Experience helps you cover your bases when it comes to putting your retirement plan to work. Don't let your financial advisor learn on your dollar!

One more point about experience: It is not defined only by the number of years a person has been working. I once heard a great quote that went something like, "When hiring someone who says they have twenty years of experience, make sure you're not hiring someone who had one year of experience twenty times in a row." Think about the implications of what that means. Think of a doctor who doesn't take the time to learn new procedures, or doesn't take the time to practice with new medical technology, or doesn't attend medical conferences to share ideas with other medical professionals, or doesn't take a genuine interest in innovation in medicine, or never tries to learn anything new. That would be crazy, right? You'd never go to a doctor like that because no matter how many years of experience they have, they don't understand the latest developments in medicine that could save your life. Well, this same scenario happens over and over again with financial advisors who refuse to educate themselves about new financial products and methods for reducing risks to their clients. They're stuck in the caveman days of finance—and so are their clients. An experienced financial advisor continually seeks self-improvement and goes the extra mile to stay on top of the latest research for the sake of his or her clients.

It has always been my opinion that the best advisors are the ones who help you acquire wealth, while simultaneously helping you sustain the wealth you have acquired. You simply cannot attain the wealth you desire through cookie-cutter or outdated investment plans that are right off the shelf. That's exactly what you'll likely receive from a rookie. Your investment plan should be specifically tailored to *your* financial needs and *your* personal financial risk tolerance. And as I always say, retirement planning is not only about the investments you make; it is about your overall financial picture, spending habits, goals, and lifestyle. You cannot do one without planning for the rest.

Incorrect Diversification

You've probably heard the word diversification many times. It means not putting all your eggs in one basket. It's the idea that you want to spread your portfolio over many different types of investments. By doing this, you are helping reduce the effect that any one bad investment might have on your nest egg. For example, if you invested in one hundred different stocks, and one of those companies went bankrupt, it would be annoying—but at least most of your money would still be there because it was spread over so many different stocks. But if you invested only in two companies, and one of them went bankrupt, your portfolio would take a real hit and your retirement dreams might be ruined at that point.

One of the biggest reasons why diversification is supposed to help is because different investments will perform differently in an identical economic situation. Let's compare this to your closet, shall we? A good stylist will tell you to have a variety of clothes in your closet so you are always well prepared for every occasion. Does this mean you should go and buy twenty different styles of jeans? Of course not! Even if they are different colors, styles, or patterns, no matter how great and fantastic those amazing pairs of True Religions are, you can't wear jeans to every event. What would happen if you had to go to a formal event or to a business gathering? You wouldn't have anything appropriate to wear! The same scenario can exist if your funds are all in one type of investment— an occasion will come up and you may have nothing left in your savings.

After our economy became a mess in 2008, stocks of discount clothing stores performed pretty well because people lost their jobs and had less income. Companies that sold luxury items had a harder time because fewer people were spending money on their products. If your portfolio is well diversified, then big drops in the stock market shouldn't affect you as much because some of your investments will go up while other ones are going down. The gains and the losses will offset each other a bit.

In order for diversification to really help you, it's important to allocate your portfolio over a large variety of investment types. You can own a thousand stocks, but if the overall stock market crashes, you'll experience some serious losses. You can own thousands of bonds, but if the bond market experiences a major jolt, then your portfolio will suffer as well.

Money Confidence Investing: Things to Keep in Mind

As you work toward building a secure retirement, you will need to continuously protect your retirement nest egg from various risks. Some of these risks will come directly from the stock market, and others will come from other investments you make. Some risks will be more indirect, like working with an inexperienced advisor, not being able to keep up with inflation, or not understanding all of the fees you are being charged. To protect yourself from all these risks, you have to practice asking the right questions, pay attention to your portfolio, and when you don't understand something (like the math on your account statement doesn't make 100 percent sense), to ask questions until you do understand. This won't happen overnight. Your ability to protect yourself is something that will happen over time if you stay involved in your finances and question everything you don't understand. But you know what? It's worth it. After all, your portfolio won't protect itself—only you can take the steps to keep it safe. Most important, when it comes to your retirement portfolio, if you're going to take a risk, make sure you open your purse just enough to risk losing a few coins, but not so wide that you lose your entire wallet.

- Inflation can eat into your overall nest egg. In the US, we haven't experienced high inflation in quite a while, but a time will come when inflation will become high, and it could hit the double digits. Imagine if you are retired and are not earning money anymore. What will happen to the real value of your nest egg after five or ten years of double-digit inflation?

- Make sure you are working with an experienced advisor who has seen enough real-life situations to be able to help you.

- Don't keep your head in the sand or assume everything is ok. Check on your nest egg regularly and ask lots of questions. Your relationship with your money is much like your romantic relationships; what would happen if you paid no attention to your spouse or partner? Eventually they would leave, right? Money is the same way. If you don't pay attention to it, it could leave for good.

- Make sure you are properly diversified for your age and risk tolerance. Bring these points up to your advisor on a regular basis. It's risky to be invested into stocks only, or bonds only, or in any single investment. Even if you keep your money under your mattress, you're still facing a risk, right? Inflation! So make sure that you pay special attention to working with your advisor to diversify your portfolio for your specific situation. You can learn more about diversification in the appendix at the end of the book.

PART FIVE

YOUR INNER FAIRY
GODMOTHER

Chapter 18

HAPPILY EVER AFTER!

"We are what we repeatedly do; excellence,
then, is not an act but a habit."

—Aristotle

I choose to believe in fairy tales, the idea of a happy, prosperous ending, and a "happily ever after!" Just because things in life don't work out exactly how you expected doesn't mean you can't change things for the better. Because we are creatures of habit, once you come to the realization that you're not satisfied with where you are in your life, you *can* make a change. Whether it's your physical health, your relationships with others, or your finances, you have a lot more power to change things than you give yourself credit for.

As Albert Einstein so eloquently said, the definition of insanity is "doing the same thing over and over again and expecting a different result." This applies to everything in life. I have a close friend who hasn't yet found the right guy in her life. Whenever she does date someone, she always has the same exact problems—which she shares with me. When I look at all her actions and relationships, it's no wonder she can't find the right guy! She dates the same type of men, she does the exact same things that make her unhappy, and yet she doesn't see where the problem lies. Seriously, it's like watching reruns of the same show over and over again. You already know what's going to happen next, but the main character in the show (in this case my friend) is oblivious to what's happening. No matter how many times you watch that episode, it doesn't change! I even confronted her one day because her behavior was becoming ridiculous. She wasn't happy with me. She even stopped talking to me for a while, but all I did was tell her the truth. And, we all know that the truth hurts sometimes. But being honest with yourself from time to time is the only way to make a change and move forward.

We often do the exact same thing over and over again in our financial lives, and our professional relationships for that matter, and can't figure out why we keep falling into the same trap. I've seen clients repeat mistakes time after time, expecting that things would eventually work themselves out. Remember Mona, who was stuck with the wrong financial advisor, and kept trying to talk things out with someone who was manipulating her? Every time she tried to leave, she'd "talk things out" with him and expect that somehow everything would be different. I bet you anything that even when I advised her to focus on herself and dig deep to find out what her expectations were before getting involved with yet another unsuitable advisor, she probably didn't. Perhaps she is still repeating her mistakes. Her destiny won't change until she decides to break away from her unhealthy and unproductive habits. The only way to break bad habits is to stop dwelling on your previous mistakes or what might go wrong, and start to focus on the positive. Focus on the success you know you will have. The more you focus on the positive, the more you build your money confidence. You are training a muscle—it might feel awkward and uncomfortable at first, but the effort is worth it. After you use it a few times, your anxiety will begin to dissipate and the results you get will be better. Keep using that money confidence muscle—it will pay off in the long run!

Focus Your Mind on Success

Personally, I am all about the power of intention—deliberate, educated action to make changes and improve your life. Every single person can change their financial destiny if they want it bad enough! Because it's not only about what you do in the physical world, not all about what investments you choose, and not only about your career and how much you earn. The biggest part of your success and your future depends on what you do in your mental world first. If you think positively, and if you train your mind to refuse to think negatively or to draw you into feelings of fear or insecurity, then there's genuinely almost no limit to how much you can change your life for the better. Your attitude creates your thoughts, your thoughts create your actions, and your actions create your future!

In this book, I've shown you the importance of budgeting, explained investment basics, and given you a road map for how to ask for what you want. I've advised you on the questions you need to ask yourself when you are making a decision. Most importantly, I did my best to teach you how to think differently, because the right mind-set, and learning how to ask the right questions, is the only way to achieve the kind of future you want. But, you know what? All of it means absolutely nothing if you don't take that first step and decide to make your life better—genuinely better. Now, you don't have to do it all in one day! The best changes in life occur from small, deliberate steps that help you change your habits, and change not only the way you act but also the way you think. The only things required for change are your determination not to settle for the status quo and your determination to stick with your goals through thick and thin—through easy times and more importantly, through the difficult, and sometimes heartbreaking, times.

In many ways, making changes in your financial life is much like dieting. I've started many diets: the South Beach diet, the Atkins low-carb diet, the juicing diet, and so on. But none of them worked!

Why? Was it because they were bad diets? No. The truth is that I wasn't successful at them because I never fully committed to them. I would think about how great it would be to lose twenty pounds or how great I would look, and I would start a diet. But I came to realize that I was only starting the diets so I could say I was doing something good for myself. But I never resolved in my mind to stick to the plan. Once I made a real commitment to change my lifestyle, once I decided that my future plans were more important than freely indulging in whatever food I wanted, things changed. I was no longer getting hyped up about some diet or another just to *feel* like I was making a change. I actually *did* make a change. I was no longer only dieting but was eating healthier, exercising more, and had more energy than ever before. And you know what? Other successes followed. One little success led to many more!

As with any positive change you want to make in your life, the mental determination to make that change applies to financial planning. If you get hyped up and say, "If I only just budget right" or "If I only invest smarter" or "If I only get the right advisor," you won't get far, because it's not about one thing or another, but about changing the way you think and feel about your financial future. It's about changing your lifestyle and outlook, and doing it with 100 percent dedication.

Your Financial Intuition Zone

Many of us experience life as it comes. This can be in part because of the way we were raised. We learned about money from the way our parents talked about it, or the way our friends and others around us expressed their opinions about it, or the way society has portrayed men and women over the years. If you add in all the negative stories projected into our daily lives from TV or radio, many women can end up feeling weak and insecure. We can end up chronically worried that something's about to go wrong. We are surrounded by so much negativity that we allow it to creep into our lives—and yes, this can even affect your finances because it affects your outlook on life. If you're feeling sad or depressed, or if you're constantly worried about the economy because some clown on TV keeps talking about how things are terrible, it will affect how you feel about your finances and the decisions you make. This is why you should truly watch out for all the negative stuff that makes its way into your life—don't allow it to take over how you feel and think. I call this protecting your financial intuition zone, that spot in your mind that helps you make the right choices, calmly, without letting all the outside hoopla and negativity throw you off balance.

It's like the broken window concept that is applied to communities. If one house has a broken window that is never fixed, then chances are there will be more break-ins because the impression given to troublemakers is that the neighborhood is not being watched or cared for. In the same way, if your mental "windows" are broken and you don't fix or fortify them with self-confidence, then negativity will make its way inside. When it comes to your financial intuition, you've got to protect it and fortify it with all the inner strength you've got. Because, like a burglar, negativity and insecurities will sneak in when you least expect them. They'll ransack your house and leave you feeling lost and weak. So, to make a real change in your life, it is truly about what you do in your inner world. What you do there will project and predict what you will accomplish in the real world. If you've had a bad relationship with money or a bad relationship with financial advisors, and that makes you think that things will never change, then you can rest assured that's exactly what will happen. The state of your finances will continue to be one gigantic mystery, a shapeless mass, and something you will never resolve. But if you tell yourself, "Hey, maybe I never had a great relationship with money, but there's no reason I can't," then guess what? Your attitude will dictate your reality! Like a shapeless piece of clay, you'll be able to mold your financial situation, step by step, until it becomes a beautiful work of art that you will truly enjoy seeing.

Being in Control

Years ago, I read a book by Napoleon Hill called *Think and Grow Rich*, and the following quote connected with me: "You are the master of your destiny. You can influence, direct, and control your own environment. You can make your life what you want it to be."

You are truly in control of the choices you make. If you make the decision to commit and tell yourself starting today, "I will change everything that has to do with my finances that I don't like," and you further say, "Today is the day that I will take everything I know, including what I've learned in this book, and I will make that inner change," then you will start yourself on the path to success! When it comes to your financial well-being, you are the master of your destiny, and only you can change your life and make it what you want it to be.

The first rule of money confidence is that you have to truly desire financial well-being, and only then can you achieve it. How can you attain something if you haven't made it the object of your desire? You can't. This means you have to go after what you want, kick pessimism to the curb, and not let any previous setbacks get in the way of the new you. Forget yesterday! This is about today and what you will do going forward!

What I have witnessed from childhood and throughout my life and career is that whenever someone makes up their mind to accomplish something, they WILL IN FACT get what they want. They almost *always* do.

If you've had a hard time with your finances in the past or have worked with a financial advisor you didn't like, then make a decision that from today forward, you will have a better relationship with whomever you choose to manage your money, that you will find an advisor you have the right professional chemistry with and who will be the right fit for *you*. Because once you put you and your future first, you will accept nothing less than that!

More importantly, if you've never been able to save enough or you lost quite a bit in the market crash of 2008 (or whatever the year was that put you back financially—there were quite a few of them), learn from it, accept that it happened, and agree that you can't go back in time to fix it. Then move *forward*. So many people dwell on the misery of their losses, their painful memories, things that happened in the past, but that accomplishes nothing. If you are in a *Star Trek* episode and you can find a time machine to travel back to fix all those mistakes, then sure—dwell all you want! But since we are in the real world and you don't have Captain Picard or Captain Kirk to help you find that precious time machine, why not focus on the present and find your future instead? What's done is done, and you need to let go of it and think about the future, and how you will start making the right choices for yourself *today* and get yourself on the right track.

Love Your Future

You have to encourage yourself to love your future, and that means loving your finances. It also means loving to learn more and more about what you can do to have a better financial life. OK—maybe you don't have to *love* your finances, but at least have a cordial relationship with them. You know . . . invite your money for tea regularly, ask it about how things have been going, if it has any news for you. Your money is like a good friend—it wants to be in your life, but you've got to make a regular effort to be there for it and to make sure it's all right. Having that positive energy, having that positive attitude toward your money, and being proactive is how you will accomplish whatever you want to accomplish when it comes to your finances and future well-being.

If you look through history, over and over again you'll find people who were able to accomplish what they wanted against difficult odds. Even though they had different situations and different goals, what makes them alike is that they all believed wholeheartedly that they were going to accomplish their dreams. They saw what their future held, and they *loved* their future enough to work for it. This is exactly the same determination and faith in your future that you've got to find within yourself in order to achieve the kind of life and retirement you want. When it comes to your finances, regardless of where you are now, regardless of how old you are, *today* is the day you will begin to shine. The light may start out faint, but it can quickly grow into a roaring fire of determination if you feed it the fuel that it needs. And that fuel is made of confidence, the desire to succeed, and the refusal to simply do what everyone else does. Today is the day you will start to conquer all your fears and will begin to master everything you have learned about yourself, your money, and your future. If you want it badly enough and stop dwelling on the past, nothing can stop you.

Esther's Story

Let me tell you one last story that embodies what a positive attitude and the desire to succeed can achieve for you. I met one of my clients, Esther, several years ago. She was sixty-one and in a bad situation. When I first met her, I saw that she did not have much in her 401(k) and not that much in overall assets for retirement. She had made mistakes, lots of mistakes, but she wanted to make a change. I told her, "What's done is done," and if she decided to change, then she could still achieve a lot for her retirement. And surprisingly, on her own, she had already prepared herself. She knew it didn't matter what had happened in the past; she had already accepted it, and told me that she was meeting with me to change her life. She didn't want to think about the past and wanted to plan for the future.

Even though she didn't have as much in assets as she could have, she was confident that she could build them up again. She wasn't sure how she would do it, but she knew that she would. The crash of 2000 (the tech bubble) had left her with only about $80,000 at that time, and she was still working and contributing to her 401(k). She started looking at her savings, and mind you again, this is someone who at the time was sixty-one. Most people in her shoes would be sitting in sorrow, thinking it was too late for them to do anything about it. But not Esther! She had made a conscious decision to be positive in her way of thinking, and made a commitment to herself that she would do whatever was necessary and sacrifice her lifestyle in the short term. She wanted to take the right steps and get to her ultimate financial goal. Well, guess what? She is now sixty-eight and has over half a million dollars in retirement assets! Not just because of her contributions or market returns, but because her positive attitude brought her more than she could imagine. It's amazing how things can align themselves in your favor if you take the first steps forward.

So here is what happened. She contributed $15,000 a year to her 401(k) (she had almost doubled it from the previous contribution amount), and on top of that, she added substantial amounts to her savings, because she became fanatical about budgeting. She was also able to build up an emergency fund by adding almost $6,000 to it every year. And she was the one driving the whole process forward—because she realized it was her life and her destiny. But here's the real kicker: She made a great discovery. As she was going through all of her old paperwork and statements, she found paper certificates of shares that her mother, who had passed away a few years earlier, had purchased several decades earlier. When her mom passed away, Esther was unfortunately so distraught that she never looked through all of her financial documents. Her mom had Alzheimer's, and for the last eight years of her life (and even well before the onset of her illness), she never talked much about her finances. She had casually mentioned some shares she had from the old phone company where she worked, but Esther never took it seriously.

This was a big break for Esther, and a bittersweet turn of events. It didn't only help her find money, but helped her find closure. In a way, it was almost like a final gift that her beloved mom was able to give her, and it couldn't have come at a better time. If she had not sat down to look at her financial papers, didn't decide to get organized, then she would have never found those certificates. The only reason she made the discovery was because she had made a commitment to herself to be organized and to make her life genuinely better. I remember telling her at the time that the only thing cooler would've been if she had found the certificates in her couch cushions or under the mattress. Two years after I began working with her, at the age of sixty-three, she found the stock certificates that were then worth—drum roll please—just under $280,000! At that time, that discovery tripled her net worth.

But her late mother's shares didn't magically appear. I know these things are not a coincidence. I do believe in the power of intention. If Esther had not gotten herself on the right track, I have no doubt that she would have never remembered the shares, because the certificates would have remained stuffed away in the old dusty boxes in her garage that throughout the years she couldn't bear to face because of the memories. Imagine if there had been a fire and all those boxes burned—a mini-fortune would have been lost forever. But because she looked at her future with a new attitude and then applied positive action, it all worked out.

I'm not saying this kind of event happens often. But what I *am* saying is that positive, deliberate actions to improve your future will definitely help you uncover opportunities you didn't know existed. Through careful budgeting, you might find that you can save a whole lot more money than you thought. By reviewing your 401(k) or other account statements, you might find that your investments have seriously underperformed over the years. Whatever you do, you will find additional money simply because you'll be able to take advantage of opportunities that you couldn't before. It's because you will now know everything about your financial situation, and will be able to make well-thought-out, educated decisions.

This Is YOUR Fairy Tale

I did say earlier that I do believe in fairy-tale endings. I may not believe the magic and all the fluffy fuzziness, but to me, fairy tales are inspirations of what *could* be. They are the final result of hard work and preparation, and of being on the right mental track! That is how our destiny and our real-life fairy tales are written! Many times we look at successful people, self-made millionaires, and we think, "Wow! I wish I could have that level of success! I wish I had enough money to retire so I could do what these successful people have done. I wish I could have their life, their business, their career . . ." Well, it's time to stop wishing and time to start doing. You have your future in your hands, and you're the only one who decides what happens next. How will you write your fairy tale? How will you reinvent yourself? How secure and independent will your retirement be? If you believe, truly believe that your life can and *will* be better, if you love yourself and your future, and if you take action, then there's no reason, no matter where you are in your life, that you can't make the right plans and help your dreams become a reality. I know you can! You know you can! So, make the commitment to yourself, and go ahead and live happily ever after. It's all within your reach! You are not helpless and insecure. You have an incredible power within you: money confidence. With this power, you can walk into any office and get the answers you need to make the right decisions for yourself.

I would like to leave you with three essential money confidence rules to remember every time you think about your money:

- Do not let anyone take your money or your purse. You worked hard for it, so only hand it over when you know what you're paying for.

- Toughen up! When it comes to your professional relationships and more importantly, your money, think about this and what it means.

- Love your money. It can do a lot for you and your family; don't just have a casual relationship with it; have a long-lasting friendship so it will want to stay with you forever.

The most intelligent people in the world always have something to learn from somebody else. I want you to be able to look back on the you of today with a smile and think, *This was the day I gave a gift to myself. The gift was changing my mind-set so I could start living in the present.* After all—it is all about the present day and what we choose to do with it. So don't hesitate, embrace this day.

I want to leave you with two words from one of my new favorite songs. They can mean whatever you want them to mean to you.

Let's Go!

Appendix

MUTUAL FUNDS— THE BASICS

Mutual funds are a nifty little tool that can make your life easier if you know how to use them correctly. They can become a headache if you happen to invest in those that have high fees and consistently underperform the general market. They may or may not be right for your situation, and you definitely want to speak with a financial advisor before making any major decisions. But in either case, it's important to have a general understanding of mutual funds and how they work.

A mutual fund is essentially a huge pool of money. Many investors buy into it by investing their money in the fund, and then the mutual fund manager will invest all the money according to the fund's overall strategy. The pool of money managed by a typical mutual fund can be hundreds of millions or even billions of dollars, with thousands of investors, and the pool of money is managed as one big portfolio. Because of this, all the investors are pretty much invested in the same way, and share in the profits and losses proportionately. For example, you might have $1,000 invested with the fund, while another investor could have $10,000, while someone else might have $500,000 invested. And as the fund makes or loses money, you all share in it together. So if the fund makes a 5% return, you'll make $50 on your $1,000 investment, while someone with $10,000 invested will make $500 on their money, which is still 5%, same as you (of course, this is a static example that doesn't take into account any charges or fees you may incur due to fund management or redemption). The easiest thing you can compare mutual funds to is a buffet. Instead of ordering one entrée, you get a little of everything. Each buffet at each restaurant is different; you may have a brunch buffet or a seafood buffet or a dessert buffet, depending on what style of food you like. When it comes to mutual funds, the style is based on what type of risk you are willing to accept, and the kinds of assets you would like to invest in.

An Easy Way to Invest in Many Investments at Once

The great thing about mutual funds is that, in a lot of ways, they have the potential to make your life much easier. The fund itself can hold hundreds of different stocks, bonds, or other investments in its portfolio. When you buy a mutual fund, what you're doing is buying a tiny piece of that mutual fund's portfolio and therefore tiny little pieces of stocks. So if you invested $100 into a mutual fund, you might have ten cents worth of stock in Coach, ten cents in Apple or Microsoft, another five cents in Revlon, and so on. By doing this, you saved yourself lots of time because you didn't have to research each and every company on your own, and you are easily spreading your money over a whole lot more investments than you could if you tried to buy all of them one by one.

Understanding Mutual Fund Lingo

You can get a rough idea about what a mutual fund does based on its name. Definitely don't stop your research there, but here are some basic terms that often come up in mutual fund names:

Growth Funds: These types of funds will usually buy stocks of companies that are currently expanding, and companies that tend to reinvest a big chunk of their profits into growing their businesses. These companies are not as likely to pay dividends, and when you buy this type of mutual fund, you are focusing more on the potential growth of the investment rather than the current income.

When you're younger and have more time until retirement, growth funds would usually make up a larger portion of your portfolio (under normal circumstances) because you are focused on building up your nest egg. They are riskier and their prices can fluctuate, so you'd want to have a long-term time frame when holding them, because you are accepting more risk for a potentially higher return. As you get older and closer to retirement, you could still have a part of your portfolio in this kind of fund, but you would typically decrease their proportion in your overall portfolio because you can't afford to take on as much risk. If you're one year away from retirement, for example, and have 100% of your portfolio in growth funds, and stock prices drop, you could experience a big hit to your money with no time for your portfolio to recover.

After you retire, these kinds of funds typically wouldn't be in your portfolio anymore, because at that point your focus is on your money generating income for you, rather than trying to make your portfolio grow. But that, of course, would depend on your overall situation and your wealth. If you were no longer working, and the stock market went through a jolt, having a large part of your money in growth funds could be a disaster. Think of a growth fund as a big balloon that is getting filled with water; it can grow bigger and bigger, but there is always a big possibility of it bursting. So it's important to remember that growth does not mean *guaranteed* growth.

Value Funds: These kinds of funds also focus on capital appreciation, but instead of buying companies that are growing quickly, the portfolio managers of these funds will focus on buying stocks of companies they think are currently undervalued in the market. What the managers are doing is analyzing the price of the stock and comparing it to where they think the price *should* be, based on the company's profitability and other factors. They purchase these stocks when they think there is a temporary mismatch between the price in the market and what they think the stock is really worth. Now, the important thing to remember here is that a big part of the fund's performance depends on how good the managers are at identifying undervalued stocks. So just because the fund refers to "value," it doesn't necessarily mean that the fund managers are going to be good at finding profitable opportunities.

It's common for value funds to have dividend-paying stocks in their portfolio, so when you buy a fund like this, you're betting on capital growth as well as hoping for part of your portfolio growth to come from dividends paid by the companies in the mutual fund portfolio.

Think of a value fund like buying a painting from a no-name artist on the streets of Paris. Others have heard of him, but he is not famous. You think his paintings are good and are being sold cheaper than they should be. Further, you think he may become big one day and then those paintings will be worth so much more! You are hoping for this outcome but risking that you may be wrong.

Income Funds: These types of funds are usually focused on—you guessed it—current income. Because of this, they will primarily invest in either stocks that pay large dividends, or in bonds. The major point of these funds is to give you a steady stream of regular income. These are meant to be a lower risk than growth or value funds, and can be in your portfolio at any stage in life, but you'd be more likely to own them as you get closer to retirement, because they are meant to be less risky and to provide you a more steady return on your investment. However, because the return is expected to be steadier and less risky, you'll also likely have a lot less capital appreciation.

Remember, mutual fund returns are only as good as their managers' abilities, and bad managers or dramatic events in the financial markets can hit your portfolio in big and unexpected ways. Just because you have an income mutual fund that's had a steady price and has been paying you steady dividends for years, it doesn't mean that one day it won't experience a big drop in value or an interruption in dividend payments. Keep in mind that diversification is important.

Think of investing in income funds like going to Costco. There are always those fun stations giving away free samples. In this sense you can think of the samples as dividends, and your investment as the money you spend on your shopping trip. Now, every time you go to Costco, you expect your free food samples—it's part of the shopping experience! But one day, you may very well walk in and the samples won't be there, because they're not guaranteed. In the same way, owning an income fund doesn't guarantee dividends, and they may not always be there.

Mutual Fund Fees

As I already mentioned, a mutual fund is like a huge pool of money from lots of different investors. Since the pool itself has to be managed by someone, mutual funds can charge different types of fees, which they use to pay the management of the fund.

Loads (I'm not talking about doing laundry, so don't worry.)

Mutual funds will usually have transaction fees when you are either buying or selling fund shares. If you're buying a stock, you'd normally pay a commission to your broker to make the transaction. Mutual funds use a different method by charging *loads*. These loads are calculated as a percentage of the total dollar value of the transaction, and include front-end loads and back-end loads, which are fees to buy or sell the mutual fund. Some funds will charge front-end loads, which are a percentage of the dollar amount you are investing, as a way to cover the cost of the transaction. Others will charge back-end loads, which are fees you would pay when selling the mutual fund.

The thing to keep in mind about these loads is that they hit you directly in the pocket without any relationship to the fund's performance. Just because a fund is charging a high load doesn't mean it will necessarily do better than another fund. In fact, if you think about it, loads directly decrease your returns. For example, if you invested $1,000 into a fund with a 3% front-end load, you would immediately give up $30 for the transaction ($1,000 x 3% = $30), so now your account would have $970 in it, and it would have to grow by $30 for you to break even.

Other funds don't charge a load at all. There are lots of funds out there with different fee structures, and this is something you definitely want to consider carefully. You can find information about specific funds in their prospectuses, or you can ask your advisor to help you obtain this information.

Management Fees

These fees are regular fees (calculated as an annual percentage of your account value) that are used to pay the fund managers for their services in managing the portfolio. So if you have $1,000 in a mutual fund and it charges a 2% annual management fee, you can expect to pay about $20 per year.

12b-1 Fees

These fees are also charged as a percentage on an annual basis, and are meant to help cover the costs of the mutual fund for advertising and distribution to new potential investors. These fees usually range from 0.25% to around 1%, and not all funds have them, but they can hit your account and can add up over many years.

As you can see, mutual funds can have a lot of fees associated with them. Some try to limit these fees, while others end up charging quite a bit. That's why you should always carefully understand the fees that a mutual fund charges *before* you invest. Think about it this way: If a fund charges a lot of fees, it automatically means that any growth in investments you get will be that much smaller because you're already losing money in fees. This means that you could potentially accept a smaller return in another fund that has fewer fees and still earn as much because you're saving money by paying less in costs.

Just remember, there's no such thing as a free lunch. Whether you're paying up front, at the end, or in the middle, you are *always* paying. This is not necessarily a good or a bad thing, because what matters is how much your portfolio grows when all is said and done. It's like going on a cruise: Some cruises are all-inclusive, but that doesn't mean that all costs were not calculated ahead of time and included in the cost of the ticket. Keep in mind that you have to consider all of this before making a decision to buy any mutual fund.

Things to Keep in Mind

Overall, there is a lot to know about mutual funds, and the information in this section barely scratches the surface. But there are two major things you want to keep in mind as you ponder the mutual funds in your portfolio: 1) what kind of investments they make, and 2) what kinds of fees they charge. These two questions will go a long way in helping you make better decisions.

Don't forget that mutual funds can be as risky as stocks. Depending on their strategy and the kinds of investments they make, you could end up losing a lot of money, as you could with an individual stock. It's important to remember this as you decide how to allocate your portfolio, because you don't want to invest your money thinking that it's safe simply because it's in a mutual fund. Work with your advisor to see if—and what kind of—mutual funds are right for your specific situation and your risk tolerance. Always make sure you know exactly what amount of money might be taken out of your purse—like the fees you'll pay and the potential losses you're exposing yourself to.

MUTUAL FUNDS AND DIVERSIFICATION

As I've worked with many clients over the years, I've noticed a consistent problem: Most people don't understand how diversification works, so they end up placing their retirement portfolios in risky situations, all the while thinking they're doing the right thing.

I've noticed the biggest misconception about diversification is when it's viewed in the context of mutual funds. Many people think that simply by buying mutual funds they are well diversified, but few people realize how proper diversification is supposed to work. Their lack of understanding, and a lack of clarity on the part of the financial industry, has gotten some people in a lot of financial trouble. During the crash of 2008, many people thought they were safe because they were invested in mutual funds instead of individual stocks, but their mutual funds weren't diversified. As you work with your financial advisor to build your nest egg and allocate your money, keep the following information in mind, especially as you get closer to retirement. We'll take a look at diversification in more detail.

Mutual Funds—A Way to Spread Your Bets

Investing in mutual funds is a good way to spread your bets across lots of different investments, such as stocks, to help minimize the risk of any one stock destroying your portfolio. But there's a difference between spreading your bets and diversification. For example, when you buy an individual stock, you're making a bet that a specific company is going to be profitable and your stock will go up in value. What happens if that company isn't successful and goes bankrupt? You'll lose your entire investment. That's where mutual funds come into play, because they're a great way to lower the risk that any single investment will completely destroy your portfolio. This can be compared to making bets on the roulette table in Vegas.

Think about it this way: What would happen if you went into a casino with $1,000, walked up to the roulette table, and bet the entire amount on one number, all at once? Of course, you could be right and win a heck of a lot of money, and spend the rest of the day partying and drinking mimosas. But I'm sure you would agree that making this bet would be pretty risky because you could also instantly lose everything in one fell swoop, right? So instead, you might bet a couple of bucks on a few numbers here and there, and maybe put $5 or $10 on red. Or you might go to the slot machines and play a couple of penny games or you might play a few hands of blackjack. What happens in the second scenario is that you're spreading your money across many different bets so you don't risk everything you have on one single event.

In the same way, if you were going to bet your entire retirement savings on one stock, you *could* be 100% right and end up rich and retire in a mansion, or you could end up losing absolutely everything. The real point of a mutual fund is that you're trying to lower your risk by avoiding the possibility of losing everything if you were to place all of your trust in one investment. Instead, if you make lots of small bets, it's unlikely that every single one of them will be a loss.

Some stocks within the mutual fund will go up in value. Other stocks will go down. But the idea is that even if some of the companies in the mutual fund portfolio go bankrupt, it won't completely destroy your nest egg. Of course, that's the idea, but simply buying a mutual fund doesn't guarantee that you made the right decision.

Diversification Is NOT the Same Thing as Spreading Your Bets

As I just mentioned, mutual funds are a great way to spread your bets across lots of investments so your portfolio isn't dependent on any single stock or bond. But here's where most people make a huge mistake: They assume that spreading their bets or not putting all their eggs in one basket automatically means they are diversified. It does not.

Here's how diversification is supposed to work: As I mentioned in chapter 15, when you buy a stock, you're buying a piece of ownership in a company. There are thousands of companies out there, and they operate in different industries. Some companies are in real estate, others are in retail, others are in manufacturing, some are technology firms, and so on. Now, this is important: Different industries are affected differently by the overall economy. For example, when the economy drove off a cliff in 2008, stocks of banks were hit hard, because many of them issued or bought mortgages that would end up pretty much worthless. So investors were rushing to sell their bank stocks because they expected these banks to experience huge losses. In the same way, companies that were involved in home construction were also hit hard because if the economy was in a recession, then fewer people would buy houses, and construction companies wouldn't be making profits. So, investors started selling the stocks of these companies as well, and the stock prices fell. During the same time, stocks of companies that were in the business of selling cheaper everyday products did better! Discount clothing stores and discount retailers saw their stock prices increase during the economic mess. That's because as the economy was faltering, and people were being laid off left and right, folks weren't willing to spend as much on clothing or other items. So investors started buying up their shares.

The idea behind diversification is to spread your portfolio across lots of different investments that react differently to what's going on in the economy, and help balance each other out. So if, let's say, one stock goes down by 20%, another one, in a different industry, might go down only 10%, while a third one in yet another industry might go *up* by 5%—*all at the same time.* That's why buying mutual funds without taking the time to understand what their strategy is can be dangerous and can give you a false sense of security. For example, many mutual funds will invest in technology stocks only. Others might invest in retail stocks only. Some might invest in real estate stocks and some only in small growth companies that haven't proven themselves. So if the mutual funds where you allocated your savings invest in stocks of companies within the same industries, then all you're doing is spreading your bets. You're definitely not diversifying your portfolio.

When you're selecting mutual funds for your portfolio, you have to check the kinds of investments the mutual fund makes. You can pull up their prospectuses online, and then read about their general investment strategy as well as take a look at the most recent allocation of their portfolio. That's the only way to truly understand what the mutual fund is doing, and the only way to see if it fits your comfort level and if it will help you diversify your portfolio.

Full Benefit of Diversification

In the previous section, I only talked about the idea of diversification from the standpoint of stocks. I explained the idea that shares of companies in different industries don't always react in the same way to economic events and will sometimes move in opposite directions. But the discussion of diversification doesn't end there. You see, even if you buy several mutual funds and diversify across lots of companies and lots of industries, you're still facing a diversification problem, because your portfolio is 100% in stocks. The issue is that stocks are all in the same asset type—equities. As I mentioned in chapter 15, when you buy shares in a company, you're buying a small piece of the ownership, or in other words, a small piece of the equity. At a certain point, no matter how many stocks you own through your mutual funds, you reach a limit as to how much more you can reduce your risk, and the only way to diversify your portfolio further is to invest in other asset types that are different from equity. Examples are fixed income (bonds) or money market accounts.

The reason for doing this is that in the same way different industries react differently to the economy, different asset types will react differently to economic developments as well. So a good mix of stocks, bonds, money market funds, and other asset types can give you even better diversification. You can go a step further and diversify even more by adding funds that invest in foreign stocks and bonds as well so your portfolio isn't strictly based on the US economy but is also diversified geographically across the economies of other countries.

Diversification and Age

Here's one final important note about diversification: Proper diversification is meant to decrease the overall risk to your portfolio, so it's important to pay more and more attention to this as you get older. I've seen women in their early sixties who had the majority of their money in mutual funds that invested in small-cap growth stocks because no one told them otherwise. They had no business being in such risky allocations, but they thought that because they were invested in mutual funds that they were safe, all the while having their entire retirement savings exposed to humongous risk. In the same way I've seen people invested 100% in bond mutual funds, and they also thought they were safe. Sure thing, right? They were happy because they were getting a good dividend payout. But the bond funds they owned only had lower-rated US corporate bonds. They didn't realize what a dangerous situation they were in. What if interest rates went up and caused their mutual funds to fall in value? What if there was another credit crunch like we had in 2008? That's why as you get closer to retirement, it becomes more and more important to carefully plan out your allocations to make sure you're not exposing yourself to unnecessary risks by being stuck in only one asset class.

Things to Keep in Mind

Diversification is not as simple as buying up a bunch of mutual funds. You need to figure out exactly how much time you have left until retirement, if you'll continue to work part time afterward, and what your comfort level is when it comes to losing money. Doing all of those things, and working closely with an advisor who will take the time to explain all the pros and cons to you, is what will help you figure out the proportion of the various types of funds you should have in your portfolio.

- Diversification is not the same as spreading your bets.
- Different companies in different industries will react to economic developments differently.
- It's important to consider how you are allocating your money across various asset types as well. Different asset types will react differently to the same economic events.
- The closer you get to retirement, the more important it is for you to be diversified intelligently, in a way that helps lower the overall risk to your money.

THE BASICS OF BONDS

I t's important to know a bit about how bonds work because they could end up in your portfolio, especially if you happen to invest in mutual funds that invest in bonds as part of their investment strategy.

A bond is an IOU. It's a way for companies, the government, and government entities to borrow money. You give the bond issuer your money, and they give you their promise that they will make regular payments to you, the bondholder. This may sound kind of like a car loan or a mortgage, but it's not the same thing. With a car loan, each and every single payment will be the same, and after you make your last payment, you don't owe anything else. But with bonds, payment terms can vary quite a bit, and they can have different ways of paying you back. Usually, a bond will have regular payments of interest, and one final payment of the principal. So, for example, if you buy a five-year, $1,000 bond that pays 7% interest, you can expect to receive $70 per year for five years (the 7% interest), and when the five years are up, your $1,000 will be repaid in one lump sum payment. So the company or the government (from which you bought this bond) gets to use your $1,000 for five years, and you get to earn the 7% interest rate. At the end of it all, you get your money back.

In the simplest terms, companies and governments need money to use in different projects, so they issue these IOUs so they can accomplish their goals and you earn something on your loan to them. What is important is that you realize that a loan is a loan. Things could go bad, and you might not get your money back.

Bond Types

Overall, there are many different types of bonds out there that are designed for different purposes and can have different overall terms.

Payment Terms

One aspect in which bonds differ is in how they make payments to the bondholders. Some bonds will only pay you regular interest until they mature, and will repay the principal as one payment at the very end. Other bonds will work like a car loan, where every single payment will be the same, and every payment will consist of interest and some principal. So there's no lump sum payment at the end because you're getting your principal back regularly, piece by piece. There are also so-called *zero-coupon* bonds, which have no monthly payments at all and will instead accrue interest over the life of the bond. You would receive one lump-sum payment at the end of the loan, which would contain the principal as well as all interest together, in one big payment. Overall, bonds can vary a lot in their payment terms, so make sure you clearly understand what those terms are before you invest your money into a bond.

Bond Duration

Bonds can also vary based on their durations (from a year to several decades). If you've considered buying a bond before, you may have noticed that longer-term bonds will usually have a higher interest rate. There's a reason for that, which I'll explain shortly. But if you consider buying a bond, keep in mind that generally (if all other things are equal), a longer-term bond will be riskier than a short-term bond. That is because while your money is tied up in a long-term bond, a lot more things can happen—including rising interest rates and political instability.

Think of a bond's duration like a serious relationship and of stocks as more like dating (you can break up anytime). With bonds, time can become an issue if you want to get your full value back. With stocks, your decision to dump them depends on the price of the stock on any given day. The price of bonds can also depend on interest rates, which can take time to change. It's much easier to end a date than an actual relationship, right?

Bond Ratings

One thing bonds usually have, and stocks don't, is credit ratings. Just as credit reporting agencies will issue a FICO score for people, there are also agencies that will rate companies and governments (federal, state, city, etc.) on their ability to repay a loan. These ratings are usually done with letters and can range from ratings such as AAA all the way down to a C, or even lower. This is a way to show investors what the likelihood is that the issuer of the bond will have enough cash flow to be able to repay it. It's important to note that a rating of AAA doesn't guarantee you'll get your money back. The mortgage crisis that sent our economy into a tailspin was partly due to credit rating agencies issuing high quality ratings to mortgage-backed securities that ended up being nothing more than junk. So do take these kinds of ratings with a grain of salt.

Bond Coupon

A bond's *coupon* is the interest rate that the bond is paying. This interest rate is calculated on the original price, or *face value*, of the bond. So if the original face value of the bond is $1,000 and it has a coupon of 5%, then it pays $50 in interest per year. However, it's again important to remember that this rate only relates to the face value, and the *dollar amount* of the annual interest is set at the time the bond is issued. If you end up buying a bond in the open market, after it was issued, you may not get the same *interest rate* on your money as the coupon. This is because you may not be buying it for the original $1,000 face value. If you buy it in the open market for $1,100, for example, you'll still get the $50 that's spelled out in the terms of the bond, but for you it will be less than the 5% interest rate because you paid more than the original price. Or you might be able to buy it for $900, and if the coupon is 5%, then you'll still get the $50 per year ($1,000 face value x 5%), which in your case would be a return of more than 5% per year, because you only paid $900 for it. If all this is completely new to you, then you definitely want to stay away from bonds until you learn about them in more depth. Bonds may *seem* safe, but they are different from any other investment. They could give you disastrous losses—like any investment can.

Bonds vs. Stocks

Bonds have their own set of advantages and disadvantages. Here's something to remember: Because bonds are loans, they don't participate in a company's upside when the company does well. Bondholders are entitled only to the predetermined amount of cash payments that come with the bond, and that is all—even if the company does amazingly well. On the flip side, bondholders are often first in line if a company goes bankrupt. For example, if Little Red Riding Hood's company issues bonds and then goes bankrupt at a later point in time because wolf coats are not selling, all lenders, including bondholders, have priority over stockholders when it comes to sharing in whatever money is left. So the bondholders may not participate in the upside of the company doing well, but they're also taking on less risk than regular investors, because bondholders have priority claim to any assets the company may have in case of bankruptcy.

When you think about it, it makes sense from a risk-reward perspective. Bondholders don't get to participate in a company's upside the way that stockholders do when the company does well. If a company does poorly, its stock might drop in value, and investors won't receive any dividends that year. But the bondholders have to be paid no matter what. In that same exact way, when a company does well and the stock doubles, the bondholders will still receive the same payment they were scheduled to receive, and nothing more, according to the original terms of the bond.

Now remember, all this doesn't mean that bondholders are 100% protected if a company goes bankrupt. Let's say you are a bondholder in Little Red Riding Hood's company. The company goes bad and all she has left are a few furs, her little cottage, and a few sewing machines. Well, first, her staff has to get paid. Then she has to pay village taxes. Then all the creditors (farmers, banks, vendors who gave her credit) have to be paid. Once all is said and done, you, the bondholder, might get paid. But you can see that by the time it's your turn, there may not be much left to pay you or anyone else fully!

Bond Prices and Interest Rates

Most people don't truly understand how bonds work. So, if you have any bonds in your portfolio, one thing I want you to keep in mind is that understanding the relationship between bond prices and interest rates is important, especially if you may at some point need to sell your bonds early, before they mature.

Let's say you're back in magical make-believe land. Little Red's company, Red Wolf Coats, Inc., wants to borrow $1,000 for a year by issuing a bond and paying you 10% interest on it (which happens to be the average interest rate for these kinds of bonds based on Red Wolf Coats' credit rating). At the end of one year, you would receive $1,000, plus an extra $100 in interest ($1,000 x 10% = $100). And let's say that you look at all the risks, think about it, and decide to buy this bond for $1,000, with the expectation of receiving all your money back, plus an extra $100 at the end of the year—or $1,100 altogether.

Now, let's pretend that the next day interest rates went through the roof, and now Red Wolf Coats was selling some more bonds. Everything is exactly the same, but instead of offering 10% interest, like on the one you bought, they were now offering 20% per year in interest. That would mean that any new bond purchasers would now get $200 per year ($1,000 x 20%), while you would still only get $100 ($1,000 x 10%). So there you are, sitting with your bond, for which you paid $1,000 and will receive $1,100 at the end of the year. But if you had waited and bought the bond a day later, you would be receiving $1,200 at the end of the year. Besides making you feel like you made a mistake buying the bond when you did, how does this affect your money?

Well, if you're going to hold the bond until its maturity (until the final payment), it doesn't directly affect how much money you'll get, since you'll still receive the exact same amount of money you originally thought you would. That's important to keep in mind, because if interest rates change while you are holding a bond, and if you are expecting to hold the bond until it fully matures, then the situation doesn't affect you from the perspective of the number of dollars you will receive. The amount of money you will receive is still exactly the same as you thought it would be when you made the purchase. Yes, you'll get the same amount of dollars, but depending on what happens with inflation during that time, those dollars may not be able to purchase nearly as much as you thought. And if interest rates are rising, then inflation is likely to increase as well. But what if a week later you have an emergency and you need to sell your precious bond? Well, don't forget all the bonds that are out there that are now paying 20% per year, or $200 for every $1,000 in principal. If you try to sell your bond, which pays only $100 a year, no one will want to buy it for the full $1,000 price. Instead, you would have to ask your broker to sell your bond for less money than you paid for it in order to make it more attractive, so the person who does buy it from you can still make 20% a year.

Think about what's happening here: The person who takes it off your hands will buy it for less than what you paid for it, but will still get the $100 in interest at the end of the year. So you have to drop the price of your bond so the amount of money the buyer would get at the end of the year would still give them 20% in interest. In this case, even though you paid $1,000 for this bond a few days before, you would now need to accept only $917 for it if you wanted to sell it. This is how it works: If you sell your bond to someone for $917, and at the end of the year they collect what you were originally going to collect (which is the $1,000 face value + the $100 interest, or $1,100 altogether), they will have earned 20% on their money (the $1,100 they receive, minus the $917 they paid to you, is $183 they will receive on top of their investment—which is a return of 20%, or $183/$917 = 20%).

It's crucial to remember the relationship between bond prices and interest rates if you hold bonds in your portfolio. Bond prices and interest rates are like two friends on a seesaw—when interest rates go up, bond prices go down, and when interest rates go down, bond prices go up. Also remember that if you hold bonds until their maturity, changes in interest rates won't usually affect the original amount of cash flow that you were going to receive. However, if you need to sell your bonds early, a rise in interest rates can significantly reduce the amount of money that you will be paid for your bonds. Therefore, although bonds are considered to be safer than stocks, if you are forced to sell when interest rates have risen, you may still end up losing money simply because you needed to sell at the wrong time.

Therefore, if you do choose to buy bonds for your portfolio, you want to make sure you won't be forced to sell them if you are close to retirement. If you are in your mid-sixties and decide to buy thirty-year bonds with all of your money, you'll likely suffer if interest rates rise unexpectedly. If rates rise and you need to sell some of your holdings to cover medical costs or long-term care costs, you'll probably end up selling your bonds at a discount.

Things to Keep in Mind

Bonds are not the simple, straightforward investments that many people think they are. Bonds can be dynamic. As our financial system gets more and more complex and intertwined, bonds can react in significant ways. You could, in fact, lose lots of money in bonds, especially if you have to sell them before their maturity. You can lose money with bond mutual funds the same way you can with stock mutual funds. Generally speaking, under normal circumstances, bonds are not as risky as stocks. But what I'd like you to clearly understand is that even though bonds have certain guarantees, it doesn't mean that they can't hurt your portfolio. In fact, whenever a client asks me if a bond, or any other investment, is safe, my first answer is always, "It depends." Your personal circumstances, your cash flow needs, jolts in the economy—lots of things—can have an impact on the riskiness of an investment as it relates specifically to you.

I will leave you with one thought: Be sure of who you bond with, because once bonded, you will never know if they will ever be out of your life.

OTHER INVESTMENT TYPES

O ver the last half century, the financial industry has created many kinds of investments with unique features so they can be used for specific investment strategies. As a result, you have many choices about how to allocate your money, beyond the simple decision of what stocks or bonds to buy. Some investments are complex and can be confusing, while others are simpler and much easier to understand. The key is to realize that there are a lot of products out there to invest your money in, and they have different features that may or may not be right for your specific situation. If you understand the features and can work with your advisor to understand how they can affect your retirement goals (including returns, liquidity, and risk, etc.), then you will be able to make better decisions for yourself as you try to navigate the waters toward a well-funded retirement.

Certificates of Deposit (CD)

CDs are round disks that contain music and can be placed into your Walkman to play exactly the kind of music you want—if you're still living in the '90s! OK, OK!, "CD" stands for Certificate of Deposit, which can be purchased through many banks. Think of certificates of deposit the same way you would think about a savings account but with a slightly higher interest rate and limitations on your ability to withdraw your money. What happens with a certificate of deposit is that you give the bank some money for a certain amount of time (three months, six months, one year, or more), and the bank pays you a pre-agreed-upon amount of interest in exchange for your promise not to take the money out. Because you are agreeing to give the bank your money for a certain amount of time, the bank can pay you a higher interest rate than you would get in a savings account because the bank can better plan its own cash flow. Sometimes, however, longer-term CDs may offer a lower rate than a savings account because future interest rates are expected to fall. It doesn't happen too often, but don't be surprised if you see this from time to time.

If your plans change, and you need access to the money sooner, you can still withdraw the funds in most cases and pay a relatively small penalty—which usually equates to a few months of interest that you would have earned. This penalty is a way for the bank to encourage you to stick to the original agreement to keep your money with them for a certain amount of time.

CDs are a great place to park money that you won't need immediately but would still like to have access to in case of emergencies. In fact, having your emergency fund in a CD makes a lot of sense because you don't plan on using the money unless something unexpected happens, and you get to earn a slightly higher return because of the higher interest rate. It's a way of keeping your emergency fund secure without risking the principal, while still being able to earn at least some sort of return, even if it's little.

However, one thing you want to triple-check when putting your money into a certificate of deposit is that the CD is FDIC-insured. FDIC stands for "Federal Deposit Insurance Corporation," which is an organization designed to help protect the general public's deposits when banks go bankrupt. This way, if something happens to the bank and it has to close its doors, you have a much better chance of recovering your money.

Here is one final important note: When banks quote their CD rates, they will usually quote what a CD will earn on an *annual* basis. If the CD you are being offered has a maturity date of less than a year, you have to divide the interest rate by 12 months, and then multiply it by the number of months of the CD duration to figure out how much you will receive in interest. So if they're advertising a 2% CD for six months, that means that you will earn only 1% in interest, because the CD duration is only half of one year. So the 2% annualized rate of return that is being advertised would give you 2% after twelve months, but will bring you only 1% actual return over a six-month period. Banks quote CDs this way so it's easier to compare CDs of different maturities.

Not too long ago, one of my clients called me with what she thought was exciting news. She saw an advertisement for a three-month, 1.5%-interest CD, and thought she could earn 6% per year. She was thinking that she would get 1.5% every three months and could reinvest the money again. I felt absolutely terrible when I had to explain to her that she wouldn't earn the full 1.5% in three months and that the rate quoted was an *annualized* rate. This meant she would earn 0.375% for the three months. This is because 1.5% was the *annualized* rate that she would earn if the CD were of a twelve-month duration. But because she was only committing her money for three months, she would only earn a quarter of that amount (three months out of the year is a quarter of the year. One quarter of a 1.5% annual return is 0.375%). So even though she may have felt somewhat embarrassed about asking the question and then learning that she misunderstood the offer, she now knows how to interpret these offers correctly and won't make the same mistake again. That's precisely why it's so important that you feel comfortable asking your advisor any questions you have. There's no need to feel silly for not knowing the answer immediately or misunderstanding something, because the only way to learn is to ask questions. Everyone is a novice at one point or another, and there's absolutely no shame in that.

Exchange Traded Funds

An Exchange Traded Fund (ETF) is an investment product that is similar to mutual funds in some ways and stocks in other ways.

Like investing in a mutual fund, when you buy an ETF, you are investing your money into a portfolio that contains a variety of other investments. For example, if you bought a mutual fund that invested in certain type of stocks, every dollar you invested would be spread across many different individual stocks. If you bought a mutual fund that invested in certain kinds of bonds, every dollar would buy small pieces in many different bonds. An ETF is a similar concept in that you're buying a small portion of a larger portfolio that could have lots of different investments in it.

The one big difference between mutual funds and ETFs is that ETFs are not meant to be actively managed. Their portfolios instead mirror an index. A portfolio manager will actively manage a mutual fund, making regular decisions about how the portfolio should be allocated. The portfolio manager has to stick to certain guidelines, but he or she can make active decisions about buying one investment and selling another, how much they will buy, and other similar considerations. For example, an ETF might follow the S&P 500 index or the price of gold or the price of silver or a bond index, and so on and so on. Instead of making decisions about how to invest the money in the fund, the manager's job is to try to get the fund to copy the performance of the index as closely as possible, regardless of whether the index is going up or down.

One of the reasons ETFs were designed this way is to make it easier to diversify your portfolio over different asset classes. Remember our earlier discussion about diversification? ETFs were meant to make asset-based diversification easier to achieve. Because an investor can buy ETFs that follow all sorts of indexes, she can diversify her portfolio across stocks, bonds, precious metals, international investments, and many other kinds of assets, and can usually do so at a significantly lower cost than a typical mutual fund with comparable assets. The reason for this is because a majority of ETFs are not actively managed, since the funds follow an index and there isn't any real research or stock picking involved on the part of the fund manager. This keeps the management fees lower. In some instances these fees might only be 0.10% per year. When you compare that to a mutual fund, where management fees can be 2% or more per year, it can be a huge savings. At the same time, because there is no active management of these funds, if an asset class, like stocks, begins to quickly drop in price, no one is there to try to soften the blow. So if you own an ETF that follows the S&P 500 index, for example, and the markets begin to crash, your ETF will experience pretty much the same price movements as the index that it follows. Now, as you've probably seen, having money in a mutual fund with active managers doesn't mean they can protect you in case of a downturn in the markets, but it's definitely an important point to keep in mind when considering ETFs.

Another difference between ETFs and mutual funds is in the way you buy them. You buy a mutual fund by investing a specific dollar amount and (usually) paying loads (sales fees); an ETF is bought and sold like a stock. You would buy a certain number of shares of an ETF and pay the same commission to your brokerage as you would for stocks. In addition, you could sell them as quickly, without any sales fees (like the back-end loads in some mutual funds) other than the brokerage commissions.

Last, it's important to note that a new kind of ETF has been appearing recently. It is actively managed, like mutual funds, and charges higher annual management fees. It remains to be seen how these kinds of ETFs will fit into portfolios as they become more common.

REITs

Real Estate Investment Trusts (REITs) are financial instruments that allow you to invest in real estate without going out to purchase and manage properties yourself. REITs purchase and operate commercial real estate for profit. There are many types of REITs out there. Some invest in apartment buildings, others in office buildings, others in industrial properties, and they can specialize even further by focusing on operating specific types of buildings (like medical office buildings, hotels, and other more targeted real estate properties).

When you purchase an REIT, like with a mutual fund or an ETF, you are purchasing a small portion of the overall portfolio and get to share in the potential profits that correspond to the number of shares you own. You are buying a small piece in a portfolio of properties. One thing you will notice about these trusts is that they pay out a large chunk—90%—of their income in dividends, because they have to do so by law. When someone purchases an REIT, a big component of the total return on investment comes from the regular dividend payments that are a direct result of the income produced by the properties that the trust owns. To a degree, some of the profits will also come from the properties appreciating in value.

Having said that, it is important to understand the kind of REIT you are buying and what its drawbacks are before you decide to invest your money. There are three main types of REITs: equity (those that purchase and operate actual properties), mortgage (those that generate income by buying and owning mortgages), and hybrids (those that operate actual properties, as well as invest in mortgages). These broad categories of REITs can also specialize significantly in subcategories of property type. If you're going to invest in one, it's a good idea to research not just the REIT itself, but to have an understanding of how the property types it owns are likely to perform in the future. If the underlying property type is not expected to perform well, then it will directly reflect on the share price of the REIT as well as its ability to make dividend payments. Like with stock, if a company whose stock you own does not do well and cannot generate income, the stock price will likely suffer. In the same way, owning REITs that have properties that are not generating income and have high vacancy rates because of a bad economy or overbuilding is likely to make the REIT share price suffer.

Another thing to keep in mind about REITs is that there are two ways of purchasing them. Some can be purchased like a stock, within your brokerage account. Other REITs, referred to as non-traded REITs, are not traded on the markets, and investments have to be made directly with the REIT itself. If you ever choose to purchase a REIT that isn't publicly traded, keep in mind that it becomes an *illiquid* investment, meaning that you may not be able to sell it as quickly as you'd like if you need to. A publicly traded REIT can be sold like a stock, directly from your brokerage account, while a *non-traded* REIT cannot always be sold easily. If there is a high probability that you will need to withdraw your money, a non-traded REIT may not be the best strategy because of the lack of liquidity.

Overall, REITs can be a useful tool if you choose to diversify a part of your portfolio into real estate, but they can also be highly risky. Keep in mind the recent real estate bubble and the effects it could have on your portfolio. That's why it's important to do thorough research when you're considering investing your money in an REIT. Work with your advisor to make sure the investment matches your portfolio goals. REITs can be attractive and can sometimes offer lucrative dividend yields. But the higher the possible return, the higher the risk you are likely taking. If you see a REIT that's offering an attractive dividend payment, don't make your decision to buy it based on that fact alone. That dividend payment could drop significantly, and the price of the shares could fall as well.

Things to Keep in Mind

As an investor, you have many options available for investing your money. There are lots of financial instruments out there, and more of them are being created all the time, giving investors more choices. However, there are two questions you always have to ask yourself: First, what are the particular features of this investment and how do they fit into my overall situation, and second, what are the risks and costs associated with these features? As with stocks or bonds, every investment has a potential upside and a potential downside. When you're considering various investment types to include in your portfolio, such as ETFs, CDs, REITs, or whatever other investment you come across, you always have to ask yourself how the features of that investment will affect you and what are the risks and costs associated with it. If you do that, then your decision-making process will become more structured, no matter what investment idea your advisor presents to you.

ANNUITIES 101

The subject of annuities is too complex to cover in one section, but I will focus on their basic features and concepts to help you get a better feel for how they work.

There is often a bit of confusion surrounding them because there are many different types, each can work quite differently, and each has a variety of features. These features can make annuities somewhat difficult to understand the first time around. But these same features make them a versatile tool that can address a number of concerns in ways that stock and bond investments can't. That's why there are a lot of suitability issues to address, and if you ever consider an annuity, it's important to understand all of the features before you commit to anything.

The Basics

Annuities are meant to be a financial product that an investor would buy with a long-term view in mind, and one of the main reasons why investors usually put their money into an annuity is to generate income at a later point in time. In the simplest of terms, some annuities can be compared to a defined-benefit pension plan. In a defined-benefit pension at your job, you put in a certain amount of money every paycheck. You then get a promise from your company that (based on the number of years you work and how much you earn in wages) you will receive a certain amount of money every month after you retire. An annuity could be set up much like a defined-benefit pension, except that it's a stand-alone product where you can invest your money with the goal of eventually receiving regular monthly payments once you retire.

Many types of annuities do not necessarily have to be turned on as an income stream, and can instead grow and be taken out as a lump sum or can remain liquid after maturity. Some retirees may not be looking for an income stream but may want to protect their nest egg against market volatility. So they choose certain annuities, such as equity-index annuities, to protect their principal and still enjoy growth potential based on index options available.

To better understand how annuities work, let's first look at some of the relevant concepts. Unlike stocks or bonds, annuities are a contract between the annuity owner and an insurance company. Every annuity will have an annuity owner, an annuitant, and in most cases a beneficiary of the contract.

In its simplest form, when someone buys an annuity (creates an annuity contract), the insurance company receives money, either as a lump sum or as a series of payments. In return, the company promises growth potential depending on what type of annuity you get. The *owner* of the annuity is usually the person who purchases the annuity contract with the insurance company, and the *annuitant* is the person who will receive the benefits of that annuity, whether it's a lump sum amount or a stream of regular payments, depending on what is chosen. Usually, the owner will purchase the annuity for themselves, to either help supplement their income during retirement or to simply have principal preservation with growth potential. In this case, the owner will also be the annuitant. However, this doesn't always have to be the case, because an annuity owner could also be an individual like a spouse or an entity such as a trust. The key is to understand that an annuity will have an owner and an annuitant, but they don't always have to be the same person.

An annuity will usually also have a *beneficiary*—the person who is entitled to receive any death benefits of an annuity, if there are any. This works similarly to listing a beneficiary on your IRA or 401(k) account, where you designate who would receive any remaining money in your account in the event of your death. With an annuity, it's much the same thing. The beneficiary doesn't receive any money from an annuity while the annuitant is alive and will receive any remaining benefits of the contract only when the annuitant dies.

How an Annuity Works

Once an annuity contract is purchased, it goes through two phases—the accumulation phase and the annuitization phase (if that phase is chosen). The accumulation phase comes right after the contract purchase. During this phase, the money that was invested into the annuity grows over time. This phase is important because it will directly affect how much income your annuity will pay out in the future (if you choose an income payout option). The growth during this phase can vary significantly based on the type of annuity you purchase and all the features you requested it to have. During the accumulation phase, most annuities will have a penalty-free withdrawal option. As long as you are over 59½, you can use that option should you need to. For example, you may put $100,000 in an annuity and may be still able to withdraw $10,000 a year (10%) after the first-year anniversary, even during the accumulation period.

Once the accumulation phase is over, you can decide to annuitize it, and the annuitant will begin receiving regular payments. This is called the annuitization phase. If this option is chosen, the size of the payments will depend on many factors, but two of the major ones will be your total accumulation value and your age when you start receiving the payments. Again, remember that it depends on the type of annuity and the reason you decided to purchase the annuity. You might decide not to annuitize it and instead take a lump sum and walk away.

Types of Annuities

There are four main types of annuities: Single Premium Immediate Annuity (SPIA), Fixed Annuity (FA), Equity Indexed Annuity (EIA), which is also referred to as a Fixed-Indexed Annuity, and Variable Annuity (VA).

Let's start with the most basic one, which is a fixed annuity. A fixed annuity is similar to a CD at a bank. What that means is that a fixed annuity will earn a predetermined interest rate for the term of the annuity, similar to a CD that would earn a predetermined rate at a bank. Let's say you purchase a five-year annuity giving you a specific interest rate for that time duration—for example 2%. That's the interest rate you will receive regardless of what's happening in the economy or the stock market. As with a CD, a fixed annuity limits what you can do with your money for a certain period of time, because it's a contract between you and the insurance company. You agree to keep your money in the contract for a specific duration in exchange for a specific interest rate. That doesn't mean that you can't take your money out at all, though. Remember —unlike a CD, there is a penalty-free annual withdrawal amount available on most annuities. But if you decide to break the annuity completely and take all your money out early, then you will have to pay a surrender charge. That amount depends on your specific annuity policy.

Single premium immediate annuities are contracts where you give the insurance company a certain amount of money and they immediately start paying you regular income payments. So there isn't an accumulation phase in this kind of annuity, because what you're doing is agreeing with an insurance company that it will immediately start making regular payments to you for a predetermined amount of time. There are several payment options to choose from, and the amount of the regular payments will depend on how long you'd like to receive those payments (the longer you'd like to receive the payments, the lower those payments would usually be).

For example, you could choose a payment option called life pay, which means that you will receive larger regular payments, but only as long as you are alive: There won't be any money paid to your beneficiaries after you die. This is an option that people with no children or other dependents sometimes choose because they would rather receive more in income instead of worrying about what happens after they pass away. You can also choose a life pay with a certain year option, such as ten-year certain, fifteen-year certain, and so on. In these types of payment options you will receive regular payments. But if you were to die before a certain amount of time passed (ten or fifteen years, for example), then your beneficiary would continue receiving the payments until that period of time is complete. So, if you choose a fifteen-year certain payment option and pass away after ten years, your beneficiary would continue to receive payments for five years after that. On the other hand, if you choose that same fifteen-year certain option but live for twenty-five years, then your beneficiary would receive nothing—because the contract will have already met its minimum requirement to make payments for fifteen years. It's important to note that in this second example, you would continue receiving payments no matter how long you live, even after the certain period elapses.

Equity and fixed-index annuities are types of annuities that depend on what's happening in the stock market but which don't directly expose your principal to the risks of the markets. This type of annuity safeguards your original principal in exchange for a lower rate of return than the money could earn if it were invested directly in the markets. This provides protection of the principal, but as you remember from chapter 16, because you're taking less risk, you will also receive a lower return—and in some cases you may earn nothing at all for a year or longer, if the markets are falling. But it also means that you are not losing anything either like you would be if you were invested directly in the market and it crashed.

These types of annuities usually work by being tied to an index. In the previous chapter I talked about Exchange Traded Funds (ETFs), which mirror an index. Fixed-index annuities are also tied to indexes, and the growth of your accumulation value will depend on how those indexes perform. Usually, an insurance company that sells you this type of annuity will add gains to your accumulation value annually. So if an index performs well, your annuity will earn a return, which will be added to the accumulation value. But unlike a straight stock market investment, this gain will be locked in. So if the market experiences a loss the following year, you would not earn anything, but you wouldn't lose anything either.

For example, let's take the crash of 2008. Someone who was invested in a fixed-index annuity would accumulate gains all the way up to the time of the crash. When the crash occurred, they would maintain whatever the accumulation value was in their fixed-index annuity as of the last anniversary date of the establishment of their annuity contract. So even though the market was deteriorating, someone with this type of annuity wouldn't experience any losses. But if the market performed poorly, they wouldn't experience any returns either.

It's important to remember that in a fixed-index annuity, the growth depends on the index options that are selected. A more aggressive allocation can provide a higher return if the markets do well, but can give you 0% if the markets are doing poorly. And as you already know, just because you're not losing money doesn't mean that you're in the clear, because your purchasing power continues to decrease due to inflation. That is why it is so important to carefully select the annuity, the index allocations, and the insurance company from which you purchase the contract. Two people can be holding the same type of annuity from different companies throughout the same exact time period and with similar indexing options, but one could earn 3% while the other could earn 8%. This is because different companies will have different methodologies for calculating returns and different allocation techniques.

The reason someone would choose a fixed-index annuity versus a fixed annuity would usually be because they want a higher potential return while giving up the rights to a fixed regular rate of return. On the other hand, someone might choose a fixed annuity because it's more important to them to earn a regular rate of return, even if it's lower, rather than take the chance that they won't earn anything at all if the markets do poorly.

Last, there are variable annuities, which are a lot like owning mutual funds within an annuity contract. It's similar to purchasing mutual funds in a retirement account, but instead you purchase them within your annuity contract. So you expose your principal to the upside and downside of the markets, and your annual return depends on how the markets perform. But it's still different than investing directly into the markets because you can choose to attach certain riders (contract options) to help protect the income benefits and the death benefit of the contract. Also, because variable annuities are tax-deferred products (you don't pay tax on the gains until you start withdrawing the money), a variable annuity could be a way for some people to save money for retirement outside of their IRA or 401(k). But of course, make sure to check with your tax preparer to see how this would affect you before making any decisions.

Although variable annuities can play a specific role in a retirement portfolio, they still expose your principal to investment risk and are similar to being invested directly in the stock market. Granted, these annuities have certain riders you can add to guarantee some features, but exposing your principal to market volatility makes variable annuities more risky. Most annuities are complex and have a variety of features to carefully consider before making the decision to invest your money. You should give special thought before selecting a variable annuity. If you choose one, make sure it fits within your portfolio objectives and that you don't have unrealistic expectations about its safety and the possible returns it can generate.

Riders

Riders are various options that can be added on to annuity contracts to fine-tune the features of the annuity to better fit an investor's specific situation. There are many different kinds, and they are too numerous to be covered extensively in one section. I'll give you an example of one of the more common ones, the income rider.

An annuity has an accumulation value where your principal grows based on the features of the annuity. You could choose to take your accumulation value as a lump sum out of the annuity and move it somewhere else, or you could choose to annuitize it and receive regular payments instead. But, as with any investment, there is a chance that your returns won't be as high as you expected, and because of that, the accumulation value will not grow as large as you had hoped. For example, if you had a fixed-index annuity and the index it was tied to continued experiencing constant declines, your principal would be safe, but it wouldn't grow, either; if you are in a variable annuity, you could have less money than you invested. The income rider can help address this situation by giving you an opportunity to choose a different rate of return if that were to happen. But it comes with some strings attached.

Let's pretend you are fifty-five and you purchase a fixed-index annuity. You add an income rider that happens to guarantee a rate of 6% per year. Let's say you started by investing $100K. After ten years, your accumulation value has grown to $150K, based on the returns of the indexes (not from the income rider). You could choose to take that $150K out as a lump sum amount and put that money somewhere else. But since you had an income rider that guaranteed a 6% return, you also have another choice. At a 6% annual return, your guaranteed income value (similar to accumulation value) would have grown to about $179K, which is more than the $150K that your accumulation value reached in mutual funds in this example. At that point you could choose to annuitize that $179K guaranteed income value for a regular stream of payments instead of taking the $150K accumulation value as a lump sum. However, you cannot choose to take that $179K as a lump sum amount.

As the example above suggests, the income rider is a good way to guarantee that your principal can grow at a predetermined rate to give you a higher amount to annuitize into regular income payments during retirement, should you choose to do so. But as with everything, options do cost money, and an income rider will cost a certain fee per year, like any other riders you might decide to add.

Overall, there are many different riders to choose from that can alter the features of an annuity and will address the different needs you may have. There are, for example, death benefit riders that work by protecting and adding growth to your principal. This is why it's important to understand what your needs are and select riders that will address your specific concerns.

The Role of Insurance Companies

A big part of selecting an annuity is selecting the right insurance company to work with, because the stability of the insurance company plays a role in the safety of the annuity. That's why it's important to research the insurance company to ensure that it is reputable, stable, and not an operation that will go out of business in a few years. Annuities are getting popular, and many smaller companies are beginning to offer them, but they do not have the same backing a bigger company has or the experience to keep their promises to their consumer.

What's important to remember about annuities is that they are guaranteed by the insurance company that issues them; but unlike a CD at a bank, they are not FDIC-insured. This makes it vital to select reputable insurance firms that are going to be around for the long term. I personally prefer that a company issuing the annuity contracts has been around for at least five or more decades. I believe a company with a longer reputation has had the opportunity to navigate the financial markets through various ups and downs in the economy, and has the benefit of experience in dealing with difficult economic environments. It's important that they have an A-rating when it comes to their financial strength, and that they have a good reputation of payouts and keeping their commitments to their clients.

Things to Keep in Mind

Annuities are a complex investment vehicle that have a lot of different options. They can have many pitfalls if they are not chosen carefully, precisely because the options they have are designed to address many different needs and to fit specific situations and address specific concerns. This is kind of like going to the store and buying a good dress—you have to find one that fits you. It may look good on the mannequin and it might look good on some people, but it won't necessarily look good on you if it doesn't fit your unique shape and personality. In the same way, an annuity has to be chosen carefully, with the right features to make sure it addresses your needs and helps you achieve your specific goals.

- Understand the strength and rating of the insurance company.
- Understand what type of annuity you are purchasing.
- Understand the terms/length of the annuity.
- Understand withdrawal options during and after the accumulation period.
- Understand how much you will be paying in fees, if they apply.
- Understand riders that are available, and which riders will address your specific concerns and goals.

NOTES

1. Jessica Arons, "Lifetime Losses: The Career Wage Gap," Center for American Progress Action Fund, 2008.

2. Current statistics show that women earn approximately between 75% and 86% of what men earn. These statistics vary based on age, occupation, education level, and how average earnings are measured. Even wider variance exists when ethnicity is taken into account.

3. Lilly Ledbetter filed a complaint with the EEOC after having worked as a supervisor for the Goodyear Tire & Rubber Company for approximately twenty years. She learned that during the entire time of her employment she was consistently paid less than her male counterparts, and she was awarded approximately $3.3 million in damages. However, the US Supreme Court eventually overturned the ruling on the grounds that the case was filed more than 180 days after the original decision was made by Goodyear Tire & Rubber Company to pay Ms. Ledbetter less, and therefore, her case was filed too late. The Lilly Ledbetter Fair Pay Act of 2009 resets the 180-day period every time a discriminatory pay practice occurs—not just from the original date of the discriminatory practice.

4. Under coverture laws, women had few legal rights and were either considered dependents of their fathers or their husbands. When a woman married, she and her husband became one entity, which was fully controlled by the husband. The wife had no legal rights to sue, own property, or make other financial decisions. A woman was simply not considered to be a legal entity under the law. Some of the aspects of coverture laws have been slowly dismantled during the twentieth century, but their effects still persist.

5. Texas State Historical Association, "Women and the Law," accessed May 9, 2013, http://www. tshaonline.org/handbook/online/articles /jsw02.

6. National Women's Business Council, "Businesses Owned by Women," accessed August 20, 2013, http://www.nwbc.gov/sites/default/files /NWBC%20Women-Owned%20Businesses_FINAL.pdf.

7. Catalyst.org, "Women in Law in the US," accessed May 9, 2013, http://www.catalyst.org/knowledge/women-law-us.

8. Catalyst.org, "Women in Medicine," accessed May 10, 2013, http:// www.catalyst.org/knowledge/ women-medicine.

9. Having worked with many women over the years, one of the most common concerns I hear is that their advisor does not listen to them or take their concerns seriously. This is one of the more frustrating hurdles that routinely prevents women from getting the answers they want, and it's a hurdle that is only reduced if a woman assertively demands that her questions and opinions be taken seriously. I have heard many stories over the years that border on absurd, but that is the sad reality. It's an absurd one.

10. United States Government Accountability Office, *Gender Pay Differences: Progress Made, but Women Remain Overrepresented among Low-Wage Workers*, GAO-12-10, October 2011.

11. According to "Graduating to a Pay Gap. The Earnings of Women and Men One Year after College Graduation," a 2012 report by AAUW, one factor behind the pay gap is that women are less likely to negotiate their salaries than men are because they feel that employers will not perceive it favorably.

12. Rapunzel is a fictional character in the fairy tales of the Brothers Grimm. She is held captive in a tower by a witch, and has very long hair that the witch uses to climb up to and down from the tower. One day, a prince finds her and she lets down her hair so he can climb up to the tower. But throughout her ordeal Rapunzel never thought to use her hair to escape from the tower and run away.

13. In the 1987 film *Wall Street*, Michael Douglas portrays a greedy and ruthless broker by the name of Gordon Gekko, who is eventually caught in an insider-trading scheme.

14. CNNMoney, "Prosecutors: Madoff fraud started in 1970s," accessed May 10, 2013, http://money. cnn.com/2012/10/01 /investing/madoff-fraud/index.html.

15. In his early nineteenth-century poem, "Marmion," Sir Walter Scott tells a tale of lies, deception, and greed that ends poorly for the instigators of the plot.

16. Bruce Bartlett, "Who Saw the Housing Bubble Coming?" Forbes .com, accessed May 13, 2013, http:// www.forbes.com/2008/12/31 /housing-bubble-crash-oped-cx_bb_0102bartlett. html.

17. Gretchen Morgenson and Louise Story, "Banks Bundled Bad Debt, Bet Against It and Won," *The New York Times*, accessed February 18, 2013, http://www.nytimes.com/2009/12/24/ business/24 trading.html?pagewanted=all&_r=0.

18. In the 1987 film *Wall Street*, Bud Fox, played by Charlie Sheen, was the reluctant hero who brought down his greedy boss Gordon Gekko (Michael Douglas). Unfortunately, he had to personally get a taste of Wall Street before realizing what a painful and ruthless game it can be.

19. In the tale of "Jack and the Beanstalk," Jack is a boy living with his mother, who asks him to take their cow to the market for sale. The cow was their only asset and it had stopped giving milk, so they had no choice but to sell it. On his way to the market, Jack meets a man who asks him to trade the cow for some magic beans. Jack goes ahead and decides that it is indeed prudent to trade their only asset for the beans. In the end, Jack finds treasure, but he could have well traded his mother's only asset for a handful of regular beans.

20. BusinessInsider.com, "FAIL: 84% of Actively Managed Mutual Funds Did Worse Than Their Benchmarks in 2011," accessed May 13, 2013, http://www.businessinsider.com/84-mutual -funds-underperform-2012-3.

21. Michael Zennie and Eddie Wrenn, "Google overtakes Microsoft in market value for first time (but it needs to work hard to catch up with Apple)," *Daily Mail*, October 2, 2012, http://www.daily mail.co.uk/sciencetech/article-2211565/Google-overtakes -Microsoft-market-value-time.html.

22. In the story "The Emperor's New Clothes," a ruler is fooled into believing that clothes made for him are invisible to anyone who is stupid or incompetent. When the "clothes" are delivered, neither he nor anyone else can see them (because they don't exist), but everyone pretends that they do see the new clothes to not seem stupid or incompetent. The emperor, not wanting to seem unfit for his office, ends up "wearing" these clothes in a parade, but really just walks around naked.

23. CNBC.com, "This Is the Worst Thing About Fake-Tweet Stock Dive," accessed May 5, 2013, http:// www.cnbc.com/id/100669021.

24. Bureau of Labor Statistics, "The U.S. Housing Bubble and Bust: Impacts on Employment," December 2010.

ABOUT THE AUTHOR

C rystal Oculee is a personal finance expert, a national financial motivational speaker, and a Personal Money Trainer™. She is also a TV and radio personality and author who has appeared on CBS News, Fox, ABC, KFI, KTLK, KRLA, KDAR, and KKLA. She has also been featured in publications such as *Entrepreneur* and *Redbook*.

In a world where many women often feel at a loss when it comes to their finances, Crystal empowers them with the tools and confidence they need to get the results they're seeking. She is passionate about helping women deal with the unique financial challenges they face. With a deep understanding of women's issues and a passion for change, she has taught thousands of women to take positive action in their lives and stand up for themselves, their money, and their futures.

Crystal has been a guest speaker at numerous events sponsored by organizations such as the National Active and Retired Federal Employees Association (NARFE), the Screen Actors Guild (SAG), the Motion Picture & Television Fund, California Women's Conference, the Los Angeles Women's Expo, An Empowered Woman, and the Guam Women's Leadership Retreat. She is the author of *Your Personal Money Diary*.

You can find more information about Crystal's work at www.Crystal Oculee.com.